ADVENTURES WITH ED

Ed on trip to Grand Gulch, Utah, May, 1988. Photo by Mark Klett.

ADVENTURES

with

A Portrait of Abbey

JACK LOEFFLER

UNIVERSITY OF NEW MEXICO PRESS

ALBUQUERQUE

ISBN-13: 978-0-8263-2388-0

12 11 10 09 08   2 3 4 5 6

Library of Congress Cataloging-in-Publication Data:

Loeffler, Jack, 1936–
Adventures with Ed : a portrait of Abbey / Jack Loeffler.—1st ed.
p.   cm.
Includes bibliographical references (p.) and index.
ISBN 0-8263-2387-1 (cloth : alk. paper)
ISBN 0-8263-2388-x (pbk. : alk. paper)
1. Abbey, Edward, 1927–
2. Loeffler, Jack, 1936—Friends and associates.
3. Novelists, American—20th century—Biography.
4. Environmentalists—United States—Biography. I. Title.
PS3551.B2 Z77 2001
813'.54—dc21

2001003998

Design: Mina Yamashita

THIS BOOK IS DEDICATED TO Katherine, my wonderful and talented wife and friend, whose patience and perseverance have nurtured the home habitat for over three decades; our daughter, Celestia Peregrina, whose love of life and the natural world is wondrous to behold; and those flame bearers who recognize our rootedness in Nature, for whom the spirit of Ed Abbey will long endure as a guiding light.

contents

preface

During the twentieth century, the human population of the planet more than tripled, wilderness shrank, the land, air, and water became dangerously polluted, and it finally became evident to many biologists that the planetary biotic community was suffering a massive extinction of species. At the same time, in spite of two world wars and myriad regional wars, many nations thrived due to rapidly evolving technology, mass production, energy availability, and conspicuous consumption—all at enormous expense to natural habitat.

Self-reliance in conscious partnership with home habitat atrophied in all but a few indigenous cultures scattered about the globe. Early on, this new milieu spawned a few individuals who resisted the temptation to conform to public opinion and sought to defend the natural world. Men like Henry David Thoreau, John Wesley Powell, and John Muir were in the nineteenth-century vanguard of American environmentalism. During the twentieth century Aldo Leopold, Robinson Jeffers, David Brower, Paul Shepard, and others were instrumental in bringing into public focus the growing jeopardy to natural habitat. The Sierra Club and Friends of the Earth included national member-ships of people sympathetic to the natural world.

In the 1960s and early 1970s individuals such as "The Fox" and environ-mental groups including Greenpeace and the Black Mesa Defense Fund emerged. Their intent was to draw attention to areas of jeopardy in the natural environment through lawsuits, civil disobedience, and attempts to rally spirited, environmentally sensitive people to actively defend habitat.

With the publication of his book *Desert Solitaire* in 1968, Edward Abbey emerged as a provocative voice crying out on behalf of wilderness that gradu-ally compelled a cadre of young outdoor adventurers to respond to the pillage of the planet in ways that threatened the corporate status quo. After the publication of Abbey's *The Monkey Wrench Gang* in 1975, environmental activism took on a new dimension. A fighting spirit pervaded groups of environmental activists that included Earth First!, whose defense of the planet against corporate and governmental pillaging of habitat was so effective that in May 1989, less than three months after the death of Edward Abbey, Earth First! cofounder Dave Foreman was arrested by the FBI and charged with conspiracy to commit sabotage. Although innocent, he was found guilty on one charge of conspiracy. Indeed many Americans devoted to the preservation of the environment have come to be regarded as enemies of the state.

In the twelve years since Edward Abbey's death, America has been privy to the terror of the Branch-Davidian debacle in Waco, Texas; been horrified by the bombing in Oklahoma City by an American citizen; been witness to the tragedy of youth gun violence as committed in Jonesboro, Arkansas and Columbine High School in Colorado; been engaged in the Gulf War; and has suffered the horrors of international terrorism at the World Trade Center and the Pentagon. These are clearly manifestations of the evil of our times. We are not a world at peace.

How do we interrupt this terrible cycle of worsening violence and contribute to a consciousness of world peace? Commercial media has capitalized on violence and terror thus captivating and degrading the minds of generations of Americans. The computer has linked much of the world through the Internet in such a fashion that the Internet has become a dominant force of virtual reality. In a time when we seem to be replacing our perception of Nature with virtual reality, it seems appropriate that this book, ten years in the making, finally see the light of day.

Edward Abbey was a great enemy of terrorism in all its myriad forms. While he was certainly a product of his milieu, he was also a natural flame-bearer in the time-honored tradition of resistance to centralized power. He was a gadfly with enormous literary talent. He was an activist who did his share of what he called "nightwork." And he was a great social critic. He once said, "Society is like a stew. You have to keep stirring it so that the scum doesn't rise to the top."

This book is intended as a portrait of Edward Abbey. It is *not* intended to invoke a wave of sabotage or violent confrontation. It is my fervent hope that those who read this book will be inspired or reinspired to tithe their time creatively and consciously on behalf of natural habitat and wilderness preservation. We are rooted in Nature. If we as humans have a purpose, consciousness lies at the heart of it.

PART I

Earth is clearly more delved in and built over than before. All its parts are trampled, familiar, full of trade. Placid farms overspread notorious deserts. Fields rebuff the forest. Herds fright off the beasts. The very sands are sown, rocks cultivated, swamps drained. Today's towns outnumber yesterday's huts. Islands are not lonely nor cliffs intimidating—everywhere are residences, peoples, governments, life. And this above all proves man's drastic growth—we so clog the universe it can barely support us; as our needs increase, we struggle with each other for them, and nature fails us.

—*Tertullian*, A.D. *150?–220*

introduction

It is a snowy day in Santa Fe, a good day to begin this book I have been entrusted to write. This is a book about Edward Paul Abbey, my best friend of a lifetime, who honored friendship and truth above all else. He was born in Home, Pennsylvania, on January 29, 1927, and he died in the Sonoran Desert on March 14, 1989. Ed was not only a great friend; he was also a great man. There are many of us who know this to be true.

Living a creative self-directed life is like running a wild river; you don't deny the current its due, but you work your own way through the rapids, camp where you will, explore side canyons that intrigue you, and relish the danger, heeding no higher authority than the truth. Few men have the strength of character to follow the truth no matter where it leads. Edward Abbey was such a man.

He was an adventurer in both deeds and ideas; he was a great naturalist, although he abhorred the epithet; he was a lover of women, married five times, and took dozens of paramours; he was a gifted writer with twenty-one books and scores of articles to his credit; he was an avid reader of literature and connoisseur of fine music; he placed profound value on friendship; he detested bureaucracy and regarded it as a disease fatal to the human spirit; he fearlessly defended both the right of the individual and the rights of other species to coexist equally within the biotic community; he melded anarchism and environmentalism into a system of thought that will continue to affect western culture for generations.

For more than two decades Abbey and I were *compañeros*. We shared hundreds of campfires and hiked thousands of miles together. Little by little, we revealed to each other the details that make a human lifetime. These revelations took no chronological form; rather, they occurred by association as happens in conversation. Ed was given to philosophical speculation, and we spent endless hours pondering any possible meaning to existence. Much of the time we kidded and razzed each other. When we disagreed, we mostly debated, rarely argued, and fought only a couple of times.

We created our own history, some of which appears in this book. It seems appropriate that it should, inasmuch as it reveals the way Edward Abbey was as a fellow human being, or at least the way he was when we were together.

On a few occasions in the 1980s Ed suggested that I be his "chronicler." But this book is not so much a biography as a biographical memoir divided into two parts. In order to write it, I lived with Abbey's journals and papers, reread all of his books, and spoke with friends, enemies, and relatives. I have relied greatly on my own memory of our myriad conversations and experiences. I revisited many of our old campsites and hiked along many of our old trails.

Every now and then, I visit Ed's grave and pour him a beer while I drink one myself. The timbre of his voice is clear as a bell in my mind's ear. Other books about Edward Abbey may reveal other facets of this extraordinary man. But I have done my level best to follow Ed's own motto: "Follow the truth no matter where it leads."

I first heard mention of Edward Abbey's name in the summer of 1964. At that time I was living in an old forked-stick hogan at the base of Navajo Mountain, Utah, in the remotest part of the Navajo Reservation. It was fifty-seven miles of rough dirt road to the nearest pavement and a good hundred miles beyond that to the nearest town of any consequence. My friend John DePuy, an artist, had come to stay with me for a while. It was "Debris," as we later called him, who had told me about Navajo Mountain in the first place. After recuperating in a naval hospital from wounds he received during the Korean War, DePuy had traveled to Navajo. He had apprenticed himself to a Navajo medicine man when the naval constabulary tracked him down and took him back to Annapolis. He was discharged with a modest pension.

During his visit to my hogan, DePuy and I hiked many miles through that windswept red desert broken up by the most beautiful canyons in the world. It was during one of our hikes that he said, "You and Abbey must meet."

"Who's Abbey, and why should we meet?"

"Abbey is a friend of mine. He's a writer and a loner and he loves the desert and beautiful women," said DePuy.

"He sounds like a good man to me, DePuy," I responded, inventing an image of someone sitting in a high place, his back to a rock, a million empty miles before him, a long-legged, languorous naked lady lying spent by his side.

Time passed, and I negotiated with the U.S. Forest Service for a job as a fire lookout atop Carracas Mesa in northwestern New Mexico. There was no tower there and no cabin—just a two-acre expanse of uneven Navajo sandstone. I could just barely get my pickup truck to the top of "The Rock," as my lookout was known, and with a little jockeying, I could even get it level. That is where I lived for months at a time. At night I could see no light other than starlight and moonlight. Except for an occasional airplane, or if the wind were just right, the occasional chug-a-chug of the distant narrow-gauge railway, I could hear no sound of human provenance. I was utterly at home in the high ponderosa with the mule deer, black bear, wild turkeys, golden eagles, red-tailed hawks, bobcats, coyotes, elk, mountain lions, Stellar's jays, l.b.j.'s (little brown jobbies), ground squirrels, porcupines, rock rattlesnakes, lizards, tarantulas, tarantula hawks, ticks, ants, and wild horses running side by side.

I ate beans, cornmeal cakes, onions, and venison jerky that I prepared myself from meat of deer I had hunted, and I hauled water out of the San Juan River, which meandered through its canyon eight miles to the north, a river still pure enough in those days to drink straight from the current without fear.

I've never been less lonely and in better health on all counts.

About once a month I'd drive sixty or so miles into Durango to buy supplies, quaff some beer, and visit the bookstore, for one of the great features of life as a fire lookout is the time it allows for reading. During a typical fire season I would read about sixty books.

One day a new book was featured at the bookstore. The name of the author caught my eye. Edward Abbey, the guy DePuy had told me about a few years back. I picked up the book and examined it. Hardback. Expensive at $5.95. There was a picture of a familiar-looking Abbey on the inside of the dust jacket. Bearded, smiling, and possibly intelligent. Alive. What the hell. I coughed up the money and bought *Desert Solitaire*. Support your local author.

When I finally got back to my fire lookout from Durango, it was too dark to read. Sometimes at night I would fire up a kerosene lamp and read in the back of my homemade camper, but more often I would lie on my back on the sandstone, which still held the heat from the sun, and watch the night sky while listening to distant owls or coyotes or wind passing through the high timber. I lived in a paradise little known by most of my species, in whom I took little interest.

The next morning, after I had scanned the canyons and ridgelines for wisps of smoke and listened to the sounds of the wild, I radioed the ranger to let him know that I was on the job and that the forest was safe—from fire at least. In those days I was naive enough to think that I was protecting the trees in the forest from fire for their own sake. I had yet to witness clear-cutting from timber sales or chaining down of trees to make way for cattle or gas well drillers.

I brewed up a fresh pot of coffee on my Coleman stove, rummaged through my purchases of the day before, and settled down under the lone pine tree that had somehow rooted itself to soil hidden in a crevasse in the sandstone. I looked at my new book. It had a good feel to it and a good smell. I experienced the excitement I always feel when I crack a new book full of promise. *Desert Solitaire: A Season in the Wilderness!* I had spent many seasons in the wilderness. The title of this book thrilled me in a fashion that is difficult to express. I started reading, tentatively at first, then with increasing interest. Near the end of the first chapter, Abbey had written concerning his stint as a backcountry ranger at Arches National Monument, "I am here not only to evade for awhile the clamor and filth and confusion of the cultural apparatus but also to confront, immediately and directly if it's possible, the bare bones of existence, the elemental and fundamental, the bedrock which sustains us. I dream of a hard and brutal mysticism in which the naked self merges with the nonhuman world and yet survives still intact, individual, separate." Tears blurred my vision, and I shouted out some weird primal yell.

"Ah, Abbey, you bastard! You *know,* don't you! You know the truth! The same truth that I know! Except you maybe know it better than I do!" I laughed and cried and then I read *Desert Solitaire.*

More time passed. I spent a final season as a fire lookout atop The Rock—long enough to witness man-made mayhem committed against trees whose souls expired in some wooden agony that I could feel empathetically deep within my own bones. I watched a pair of Caterpillar tractors, umbilicated to each other by a behemoth anchor chain, dragging down trees, uprooting piñons and junipers to make way for heavy equipment designed to drill for natural gas.

That last sad season on the fire lookout, I watched the air thicken to the west. The strip-mined-coal-burning Four Corners Power Plant, between Farmington and Shiprock, New Mexico, was a presence that was killing the American Southwest. I had no idea how many other presences were planned for this land that I love. How frustrating to watch the Southwest fall prey to greed. I remember Glen Canyon before it was befouled by Lake Powell. I remember the howls of wolves in the wild. I remember when the air was pristine and the electric kachinas had as yet to hoist power lines across the landscape.

I remembered having read *Desert Solitaire* and wondered about the man who had written it, that friend of DePuy's who brandished such a mighty pen. I decided to look up Edward Abbey.

If you study the map of North America and find Arcata on the north coast of California, then draw an azimuth due east until you reach the eastern aspect of the Rocky Mountains, and from that point draw yet another azimuth south to the point of confluence of the Rio Pecos and the Rio Grande, you have a general picture of what I regard as the American Southwest. I figured that Edward Abbey was somewhere in that general region. It took a while, but I found him on the North Rim of the Grand Canyon. DePuy was there. They were eating beans, drinking beer.

"DePuy!"

"Joaquín!" says DePuy. He has always called me Joaquín.

I turned to the other man. "Howdy. I'm Loeffler."

"I figured. I'm Abbey." He stood up. He was tall. He had a good two or three inches on me. We shook hands. He had a curious way of standing in reserve. Clear green eyes on either side of his raptor's beak of a nose. He already bore the scar of a frown that would deepen as the years passed. Good teeth. Good beard. Stood square on the Earth.

"How 'bout some beans?"

"Don't mind if I do. Can I offer you guys some beer?"

They both grinned at me. The ice was broken. I went back over to my pickup, pulled a cold six-pack out of my cooler, and returned to the campfire. Abbey handed me a plate of beans. I handed him the six-pack. He handed me back a beer, gave one to DePuy, took one for himself. We passed around the church key and opened our beers. "Salud!" "Salud!" "Salud!"

We ate our beans, mostly in silence. Although I had intruded, they were both gracious with that quiet etiquette that some outdoorsmen possess who have spent a lot of time alone. After supper we cleaned our utensils. Then we sat down again around the fire. DePuy filled and lighted his pipe. Abbey lighted a cigar. I rolled a Bull Durham. We opened our second round of beers.

"Well, Joaquín," says DePuy. "What brings you to this part of the world? I thought you would be up on Carracas Mesa this time of year."

"I didn't take my lookout this year," says I. "Too depressing."

"What do you mean, 'depressing'?" says Abbey.

"Too much smog. Too many timber sales. Too many gas-drilling rigs. I didn't have the heart for it this year." I took a long pull on my beer.

"Where's Carracas Mesa?" Abbey looked me in the eye.

"It's east of here. Over in the Jicarilla country."

"Over near Four Corners?"

"Yeah."

Silence. We all drank our beer and stared into the fire. After a while I got up and went over to my pickup. I returned to the campfire with a couple more six-packs.

"For chrissake, Loeffler. Are you trying to get us drunk?" asks Abbey.

"Yeah."

"Good!"

We all three laughed and hunkered in around the campfire and started the process of getting comfortable with each other. We told lies and ruminated on the devastating beauty of Nature. We listened as dusk turned into night and existence fit within the glow of the campfire.

There is always a certain shyness between people who have heard of each other for years and then finally meet. There was a shyness between Abbey and me. For a while he wasn't particularly talkative, but as the stars eased through the night sky and we sipped our beers, a camaraderie began to grow. DePuy, a good friend to both Abbey and me, philosophized as only DePuy knows how. Little by little, our attention turned to the state of the American Southwest, a landscape dear to all three of us.

"It's not like it was," says I.

"It was pristine. It was the pupil in the eye of God . . . the supreme moment when cosmic imagination crystallized into perfect form," says DePuy.

"It's the best place I know where a good man can get beyond anthropomorphism," says Abbey.

"And now the Gaseous Vertebrate has farted," says DePuy.

"Do you refer to the Four Corners Power Plant?" says I.

"I do," says DePuy.

"I remember Glen Canyon," says Abbey.

"So do I," says DePuy.

"Me too," says I.

"And now they've put in that goddamn concrete plug above Lee's Ferry," says Abbey. "I hate that dam."

"I wonder how hard it would be to blow it up," says I.

"You sound like an anarchist," says Abbey.

"Well, what the hell. Don't we have the right to preserve the face of God from politicians?" says I.

"It's not just our right. It's our duty!" says Abbey.

"Hear, hear!" says DePuy.

"Salud!" says I. "I think there's another two six-packs in my pickup. If you're interested, that is."

"If I give the impression that my interest is waning, I apologize," says DePuy.

"When it wanes, it pours," says I.

"Oh, Christ," says Abbey, grinning. "Go get the fucking beer and shut up!"

And so it went. Abbey pointed out that we were only renting the beer long enough for it to pass through our bodies before we selected to redistribute it to the worthy vegetation. Or to the dismay of a community of red ants. It turned out that Abbey felt great antipathy for red ants. Maybe that's why he pissed on red ant hills. I know that twice in his life when he was out camping, ants crawled into his ears. If he had to sleep on the ground, he stuffed cotton in his ears. He hated red ants. Red ants hated Abbey. Abbey hated uniformity that denied the spirit of individualism.

That night, with DePuy's help, Ed Abbey and I began to become friends. When the fire had burned low and DePuy had turned his attention inward, Ed and I took our first walk together, both of us needing to work off some beer before turning in for the night. And because we were curious about each other. Our conversation wasn't particularly profound, but we let each other know that our respective campfires would always be open to each other. We walked a few miles that night at an easy pace. The first of thousands of miles we were to walk together.

Many years later, just before Ed was to head down a trail only he could follow, we figured we had hiked the equivalent of the breadth of the continent together, involved in conversation that was utterly without limits. We were *compañeros*. And as long as I continue to live, we shall be.

chapter 1

Edward Abbey was born in the tiny village of Home, Pennsylvania, on January 29, 1927—born into a heritage that had already tapped roots into Appalachia.

His paternal grandfather, Johann Aebi, emigrated from Switzerland in 1869 at the age of nineteen. Herr Aebi had received his formal education in a French academy, where he learned English, French, and German. He was also fluent in several Swiss dialects. When he arrived in the United States, he changed the spelling of his last name to Abbey.

Johann Abbey began life in the New World as a Pennsylvania coal miner but soon turned to farming. He met and married Eleanor Jane Ostrander, and together they had eleven children. Johann Abbey was a tall, powerful man who, even in his sixties, could "shoulder two bushels of wheat from the ground while standing on a bushel measure." He played both the flute and organ, and sang and yodeled. He was avidly interested in natural history and seemed "to know everything about trees and plants, animals, birds, bugs and bees." He never went to church, although he read from the German Bible.

One day Johann Abbey read a newspaper notice advertising for an experienced farmer to assume responsibility for five hundred acres of cultivated land in Indiana County, Pennsylvania, to try a hand at experimental farming. He applied for the job, and soon the whole family as well as the pigs, chickens, and other livestock moved northeast from the banks of the Monongahela River to the farm near Creekside, Pennsylvania. He farmed successfully for several years, but as his sons grew to manhood and left home, Johann found five hundred acres to be too much to handle. He bought a smaller farm of 140 acres, and it was there that his wife, Eleanor, died in June 1926. Johann fell prey to the relentless pain of kidney stones and, five years later, died of pneumonia at the age of eighty-one.

Paul Revere Abbey, the youngest of the eleven Abbey children, was born on February 11, 1901. He was attracted by the woods around the farm and remained a woodsman his entire life. His mother, Eleanor, loved to both read and write poetry.

Paul grew up in a self-sufficient family. Eleanor Abbey was a fine seamstress, crafting clothes for all the family, knitting stockings, socks, gloves, and caps and making beautiful quilts. When she was a girl, she had worked for a wealthy family and learned the art of cooking. "It makes me drool to think of her baked shad roe, oysters, turkey stuffing, johnny bull pudding, and caramel cake," recalled her daughter Ida.

Saturday was baking day, when she baked a dozen loaves of bread, fancy rolls, six or more pies, and a couple of cakes. We always had fruit and vegetables, which Mother canned by the gallons, and jelly, jam, and preserves. When Dad butchered, she made lard, sausage, headcheese, and many other things. Nothing was wasted—even the pig's feet, which were pickled, and liverwurst made from liver. Mother raised chickens under the old hens and took care of the milk, which we girls milked. It was kept in large crocks in troughs in the springhouse, and the cream skimmed when it rose. It was churned in a dasher churn for butter.

Eleanor Abbey was a strict Methodist and believed implicitly in the Bible. She allowed neither liquor nor playing cards in her home. Her youngest son, Paul, was shaped in part by this homely milieu and in part by his sensitivity to the flow of Nature. His sister Ida remembered him as a lumberman, naturalist, and rock hound. Paul Abbey was also afflicted with wanderlust and first left home when he was only sixteen years old. For seven years he traveled the country from one end to the other, fascinated by everything he encountered.

He made his first trip west at the age of nineteen and was spellbound by the high desert country west of the hundredth meridian, where the sense of space was boundless. He traveled through the South and encountered the Ku Klux Klan, who inveigled him into their fold until he discovered that their spirit of rebellion was dark with hatred for the Negro, the Jew, the Catholic. After hearing and meeting Eugene Debs in Youngstown, Ohio, he thought of himself as a Socialist.

In 1925 Paul Abbey married Mildred Postelwaite, whose family was highly regarded in Indiana County. A year and a half later Mildred gave birth to Edward "Ned" Abbey, the first of their five children. In 1928 Howard ("Hoots") was born, and a third son, John, was born in 1930. With three small children and the country in a depression, Paul Abbey was called upon to look for work wherever he could. The look of hard times carved the countenance of many a head of household across the nation.

Paul Abbey was a crack shot and a good salesman. He used these characteristics in pursuit of an adventure that took his growing family through much of Pennsylvania and into New Jersey during the summer of 1931. With a squad of National Guardsmen who were all expert riflemen, the Abbey family followed a trail of marksmanship quite literally, since many roads were as yet unpaved. In spite of the depression the Abbey family spirit of adventure ran high. Paul sold nameplates and other sundries along the road to provide the money necessary for survival. Paul, Mildred, Ned, Hoots, and Johnny lived in a tent that summer. In contests of marksmanship Paul's keen eye and steady hand ranked him as one of the best shots in Pennsylvania.

Mildred Abbey tended her three young sons as they traveled generally eastward, camping each night, cooking over campfires, hauling water from nearby springs, relishing the daily foray into the unknown, content to live in the present, trusting in their collective will to survive.

Mildred kept a journal that gives a vivid account of that time:

The first big storm hit us last night. Thunder and lightning and wind! Ned and Hootsie had gone to sleep and I took J. C. [the baby] and crawled into the car while Paul did what he could to make the tent windproof. Then he got into the car, too and stayed until the storm abated. And how it stormed! This morning there was a big dead limb on the ground outside, which, if it had hit the car would have ruined us and our outfit. But we didn't even hear it fall and were probably sitting blissfully in the car, eating Ida's candy and laughing at the storm when it happened. . . .

The grass is thick and green and short. We get our drinking water about a hundred yards down the road. Paul dug out a spring right here in the orchard and Hootsie threw stones in it a few minutes ago so it's quite muddy now. He also emptied my vinegar bottle into an old tin pail to make "mayonnaise"; threw mud into our "refrigerator" on top of the butter; spilled water around in a lot of places where I didn't want it, etc. Some boy! Ned isn't nearly so mischievous as Hootsie but he's such a little grouch that strangers decide that he is the worst of the two.

Later that summer of 1931, Johann Abbey died. As the depression wore on, Paul Abbey took a job selling subscriptions to the *Pennsylvania Farmer.*

"We had sixty-seven acres here," he recalled.

I sold ten acres of it to that fellow up on the hill. We had real good bottomland. The last tomatoes I raised, I filled up seven bushel baskets with nice rounded tomatoes. Took 'em to town and sold 'em for seventy-five cents a bushel. At the same time, I was selling the Pennsylvania Farmer magazine. By the time I had those tomatoes loaded in the baskets clean and nice and sold for .75 cents a bushel, I'd go off on my subscription route for the Pennsylvania Farmer. I'd go to people's farms to tell them when their subscriptions had run out. And by that evening, I'd made another five dollars. So I didn't plant any more tomatoes.

I raised the family with the Pennsylvania Farmer through the depression. And it was a depression. I really sold the Pennsylvania Farmer. I made money selling it. I didn't argue with anybody. If someone didn't want it, I went to the next guy. That's all there was to it. They all knew the paper. It had been in circulation for years. I worked the panhandle counties down in West Virginia. They hadn't been worked for a good while but all the farmers knew the paper. I would stay down there for maybe a couple weeks at a time. Twenty-five—thirty dollars a day.

When the Great Depression was followed by World War II in 1941, Paul and Mildred Abbey bought a farm of 120 acres and a seventy-five-year-old farmhouse on Red Dog Road near Home. Their family had grown by two more children, their daughter Nancy and their son William Tell Abbey. Paul Abbey worked the land to support the seven Abbeys.

We raised tobacco down here one year. Nancy and I planted vegetables and they all grew. We learned how to plant without stooping. I would walk along and punch the soil with my heel and Nancy would follow along and drop in the seeds. Billy would shovel a little dirt on top. Nancy would go down every day and squash all the bugs on the beans.

I trapped all up and down this stream. I had 140 traps set one year. I'd get muskrat, mainly. Skunk. Possum. Coon. I'd get a fox, occasionally. Mink.

The farm greatly influenced young Edward Abbey. His body was strong and well-knit and his curiosity profound. He learned to read by the age of four and thereafter read incessantly. His sister, Nancy, recalls his cunning:

There was an orchard up there on the other side of Red Dog Road where Ed would escape when work was to be done. He'd go up into the trees and read. Our dad swears that he knew that Ed was up there. One time, Dad was working in the strawberry patch up there. Dad said, "Ned will you go get me a hoe?" Ed said, "Where is it?" And Dad said, "You mean to tell me you've lived on this farm all these years and you don't know where we keep the hoes?" Ed said, "Yes, and I'm proud of it."

Paul Abbey was a handsome man, tall with penetrating eyes. More than one Appalachian lass looked on this outspoken rebel with favor. And more than one neighbor was put off by his politics. Little by little, Mildred Abbey grew embittered by the hardship imposed by his lifestyle of socialist self-sufficiency. There was rarely meat on the table, and that came mostly from hunted squirrels and rabbits.

She responded gracefully, tapping into her personal reserves of energy and imbuing all her children with a sense of her will. She was as devout a Presbyterian as her husband was not, and while she didn't demand Christian faith of her children, she insisted that they comport themselves according to her own spirit of morality and ethics. This tiny woman was loved and respected by all and year after year inspired not only her own family but also the members of her community with her wit and perseverance, her sense of duty to the common good, her wisdom. Generations of Presbyterians in

Home, Pennsylvania, were moved by her musical talents as she directed the church choir and played the church organ. Abbey's taste in music was shaped by falling asleep as a child listening to his mother play the music of Mozart or Bach or Handel.

Ned lorded his intellect over his younger brother Hoots, and their rivalry seemed endless. Because they were closest in age and strong as young stallions, they fought, argued, and competed. While Ned may have had a modest edge intellectually, Hoots was tougher. Both were fearless. In their myriad fights, Hoots generally emerged victorious. He recalled that Ned was a faster runner, and when the chips were down, their blood ran thick. Ned would never back down.

One time Ned and I were going to high school in Indiana, just walking down the street. We were about to cross the street where we had the right-of-way and this car pulled up with the hood right across the crosswalk. I started to walk around the front of it and Ned, with his big long legs, just stepped up on the hood and walked across the hood and down the other side. He didn't even look back. Nobody said anything. It just took everybody by surprise.

He would do what he wanted to do when he wanted to do it. He didn't like policemen. I know that.

Hoots reiterated the tremendous political influence Paul Abbey held over his children.

Dad was a socialist, which was sort of anarchistic in a way. It went against the prevalent theme in this country. He influenced all of us. I went along with Dad's ideas about spreading out the wealth. The rich people had all the wealth and there were too many poor people. Now I see the fallacy of that. In a true communist society, it would be like a bunch of ants in an anthill. Everybody's the same. People aren't the same.

It was Hoots's destiny to do most of the chores around the farm. "Ned shirked work at every opportunity. He believed that manual labor was beneath him." Ned was determined to pursue his own interests first. Baseball was a passion for the Abbey boys, although the Little League had yet to emerge. All the boys had learned to throw well by practicing with rocks from an early age. Hoots played first base or right field. Young brother Johnny was an infielder. Ned was both pitcher and organizer for their pickup sandlot baseball team. Their team challenged other teams around Indiana County.

The Abbey children attended Rayne Township Consolidated Elementary School, where Mildred's father, Charlie Postelwaite, had once been the principal. They later attended high school in nearby Indiana, the county seat. And most of them attended college for at least part of their academic careers at Indiana State.

Young Ned Abbey had a bent for drawing and a good ear for music. He wrote incessantly and well and was regarded as a talented youngster by many of his teachers. Ned became a good cartoonist. His cartoons were thematic, featuring a hero who combated evil, generally manifested in a villain whose elongated thumbnail served as his dagger. Abbey was as independent as his milieu would allow, but not so independent that he could completely shirk his chores on the farm.

He wrote a mini–epic poem in 1948 that recounted much of what he had seen thus far. About life on the farm he wrote:

> There was lots of work, I remember that,
> Hoeing the corn through the sweltering summer,
> Chasing over hills for fugitive pigs,
> Steering the cultivator through knee-high corn,
> Pitching manure in the fragrant springtime,
> Shocking wheat and pitching hay,
> Plowing up potatoes and grubbing for them
> In the loam on hands and knees,
> Cutting corn and husking corn,
> And piling fodder on the wagon,
> Digging holes and setting posts
> And stretching wire for miles . . . and miles.
> There was always an abundance of work

And never a shortage of tasks and chores.
I knew then that I hated life on the farm.
Now, of course, I'm not so sure.

One of the most significant accomplishments of Abbey's youth was his invention of the portable pigpen. This contraption was about twenty feet square, mounted on wheels so it could be moved from one patch of ground to another as the need arose.

In 1944 the war was raging in Europe and the South Pacific. When he was but seventeen years old and soon to be drafted, Ned was bitten by the Abbey wanderlust. With twenty bucks in his pocket and a bindle of sorts, he stuck out his thumb and hitchhiked across America. He made it to Chicago, a city he instantly disliked. In Minnesota he was picked up by a homosexual shoe salesman whose advances he adamantly resisted. He continued on his journey.

Across a continent I once traveled all alone,
Thinking red thoughts and riding on a thumb
Of great Ambulatory prowess. I met a man
In Madison who told me of a man in Laramie
Who knew a man in Jacksonville who had a cousin
By the name of Simp Salabaster who imagined
That he was a flower of some kind.
He was.

In old Pierre I met a man who played the guitar
And sang a song about a beautiful virgin girl
Who wandered in a park one evening and stretched
Out on the grass and fell asleep and dreamed
That she was a whore and when she woke up
Several hours later and found a two-dollar bill
On the Grass beside her she realized that
She was.

Ned ran out of money in South Dakota and spent ten days bucking wheat under the hot sun of the northern plains. He continued on to Wyoming and caught his first glimpse of the Rocky Mountains on the far horizon. That magnificent range lured him like the song of the siren and changed his life. Although he was offered a job on a ranch in Idaho, his forward momentum carried him westward until he reached the Pacific Ocean. He had spanned the breadth of the continent.

> In Seattle I met a man who told me a story
> About a little boy of unusual imagination
> Who liked to toddle out onto the state highway
> Every morning and lie down on the concrete
> And pretend that he was the tragic victim
> Of a traffic accident. One day his mother
> Went out to get him and found that
> He was.

He headed south to Portland and beyond and finally caught a ride with a con man named Fern. Fern taught him how to siphon gas from parked cars. Fern also committed a robbery, and he and Ned went on the lam. Farther south, Fern stopped the car so that Ned could take a leak. When Ned returned, the villainous Fern had driven away, taking all of Ned's gear and money with him.

Ned was left with his jackknife and a dime. He bought himself a cup of coffee, which he heavily fortified with sugar and cream. This liquid meal sustained him long enough to find a job knocking pecans out of a tree. A day's worth of nut busting gave him the wherewithal to get to Stockton, California, where he found work in a cannery, hauling crates of peaches to women who peeled and pitted the peaches prior to canning. After two weeks he had saved enough to quit and light out for the south country, forty bucks to the good and considerably wiser, a strong young man with adventure in his heart. He passed through Yosemite and Fresno and traveled south to Bakersfield and onward to Needles.

Needles in the summer is one of the hottest places in America. The Mojave Desert landscape is weird, eerie—pinnacles of stone pointing up into the awesome heat, human survival made possible only by the presence of the Colorado River.

Ned stood the day long, trying to thumb rides from the few cars that drove eastward into Arizona. The meager shade of the mesquite kept him from succumbing to sunstroke or heat exhaustion, but by nightfall he had failed to hitch a single ride. Far from forlorn, he struck up a conversation with a Negro hobo refugee from the previous decade. The two of them cooked up a meal, and the old hobo told Ned that there was a way to travel for free if hitchhiking didn't work. They were going to hop a freight. Anyone who has never hopped a freight has missed one of life's more provocative moments. It is not for the faint of heart or for the uncoordinated. You run alongside the rolling freight car, all too aware of the steel wheels rolling ever faster along the tops of steel rails. You carry your bindle in one hand, grab hold of the edge of the freight car door with the other, test the tug of the increasing momentum, throw in the bindle, and close in a mighty leap of body and faith, pulling yourself up into a dark interior inhabited by . . . ? Ned made it with the help of his hobo mentor and soon fell asleep as the train clattered through the night.

> Halleluiah! I'm a bum!
> I too
> Have hopped freights
> Ridden boxcars
> Coal hoppers
> (Tho never the rods)
> Crept through railroad divisions
> Outrun station guards
> Fallen on cinders
> And seen the land
> From a side-door Pullman.

They got as far as Flagstaff, where Ned was arrested, hauled off to jail, and tossed into a tank that smelled of vomit, piss, and the deadly breath of wasted winos. A special cell had been set aside for a madman who howled like a dog in the night. Ned wasn't afraid of the sick old men who were his cell mates, but he was stunned by the conditions in the jail.

The next morning Ned was taken before the judge and fined a dollar for vagrancy. Then one of the cops took him to a restaurant and bought him breakfast with the buck he had been fined, deposited Ned at the eastern outskirts of Flagstaff, and told him never to return.

Hitchhiking was fruitless, and Ned spent a cold night shivering beneath the high-country pines. He was now seven thousand feet above sea level, and the nighttime air was thin and icy. The next day he hopped another freight train, solo, and by afternoon he was staring into the mysterious red canyons of New Mexico.

By late afternoon the freight train had arrived in Albuquerque, which in those days had a population of less than forty thousand. Ned departed the moving freight train, walked through the tough end of town to the bus station, and bought a ticket for Home.

My days have been so wondrous free
So wondrous free
So wondrous free
I think no one will ever see
Such liberty
Such liberty.

A year later, in June 1945, Edward Abbey was drafted. The war had dragged on for nearly four years. Abbey and his fellow recruits were certain that they were going to be part of a massive invasion on the main island of Japan.

Any recruit with a modicum of intelligence and imagination cannot but wonder, "What in the hell am I doing in the army? Do I really believe in this cause enough to relinquish my life?" This became a condition of Abbey's and his fellows' thinking as they prepared for a military landing in which their ranks were sure to be decimated, possibly halved, conceivably annihilated.

Then on August 6, 1945, the newly named U.S. Air Force dropped an atomic bomb on the Japanese city of Hiroshima, killing tens of thousands, mostly civilians, in a horrendous moment of infamy that staggered the spirit of mankind. Three days later they did it again to Nagasaki. The era of depersonalized, nonselective, amoral warfare had arrived.

Abbey and his fellow recruits were spared the invasion of Japan—but at what price! On some fundamental emotional level Abbey was victimized by inner conflicts, horrified by man's lack of restraint in inflicting mass mayhem.

Relieved, dazed, sick at heart, Abbey was sent to Italy instead of Japan, where irony fated him for the military police. He was issued a .45 automatic pistol and a motorcycle named "Crash" and charged with the tasks of policing his comrades and thwarting the ubiquitous black marketeers of liberated Italy.

In early 1946 Abbey wrote a letter to his family describing life as a soldier:

Napoli
February 27, 1946
Dear Family,

There's not much that's new to write about. I'm still riding "Crash" (motorcycle) and becoming more reckless each day as my skill grows.

The big change is our relations with our Allies. The 803rd no longer rules Napoli. We are not allowed to arrest Limeys (British) or Ginnies (Italians) anymore except when they are fooling with American lives or property. And there are far less Americans around here now since so many Army outfits have moved north to Leghorn and Rome. Raids are being continued, however, for Army property continues to disappear. Let me describe a typical raid:

"Well, men," says the C.O., grinning as he repeats the old introduction. "This is it. Tonight we raid the town of X. We leave here at 2400 hours. At 0130 we pick up 50 carabineri (Italian police). At 0200 we meet companies B, C and D and proceed together to town X. At 0300 we hit them. Co. A is assigned the northwest sector of the town. Every house and building will be searched. Any questions?"

At midnight, we pile into trucks and begin the long rough ride to X, which by now we have found out to be Aversa, a town about the size of Indiana. Aversa is Off Limits to Allied troops and has a bad reputation. I thank myself for drawing a Tommy-gun.

We arrive on time, block the main roads leaving Aversa, and split up into groups of four, three M.P.'s and one carabineri. The carabineri are necessary formalities for every raid. They are really search warrants on legs. We're not supposed to break into Italian homes without one of them.

We start down a black unlighted street. The town, except for a few dogs, seems sound asleep. We are on the alert tho, for Aversa is infested with AWOLs and AWOLs are usually armed.

With me are Deer and Morrow. We three always work together, for we are all completely uninhibited and like the same thing, violence. Deer, in particular, is the kind known as "Ginny-happy." He'll beat an Italian senseless just for the sport of it.

We stop in front of a big house that looks reasonably prosperous.

"Let's go!"

"O.K."

We kick loudly on the door.

"Abri!" I say, being the linguist of the trio. "Abri presto! Este le polizia militere! Subito! Abri!"

There is a faint stirring within. Deer, the impatient one, throws himself against the door. It groans painfully. Again. Crash! In we go. The interior is as black as a supply sergeant's heart.

"Luce!" I shout, "luce?"

Morrow snaps on his flashlight and finds the light switch. We find ourselves in a typical middle-class living room, richly cluttered with bric-a-brac, furnished in atrocious taste, something like the old Victorian manner. The walls are nearly covered with those horrible Italian religious pictures showing a tortured Christ with a huge gray heart shining thru his chest and blood all over the place.

We start tearing the place apart. In a moment the usual short, fat Italian matriarch waddles in, anguishedly crying, "Mamita mia! Mamita mia!"

"Dove el cigarettes?" I ask in my beautiful Italian. "Dove pistola? Dove penesilen? Dove soldat negro Americani?"

"No got! No got!" she wails.

"She's a liar," says Morrow, lifting a carton of Camels from a flower vase. She sure is. In the next room we find a pretty little .38 revolver under a pillow and in the kitchen, stuffed in the oven, we find three Army field jackets, brand new, with tags still pinned on. We're quite elated. Aversa promises to be a good town.

The next house yields nothing but a G.I. fuel can.

"We gotta get somethin here," says Deer, "ask the old man where the wine cellar is. I'm thirsty."

"Same here," says Morrow.

"Dove sesti le cace vino?"

"Ah, pizons, es aqui . . ."

The old man leads us down an ancient stairway, down and down, until finally we enter a large cave-like room. Three huge wooden casks nearly fill the place. Deer tugs vigorously at the plug in the bung hole but fails to get it out.

"Well, there's an easier way," he says, pulling out his .45 and firing into the end of the barrel. The good red wine spurts forth like arterial blood. We gather round the wounded cask.

In the courtyard of the next place we are greeted by a huge black mongrel. It makes a vicious lunge at Morrow, nearly knocking him over. In an instant, two .45s and a sub-machine gun are pointed at that miserable dog. His life hangs by a canine whisker. More courageous than intelligent, he charges again. The courtyard resounds with gunfire, the dog spins in midair as if kicked, and flops lifeless to the ground. T.S., Fido . . .

Supercharged with vino and flushed with our heroic victory over the cur, we invade the terrorized household. Mamita mia!

We go our merry way, breaking down doors, frightening little children, insulting signorinas, kicking dogs, sampling vino, and occasionally confiscating a little American property.

It's nearly dawn before we run into our first AWOL.

"Hey," yells Morrow as we're searching a young girl's bedroom, "there's somebody under the bed."

"Well, drag him out."

"He won't come."

"Use your persuader."

"Don' shoot, boys, don' shoot, ah's a comin'."

A well built Negro crawls out, dressed in civilian clothes.

"Buon giorno," I quote with quaint humor.

"Boys, ah am askin' youall to consida'. This gal heah is mah wife, practically, an' we is leadin' a quiet peaceful life. We ain't botherin' nobody . . . please, ah asks youall, let us alone, let us alone. Don' take me away, please, it won' hurt youall to lemme go and if youall arrests me yall break this lil' gal's heart . . . please . . . ahbegs yuh . . . (the girl is weeping miserably by this time) . . . please, boys, considah' . . . please . . ."

Deer, the true M.P., reacts in his typical manner.

"Let's see your pass, nigger."

"Don't be silly," says Morrow, "he's probably been AWOL for a year. Come along, you, we're going for a ride."

My heart bled for him as we led him away and I cursed the fate that made me an M.P.

Rebel?

What's the use.

This letter should be entitled, perhaps, "Confessions of a Gestapo Playboy." There's no denying it, we often act like Nazis.

After a raid, I usually have a moral hangover that's far worse than the alcoholic type. Oh well, I must avoid boredom.

Achtung!

Ned

In the autumn of 1946 Paul Revere Abbey volunteered through the Brethren Service Center to go as a horse tender on a United Nations shipment to Italy.

In all, thirteen horse tenders, including Paul as foreman, loaded 325 horses aboard the cargo vessel *Wooster.* Most of the horses were ailing, having survived on short rations in a stockyard for two months. The horse tenders did their best, but one after another, horses became gravely ill and died, their carcasses slung by winch up and over the side into the heaving sea. For fifteen days of horse frenzy, sickness, and death, the veterinarian was at a loss. Finally, with the help of Paul Abbey, he performed an equine autopsy. The stinking innards revealed the presence of the dreaded botfly larva, which had infested the horses' intestines. In all, forty-five dead horses were committed to the deep before the *Wooster* wended its way through the still-mined Mediterranean Sea to reach Trieste. The seagoing cowboys put in for a bit of shore leave, and Paul Abbey and a friend hitchhiked to Gorizia, on the Yugoslav border, to visit Ned. He had no idea they were coming. They dropped in on him unannounced on Thanksgiving Day to have dinner with him at his army mess. It was guest day, and the hungry children took advantage of it. "What pathos," Paul recalled, "to watch the little war orphans impatiently awaiting their turn to be served, and the soldiers, unaccustomed to the task, helping them manage their food."

After dinner they walked into the hills for a view of the city and the surrounding country, with the Julian Alps in the background. They took a taxi into Trieste, which cost the equivalent of forty cents apiece for the forty miles. Ed obtained a three-day pass and stayed with them on the ship until it sailed for Venice.

His father's visit gave Pfc Abbey a lift in morale as he entered the "short-timer" phase of his military career. He had seen the Alps and observed the beauty of Italian women; he had served his country. But on leaving the army in 1947, he wasn't given a good-conduct medal—a fact of which he was proud.

By mid-February he was a free man, a veteran of the U.S. Army, just twenty years old.

chapter 2

THE DEVIL'S MANIFESTO

Do not flee, fools!

I am Lucifer, the rebel, the defiant one.

Listen to me:

I preach the gospel of sweet anarchy.

I say unto you—do as you please!

Ignore the graybeards, scorn the saints, revile the

revivalists, spit upon the moralists!

Tear down the walls, destroy the fences, bridge the moats, shatter the prisons!

Strangle the priests, hang the ministers, rape the

nuns, roast the evangelists!

Outlaw law, overrule rules, decode codes, mortify

morals, lessen mores, convict conventions!

Do all these—then do as you please!

Dance in the streets, roll out the barrels, sing

in the parks, make love in the churches!

Carouse, careen, raise merry cain . . . and when you tire,

come down to Hell, where we'll play games

through all eternity.

—Edward Abbey, age twenty and a half

Are anarchists born or made? To me there is no doubt whatsoever. Anarchists are born. If government, oligarchy, corporations, power mongers threaten, anarchists will rise and seek to thwart them.

Perhaps the anarchist responds to some atavistic urge to protect freedom. There is an arbitrary line that must not be crossed by any authority, especially one empowered by an economic oligarchy. The anarchist, the free man, knows where this line lies and guards it well. When this boundary between freedom and serfdom is breached, wrote the young Edward Abbey, "the good anarch suspends his moral allegiance to the State, disavows his duties as a citizen, and refuses to obey the law."

Abbey regarded total personal liberty not as a privilege but as the right of every human being *so long as one man's liberty did not encroach on another man's liberty, or woman's.* Wrote the twenty-four-year-old Abbey, "My own liberty is to a high degree dependent upon respecting the rights of others, thus limiting my own liberty in order to secure and increase it." Granted, there are fine lines and hairs to be split in this interpretation of personal freedom—enough to drive any passionate, well-intended soul into a state of confusion or neurosis. Yet most good people rely on their native intuition to determine the difference between right and wrong. To an evolved human, these distinctions are clearly discernible.

In 1913 the celebrated anarchist Pyotr Kropotkin wrote,

> The anarchists conceive a society in which all its members are regulated, not by laws, not by authorities, whether self-imposed or elected, but by mutual agreements between the members of that society, and by a sum of social customs and habits—not petrified by law, routine or superstition, but concordance with the evergrowing requirements of a free life, stimulated by the progress of science, invention and the steady growth of higher ideals. No ruling authorities, then. No government of man by man; no crystallization and immobility, but a continual evolution—such as we see in Nature.

For over thirty years I have had this provocative quotation pinned to the wall of my studio. Abbey read this declaration time and again and found no fault with it. We discussed Kropotkin in great detail. I told Ed how Allen Ginsberg had once read this statement on my wall and took umbrage at Kropotkin's allusion to "the progress of science."

"He did?" responded Abbey, nonplussed. "Doesn't he realize that it's not science but its application that can be villainous? You can't deny human curiosity. Science is a fine tool of the intellect."

Abbey had the highest regard for Prince Kropotkin, who demoted himself out of the Russian nobility and was exiled from Russia for decades because of his anarchist stance. Edward Abbey was a born anarchist. His love of freedom was inherent. He was fortunate to have been equipped with a great intellect and indefatigable curiosity. Throughout his childhood he read incessantly, and he began to write frequently at a young age.

> *I got interested in books and writing when I was a kid. I first discovered the creative impulse when I was a scorekeeper for our local baseball team. I did some creative scorekeeping, particularly trying to bolster my batting average. In my adolescence, I began to read some classic American literature. I had a couple of good teachers in high school who introduced me to Hemingway, Thomas Wolfe, Sinclair Lewis. I read a lot. I read and read and read probably hundreds of books during my teenage years.*

Paul Revere Abbey frequently quoted Walt Whitman. His son Ed probably heard "Uncle Walt's" maxim: "Resist much—obey little," when still a boy. Small wonder that individualistic, freedom-loving, bright young Ned, whose cultural environment was shaped and bent by the Great Depression, whose collar was basically blue and whose spirit was fired by the musical repertoire of the Wobblies, should recognize within himself the soul of the anarchist.

Abbey ruminated long on his military career. He was enormously impressed by the degree of authoritarianism the government of the United States had manifested in the name of liberty for all. Many conscriptees have reeled at the barrage of some master sergeant's barking, "Your soul may belong to God, but the rest of you belongs to the army. If you forget this, your ass is grass and I'm the lawn mower. If you get so much as a sunburn, *you* are damaging gov'mint property!" This philosophy was antithetical to Abbey's spirit.

Shortly after his discharge from the military, Abbey enrolled as a student at Indiana State Teachers College in Indiana, Pennsylvania, only a few miles from Home. Here he wrote and posted a letter calling for the ending of conscription by either burning draft cards or returning them to President Harry Truman:

A LETTER TO ALL STUDENTS AND FACULTY MEMBERS
HOLDING DRAFT CARDS:
Tomorrow, the anniversary of Abraham Lincoln's birthday, several thousand American men are going to attempt to emancipate themselves

from peacetime conscription by publicly ridding themselves of their draft credentials, either by mailing them to the President or burning them in public bonfires. This sounds like a foolish, crackpot scheme but it's not. It's much worse than that—it is a form of civil disobedience. That's something rather old-fashioned but in times like these, when America's government is diverting the major portion of its expenditures to armaments and our military leaders are trying to fasten permanent peacetime conscription to the nation, then, as Thoreau said, "It is not too soon for an honest man to rebel."

These men are certainly honest and sincere, and they are rebelling, not only against what they consider a violation of personal liberty, but against the slow and deadly drift towards World War III which an international armament race and universal conscription makes almost inevitable.

Among the men taking part in this national demonstration tomorrow are:

Rev. Donald Harrington
Community Church
New York City

Professor Milton Mayer
University of Chicago

Prof. Paul Schlipp
Northwestern University

Dr. Scott Nearing
(Economist, writer)

If you are aware of the dangers of peacetime conscription, tomorrow is the time to do something about it. Send your draft card with an explanatory letter to the President. He'll appreciate it greatly, I'm sure.

Signed: Edward Abbey

That very same day Abbey wrote for a freshman English class an essay titled "On the Necessity for Civil Disobedience":

> Just why should such apparently eminent and civic-minded citizens have committed themselves to such a drastic and ill- and *extra*-legal act, a kind of staged exhibitionism that seems like the show of a California-bred crank? Do they not realize that they will attract the suspicious eyes of J. Edgar Hoover, that they are violating Public Law Number so-and-so, enacted by the duly elected representatives of the people and according to an accepted provision of the Constitution of the United States? In short, are they crazy?
>
> That must be it. These men are crazy, "freedom-crazy," you might say, a disease acquired by reading too many books and doing too much thinking and believing too little of the national gospel. This affliction is not widespread but it is very difficult to cure and it is often fatal, as in the cases of Socrates and Bruno and Matteotti and John Brown and Sacco and Vanzetti. Prevention is much easier than curing.
>
> These men, and probably a few million others not taking part in the demonstration, are against peacetime conscription because they love freedom, and second only to that, peace.
>
> They feel and think and say that peacetime conscription is a direct and unforgivable violation of personal liberty, a major step towards the Prussianizing of America. They hold that forcing a man, against his will, to undergo peacetime military training, is fundamentally fascist. They fear and oppose placing more power than ever in the hands of the militarists, because that in itself is a threat and menace to free men. It's hard to say more. You either feel it or you do not. Maybe the freedom disease is manufactured in the bones, like red corpuscles.
>
> Love of peace is the second big reason. These men do not believe some of the things they are told, such as the theory that a huge mass army would preserve our country in an atomic war, or the more popular fallacy, that it would frighten war away. No, these contrary professors and preachers are certain that peacetime conscription, accompanied by a big armament program, leads by its own fatal logic to bigger, better war . . . sooner.

There you have it. In support of the ideas in the above two para-
graphs a handful of Americans are risking plenty. These draft card burners
think they can arouse the nation by defying Washington. Foolish? Perhaps. What do you think? Better yet . . . what are you *doing?*

Abbey's letter was the first piece of his writing to catch the eye of the Federal
Bureau of Investigation, which was just coming into its own in patriotic postwar America. J. Edgar Hoover, master of paranoia (who would soon share that
mantle with Senator Joseph McCarthy), initiated a witch-hunt that lasted for
years. At the age of twenty, Abbey had already been recognized as a potential
candidate for the stake.

There is no record as to the success of either Abbey's letter to the students
and faculty in Indiana or of the essay he wrote for his English class. But they
were most satisfying to Ed himself. His career as a gadfly was launched.

In early 1948 Abbey became an undergraduate at the University of New Mexico
in Albuquerque. The Southwest had preyed on his imagination ever since the
long hitchhike through America that had been his rite of passage. Midcentury
New Mexico was empty enough for the likes of Abbey. The University of New
Mexico was a perfect environment for him—a university on the edge of a
desert wilderness. Funded by the GI Bill, he majored in English and philosophy and began to meet fellow students with whom he would share ideas and
explore the Southwest, two of whom he would marry—and divorce.

Abbey owned an old Chevy, in which he commenced his serious explora-
tions of the Southwest. He began with the Sandia Mountain Range, at the base
of which sprawls Albuquerque. Ed told me of a time when he and a gang of
fellow students decided to climb Sandia Peak. They had been drinking and
decided at some point before midnight that the time had come to scale that
mighty mountain, whose name is Spanish for watermelon. On closer examination, the "watermelon" revealed mighty jagged scarps that could take a terrible
toll on living flesh and bone. Maybe a dozen began the journey up the mountain, but only two climbed all the way to the top sometime before noon the
following day. Ed Abbey was one of the two who made it. After he told me the
story of this climb, he turned and grinned at me and, pointing his forefinger to
the sky, said, "Resolve!" That word was a battle cry throughout his life.

He explored Puebloan ruins at Bandelier National Monument in the Jemez Mountains downslope from Los Alamos, home of the Manhattan Project and the family of A-bomb founders. Farther to the northwest he explored Chaco Canyon, with its array of ruins recalling a civilization whose descendants now inhabit pueblos along the Rio Grande and westward at Laguna and Acoma, New Mexico. He wandered north to Aztec Ruin near the banks of the Rio Animas, the River of Spirits, where an enormous kiva has been restored. He breathed the clear air of the high country and looked into canyons so filled with mystery that he ached to explore every one of them. He looked across plains at distant mountains and longed to plumb their mysteries.

He headed south into Mescalero Apache country and went trekking in the White Mountains. There he could look west past the Trinity Site, where in one blinding flash, illuminating the night sky of southwestern New Mexico, the Atomic Age had had its genesis. It would be this area around the White Mountains, near the northern edge of the Chihuahuan Desert, that Ed Abbey would use as the setting for his novel *Fire on the Mountain*.

Abbey fell in love with a young woman named Jo and became involved in student politics. Henry Wallace, a left-wing Democrat, epitomized the "common man" philosophy of the New Left. Wallace had served as vice president under Franklin Delano Roosevelt and would have attained the presidency had Roosevelt died a few months earlier. Instead he became the editor of *The New Republic* and in 1948 helped found the left-wing political alliance called the Progressive Party. He ran for president and gained a million popular votes but none from the electoral college. Abbey backed Wallace and tried to organize students on Wallace's behalf.

At the end of the spring semester of 1948, Abbey moved to Taos, New Mexico, where he spent a "wonderful and beautiful summer," falling in love three times and learning to dance "La Raspa," an energetic Mexican folk dance. He made new friends, including Richard Volpe, who would influence his life over the next few years, and wrote poetry and short stories.

He climbed Wheeler Peak, a mountain sacred to the Indians. From the thirteen-thousand-foot summit he could see 150 miles in those not so long ago days before the smog worked its way even to the northern reaches of the Río Grande del Norte.

By autumn Abbey would return to Pennsylvania, but not before he went to Venice, Florida, campaigning for Wallace. Then he descended into hell. He went to work in the General Electric plant in Erie, Pennsylvania, and earned modest wages for menial, mindless work. A GE supervisor recalled that Abbey was just an average employee who took excessive time off. When he quit, he gave as his reason, "I'm leaving town."

He returned to New Mexico in time to begin the summer session at the University of New Mexico. He moved in with his friend Dick Volpe and "listened to Christopher Salmon in the morning, swam in the afternoon, and chased girls at night." He played his flute, a practice that gave him enormous pleasure throughout his life.

At one point he and a few friends decided to drive to Los Angeles, where he had never been. They stopped to peer into the Grand Canyon, and Abbey couldn't resist hiking down into its bowels into a branch called Havasu Canyon. He didn't climb out again for five weeks. He lived there by himself, acquiring a bare minimum of supplies from the friendly Havasupai Indians. He kept his own company, ranging the fascinating, mysterious side canyons, swimming in the sacred waters of Havasu Creek, or paddling in the *tinajas,* natural basins filled with water. He very nearly met his end when he clambered down a canyon only to discover that he could go no farther and came within a hair's breadth of not being able to climb back out. This was for him a metamorphosis, where his spirit melded with the sense of place, where Abbey's soul adhered, once and for all, to the desert dust, the red rock, the piñon-juniper wood bark, the clear air, the wildness of the American Southwest. Years later he would publish a provocative account of this strange, almost eerie adventure in his great classic *Desert Solitaire.* The sojourn in Havasu Canyon was the beginning of his endless oscillation between solitude and society, and he was rarely totally happy in either set of circumstances. Always longing, forever turbulent, never at peace.

When he returned to UNM, he reveled in what he called his playboy days. He found women irresistible and fell in love repeatedly. Ed once told me that he had never made love to a woman he didn't love "at least a little bit." He spent time with his friend Bud Adams, went "charging into town every morning at 70 mph in a black Lincoln Continental," rode horses, and courted women. When Adams got married, he moved back in with "Volpe & Co."

and later with Alan Odendahl, with whom he shared a car.

At some point in his undergraduate days he met Malcolm Brown, who was to remain a friend for life. Malcolm knew all five of Abbey's wives. Early on, he recognized in Abbey a great love for the natural world and his abiding anger at extractors and developers who threatened that world.

Abbey was temporarily seduced by academe. As a young student of philosophy, he gained respect for an array of philosophers, including Pythagoras, Plotinus, Anselm, Bruno, Spinoza, Schopenhauer, and Henri Bergson. He had a special affection for Bertrand Russell because Russell wasn't an armchair philosopher but an activist!

Apart from philosophy, Abbey regarded himself as an unreliable scholar and failed both Spanish and handicrafts.

In 1949 he began work on his first novel, *Jonathan Troy*, which would eventually be published by Dodd, Mead. That same year he met Jean, a fellow student, and began a long affair, which he regarded as "deadly serious and troubling from the beginning." They would remain central to each other's lives for nearly two years. Marriage began to loom in their fantasy world. They traveled to visit their hermitlike friend Dick Volpe in his cabin near Red River, high in the Sangre de Cristos. Abbey described this as a beautiful and unforgettable place, "where Volpe kept a horse and had a pasture and a barn. There were aspens and pines and a snowfed brook ran nearby."

On another venture Abbey and Jean drove to Bluff, Utah, with the intent of visiting Monument Valley. But they ran low on gas and water and had to turn back.

In August 1950 Ed and Jean were married by a

sententious swine of a High Church Christing preacher who calmly after the service refused my champagne and accepted, without offering any change in return, my ten dollar bill. I had expected the dog to return $5 at least. No doubt he was getting even. . . . A few evenings before, he suggested that I teach Sunday School at his church. And I, to my shame, replied with loud, crass, gross, vulgar laughter. Truly, I am indicted.

They moved into the mountains east of Albuquerque near Tijeras, New Mexico, and apparently the road turned rocky immediately.

In the meantime Abbey began to develop some small reputation as a writer, contributing poetry to the *Thunderbird,* the UNM literary magazine, and writing what he himself considered brilliant papers on Shakespeare. In the autumn of 1950 Abbey became the editor of the *Thunderbird.* That same year he met the fiery artist Rita Deanin, with whom he "fell in love immediately, more desperately than ever before." He began to pursue Rita relentlessly, avoiding Jean and trying to separate from her.

Ed and Rita took a magical journey to the southern part of New Mexico, which utterly enchanted Abbey. Rita went east while Ed remained in Albuquerque to face the somber music of marriage on the edge of ruin. Somehow he found the wherewithal to continue to pursue his studies and to edit the *Thunderbird,* and somehow Jean had the strength of character to remain married to him.

There was something charismatic about Abbey, not just to women but to his male friends. Malcolm Brown, Fred Black, and others who got to know him during his days at UNM recall his face, with its piercing eyes, his energy, his seriousness. He was self-contained and self-directed. He didn't reveal much about himself, although he enjoyed learning the nature of those he selected to be his friends.

In March 1951, when he was editor of the *Thunderbird,* Abbey committed an act of literary heresy that people have never stopped talking about. He published an issue of the *Thunderbird* on the front cover of which was printed, "Man will not be free until the last king is strangled with the entrails of the last priest!" signed Louisa May Alcott. The campus went wild. Ed wouldn't rescind the issue or apologize, and his tenure as editor was terminated. Even the Albuquerque papers criticized him. Few, if any, including the FBI, recognized that the quotation was from Voltaire. Even now, over fifty years later, many recall that incident, some with glee, others still affronted.

Abbey's friend Fred Black was on the staff of the *Thunderbird.* Black rued Abbey's deed because it was both offensive to many and suspended a literary venue. Black recognized Abbey's dark humor but considered it in bad taste in light of the tri-ethnic cultural conditions in New Mexico. In a *Thunderbird* staff meeting, Black confronted Abbey.

"I told him that Louisa May Alcott had nothing to do with this," recalled Black.

Ed sat there holding his head in the fashion of "the ponderer." I went on to say that "there are no kings left, but there are many Spanish here and they are Catholic. There are priests and there is a hierarchy. This is offensive." Ed looked down his long nose and said "Goddammit, Black, these people had better learn!" "Learn what?" I said. "The truth!" said Ed.

Abbey was also condemned by many of the UNM faculty, including one of his professors who was queried by the FBI but remains unidentified to this day. He is quoted in FBI files as saying:

> Students on his staff . . . had displayed sounder and more mature judgment in trying to dissuade him from printing the cover statement. His persistence in pursuing his own somewhat pointless course seemed to me to suggest a stubborn ego, a taste for shocking the reader, a lack of maturity. . . . To me it is of importance principally as it is indicative of instability and poor judgment; Mr. Abbey may now have outgrown this phase completely.

In May 1951 Abbey was invited to speak to the philosophy students at the University of New Mexico on the subject of anarchism. The ideas presented in his paper foreshadow virtually everything he wrote thereafter. He identified Chuang-tzu, the great Taoist philosopher of the fourth century B.C., as the first recorded anarchist. He lauded Kropotkin for having introduced ethics and humanity into the deadly world of economics. He announced that painters, poets, philosophers, and other such "bums" should be free to explore as they would, drawing from the communal storehouse what they needed in order to survive because supporting the idle poor was less expensive than supporting the idle rich.

He regarded liberty as the supreme political good in that "liberty is to the spirit what blood is to the body." He strongly favored decentralization of power, stating,

> *Power must be taken away from those benevolent bureaucrats always found clustered like ants over honey in the capitals of politics and finance, and returned to the communities from which it (and they) came.*

He contended that the people should be armed and able to police themselves rather than relying on a professional police force, which inevitably serves the highest bidder. He touted the use of contraceptives, stating that the anarchist needed vast open spaces in which to practice freedom rather than having to submit to "the steady suffocation of liberty under the weight of mass overpopulation."

He called himself a barefooted anarchist, asserting that shoes were "a grudging concession to our cement civilization." And he announced his unyielding loyalty to his family and friends, quoting E. M. Forster: "If I had to choose between my friend and my country, I would choose my friend."

He was twenty-four years old, yet his philosophy was fully formed. In the future he might refine his thinking, but he stayed true to his anarchist position with an abiding resolve that was a major characteristic of his makeup.

He was a revolutionary with a sense of humor. West of Albuquerque on the horizon are several tiny volcanoes thought to be extinct. Ed Abbey couldn't resist gathering a bunch of old tires, hauling them out to one of the volcanoes, dumping them in, and igniting them, thus causing the local population to believe that a volcanic eruption was imminent.

It was in this same spirit that Abbey led nightly attacks on the billboards that desecrated the land along Route 66, the highway that connected St. Louis to Los Angeles. Although he much later called himself a scrivener who did nothing more than sit down and write about it, he was indeed an activist who did his fair share of "night work," that honorable activity intended to lead to the restoration of natural habitat.

Abbey characterized his final semester at the university as follows:

I am filled with admiration upon recalling my last semester at New Mexico University, when, in addition to being alive, I was carrying on the following activities simultaneously:

1. taking six fulltime academic courses, working hard enough to get "A's" in everything but French (that ugly language!), completing a double major in Philosophy and English, and graduating "with honors" (two projects in independent research);

2. writing 100 pages of my novel;

3. *editing, contributing to, getting in trouble with and getting fired from the student literary magazine;*

4. *working part-time in Riddle's tile factory;*

5. *separating from and trying to divorce my wife;*

6. *falling in love with and carrying on an intense affair with a crazy girl sculptor and painter;*

7. *spending the last six weeks of the semester without a roof over my head, living in a sleeping bag on top of a small hill in Tijeras Canyon.*

On May 11, 1951, Abbey received a letter announcing that he was to be awarded a Fulbright scholarship to spend an academic year in Edinburgh, Scotland, ostensibly to study philosophy and literature and to advance his knowledge of Robert Burns, the national poet of Scotland, who fascinated Ed. He was to receive the sum of fifty-two pounds a month on which to live and pursue his studies.

Burns lived a scant thirty-seven years. His father was an impoverished farmer, and early on the young poet rebelled against the existing social order. Abbey identified with Burns and was captivated by his point of view. He gave the name Burns to the most heroic of his literary characters, who would appear as a leitmotif in four of his anarchist novels.

That autumn Ed and Jean Abbey traveled to Edinburgh, bleak and gray after life in "the Land of Enchantment." Jean tried to acquire work papers so that she could augment the family income. But their marriage had worn thin, and she left Ed and came back to America well before Christmas. Abbey missed Jean, but he was still infatuated with Rita, with whom he had fallen in love before leaving New Mexico.

He continued to work on his novel *Jonathan Troy* and pursued his studies only sporadically. His journal reflects the inner sadness that marked his whole life:

I am lonely, I am unhappy. I cannot say what it is that I am feeling. There is no music for it, there is no art. . . . I know that I am alone, that I am lonely, that I am haunted by a vague cloud of sorrow and by a fading, floating image of a breathless loveliness which sings not hope to me, not warmth or happiness, nor meaning or end, but only is, only is,

and never will be more. I am heavy-tongued, slow-worded, thick and
halting and nearly dumb. I cannot say it. I am unhappy.
I am lonely. Give me your hand, whoever you are.

Abbey's thoughts frequently turned to death, not uncommon for a philosopher. While he regarded suicide as the given right of any man seeking charge of
his own destiny, his own dance with despair was never terminal. And his moth-
erly landlady, Mrs. Moore, could often cheer him up by tapping on the door
late at night and bringing him a tray of biscuits and cocoa or tea.

When he was unhappy in Edinburgh, his mind frequently returned to
the American Southwest. He dreamed of Baboquivari—a mellifluous word
that sounds like a birdcall. It refers to the highest peak in a range of mountains of the same name in southern Arizona, very near the Mexican border.
Baboquivari, known to the Tohono O'odham Indians as the home of I'itoi, a
deity partly responsible for the emergence of the tribe into this world, is also
sacred to a coterie of desert rats of mixed ancestry. Edward Abbey learned of
Baboquivari early on.

It was at Baboquivari that Abbey wanted to build his retreat, a fort to
be defended against government and bureaucracy. He imagined an adobe
hacienda with a tower where machine guns could be mounted and a guarded
arsenal filled with weapons of every nature and abundant ammunition.
There would be a library filled with great books and a conservatory supplied with every conceivable musical instrument. He would share this retreat with a few good friends—a painter, a musician, and a few revolutionary desperadoes on the lam. Women would come by invitation only. There
would be a corral full of horses and a storehouse of dried food, provender
against siege by the FBI. The hacienda itself would be constructed in a
completely defensible location, accessible only at risk to the interloper, in
the Sonoran Desert with its dangerous plants and animals. His journals
describe his ruminations:

BABOQUIVARI? Is it not a sickness, a disease, this psychic introversion
(if such it is) and is this particular daydream not a particularly vivid
illustration, objectification, concretion of it? Is the process outward,
inward; personal, social? Or both? What a crude withdrawal is this dull

blind contraction of the frightened worm, scared of light, afraid of openness, folding inward upon itself to shut out the outer. Are persons really such storms, such windowless monads, such anarchs as I sometimes seem to imagine? But what is it, really? I think, and thus I justify it, that the Baboquivarian dream is not a symptom and aesthetic expression of an unknown but powerful psychic cowardice within me, but rather the calculated and semi-instinctive response of the independent spirit, on the social plane, to the steady and accelerating growth of authoritarianism in every country in the world, an authoritarianism compounded of war and fear of war and fear of inner disharmony, of a renascent medievalism in art and thought, of the mass pressure of fastbreeding population, with its hunger and need for every inch of land.

Edward Abbey considered this defense of free men and wilderness as he sat in his garret in Edinburgh suffering the cold, moist air that drills into the bones of any desert rat. His passions raged frequently, tempered by despair; his mind relentlessly, endlessly gamboled over every philosophical terrain; he wrote myriad passages in *Jonathan Troy* and his journal; he sketched musical phrases and themes intended for massive compositions; he drew cartoons that reflected his perceptions. His being was embodied in his logo, the five-membered swastika, rolling through time and space.

Soon Abbey would turn twenty-five and reflect on what he erroneously termed the first third of his life, or "one third dead." Abbey wrote that he had lived for "25 years that I wouldn't trade for anything—except the next 25."

Much of Abbey's sense of himself in relation to the land was embodied in his dream of Baboquivari. He was a committed anarchist; he had already come to love the desert wildernesses of the American Southwest. He clearly perceived that the wilderness was ever more encroached upon by the spread of humanity and that the corporate structure of America controlled the governing body. His dream of Baboquivari would blossom in his writing and in the way he comported himself to the extent that he would come to be regarded by some as the most important anarchist thinker in America during the last half of the twentieth century.

In an age of human overpopulation, Abbey was a romantic whose interests would never coincide with those of the urbanite. He required space. He needed wilderness where he could test the strength of his resolve and cry out across an empty land. Baboquivari! would remain a battle cry, and though he would never live there, he would one day climb that distant, splendid peak.

On the winter solstice of 1951 Abbey left Scotland on a three-week trip, where he passed through France and spent time in Spain and Majorca. For part of this journey he traveled with three young men from Ceylon, who were as randy as Ed was. Ed alone abstained from purchasing the favors of ladies of the night, probably not out of any sense of morality but as a sense of aesthetics. For indeed Abbey was possessed of a sense of aesthetics. His soul was on fire, overcharged and ready to burst. His intellect ranged endlessly over any subject; in his inner ear, he heard every kind of music; he drew pictures of his impressions, a form for which he had some talent; and he wrote, keeping journals that never outnumbered the journals of Henry David Thoreau, a man for whom he had great respect.

Abbey was tremendously rich in potential at this time in his life, a warrior seeking the right battle. In Spain he was painfully aware that it had then been less than fifteen years since Franco had become dictator after defeating the leftists. It was chilling to visit a nation under the control of a man Abbey regarded as criminally insane.

Abbey's journal reflects his evolving interest in anarchism stimulated by the visit to Spain. He wrote and illustrated an essay titled "Tips for Anarchists." Near the beginning he points out that "government derives its moral authority from those whose ends it serves." He later describes a favorite melodramatic theme:

> *The harried anarchist, a wounded wolf, struggling toward the green hills, or the black-white alpine mountains, or the purple-golden desert range, and liberty. Will he make it? Or will the FBI shoot him down on the very threshold of wilderness and freedom? Obviously.*

This motif was to dominate several of his novels. He could readily imagine a man battling against himself or against other men, but he could not imagine man pitting himself against the natural world, for "the Earth was friend and home and life-source, life sustainer, life transformer, when men cooperate with Earth."

Abbey was highly complex, a system of coordinates hard to integrate. The ultimate individualist, albeit with compassion, he had the highest regard for friendship. One of the most powerful pieces of writing in his journals took the form of a prayer:

God help me, I will never sacrifice a friend to an ideal. I will never betray a friend for the sake of any cause. I will never reject a friend in order to stand by an institution. Great nations may fall in dusty ruin before I will sell a friend to save them. I pray to the God within me to give me the power to live by this design.

Ed Abbey remained true to that design all his life. When a friend was ravaged by remorse and despair, shunned by all, he was not utterly alone, for Ed was there beside him, true of heart, immensely strong in spirit.

In April 1952 Edward Abbey was twenty-five years old and had come to regard his Fulbright as a way to educate himself as he saw fit (which didn't necessarily correspond with academic guidelines). His visit to Spain had whetted his appetite for adventure, and he returned to the European mainland, this time traveling to Stockholm as the guest of a young woman and her family. His romantic fantasies were thwarted when he learned that she was engaged and was also busily studying to complete her own education. A subdued Abbey concluded his visit honorably.

After leaving Sweden, his luck improved when he met an attractive young woman from South Africa named Penelope. On his way to Vienna, in divided postwar Austria, Abbey found himself on a train passing through a Russian zone, guarded by polite young Soviet soldiers. Abbey was fascinated by their machine guns, which,

Russian made, looked efficient, simple, and well-cared for. I examined them with considerable interest, being very fond of such weapons myself. Though rifles are really much more fun, much more interesting. To me, I mean. Operating a sub-machine gun, if I remember correctly, is much like having an orgasm—sensually thrilling, pleasure quick and concentrated, but almost devoid of intellectual interest. While rifle shooting requires thought, patience, much calculation and skill, and involves precise, detailed and mathematical results and operations. Sex and logic; fire and ice; the water pistol and the .22. Where was I?

He was on his way to visit the fabled city of Vienna. The home of Mozart, Beethoven, and Strauss had lost its elegance during the war and had grown gritty and gray. He and Penelope went to a performance of J. S. Bach's *St. Matthew's Passion* that featured the famed Vienna Boys' Choir. They also attended a Communist meeting held at the Red Army Memorial in the Stalinplatz and saw more Russian soldiers, the young enlisted men lounging around looking bored in contrast to the officers, who were older, fatter, thick necked, attentive, and mean looking. According to Abbey, Russians were "the number one tourist attraction in Vienna."

One night, as was his wont, Abbey decided to go for a long walk. Needing a bit of solitude, Abbey left the room he and Penelope shared in a Soviet zone hotel.

Walking at night alone through the dim and lonely streets of Vienna— where are all the people?—I heard, seemingly from a great distance, a spasmodic wild vulpine howling, a chorus of drunken Cossacks, wild and strange, barbaric and complex, subtly beautiful. . . . I had to walk about ten blocks before I came in sight of a Red Army barracks, a huge old palace or something with sagging walls and shell-holes and blinded windows. But there was light beyond the blinds, and much noise, and every few minutes one of these short choral bursts of sound, of musical howling—there must have been a hundred men or more, but the harmony, highly chromatic and subtle, sounded as true and far more thrilling than any professional chorus. Outside—listening in. How I longed to join them, those barbarians, and share their songs and vodka, and share with them the heart's yearning for home, for the open steppes and plains, for the great skies and distant mountains of Russia—or Western America. Does it matter where? Of course that's what the strange songs were about— home and wind and vast space and wilderness and mystery—there could be no doubt about that. For an hour or more I stood outside listening, and never in all of Europe, at any time, have I felt more deeply the

trouble and longing of exile, and never have I felt, on this horrible old
continent, such comradeship with other men, as with these, my fellow
non-Europeans. And never, finally, was I more aware of what a tragedy
a war between Russia and America would be—of what our two nations
could share, could do together.

In June 1952 Abbey sailed for America, having flunked out of Edinburgh
and broken with Jean but greatly enriched by having spent nine months in
Scotland, ranged many miles about Europe, eaten well, skied high mountains,
tasted romantic love, enjoyed vicarious comradeship with Russian soldiers, and
written much of his novel *Jonathan Troy.* The vision of Rita danced before him
as he sailed across the gray Atlantic.

When Abbey returned to America, his friend from UNM, Alan Odendahl,
who was living in Washington, D.C., convinced him to take a job there with
the U.S. Geological Survey. Rita was staying near Provincetown, at the end of
Cape Cod. His family lived in Pennsylvania. Abbey himself was planning to go
to graduate school at Yale. It was too soon to head west, although his soul
yearned for the high desert. He was chronically low on money, as he would be
for years to come. Somehow Abbey convinced himself that a career in the
Foreign Service might offer an adventurous life. He made an application and
was given material for study to prepare for the civil service exam every career
officer must take before entering U.S. government employ.

The FBI began an investigation into the young anarchist's loyalty to
the United States of America. Their probe revealed that not only had Abbey
destroyed his draft card in 1948 and printed a subversive quote by Louisa May
Alcott on the front of the University of New Mexico literary magazine the year
before, he had also attended a Communist-sponsored event called the International Conference in Defense of Children in Vienna the preceding April.

The FBI, by now in the throes of the witch-hunt known as McCarthyism,
utterly missed the boat in their assessment of Edward Abbey. Not that Abbey
wasn't a politically dangerous animal, but he wasn't a communist. His anarchism was of one of the FBI's myriad blind spots.

Years later, when Ed and I were hiking one moonlit night in northern
Colorado, he recounted his recollections of Vienna.

When I found out that the FBI knew that I had gone to what turned out to be a Communist rally in Vienna, I was amazed. After all, I was chasing a pretty girl around that part of Europe. I didn't even fully realize that I had chased her into the forbidden Russian zone. I never could figure out who saw me there, how they knew it was me. It's pretty impressive how the government's got its spies everywhere. It's probably best we never talk inside.

Ed sought out Rita, who was still living and painting on Cape Cod. He had fallen deeply in love. Both artists, he and Rita were passionate about their work and each other. Rita told Ed that she wanted him to be the father of her children. This was the first time he began to imagine himself as a candidate for fatherhood or as a true partner in marriage, a soul mate sharing his life and sensibilities with a woman.

When he returned to Washington, D.C., and his dreary job, he felt trapped in a city he hated. He wasn't finished writing *Jonathan Troy.* He kept applying what he considered to be finishing touches, but the book never seemed to be done.

In the meantime a new novel had begun to form in his brain, *The Brave Cowboy,* whose hero he conceived as a sort of Don Quixote (without a Sancho Panza) riding a range fouled with billboards, highways, telephone wires. This new project roiling in his brain gave him the impetus necessary to snip the bureaucratic umbilicus, jettison the illusion of security, and leave town.

He didn't leave the East quite yet. He went to Home, Pennsylvania, to pay his respects to his parents in the tiny hamlet that seemed lodged in the nineteenth century. The autumnal wood smoke choked his heart with nostalgia, and then he was off. He boarded the Chief, the streamlined train that halved America, north from south. Abbey realized as the mighty train surged forward that another chapter in his life's journey was about to unfold. He was going to Rita, who was now back in New Mexico. He loved her. He questioned his destiny, then acquiesced. "Set me a task, my Jewish princess! Try me!—Absurdly soon!!"

chapter 3

On November 20, 1952, Ed and Rita got married in Albuquerque, New Mexico.

Marriage is one of the most difficult compacts to maintain. As Ed's mother put it, "Crises are easier to survive than the daily routine." But Ed and Rita's love was great. Two creative people, two spinning energy fields, dancing side by side, touching, fortified by love and its attendant activities. True, money was scarce, but what can you expect if you're an unemployed philosopher with a bachelor's degree to prove it? Abbey continued to work on *Jonathan Troy,* beginning a second volume, which would ultimately become the second half of the novel. On his twenty-sixth birthday Abbey wrote: "I'm as old as Keats now and haven't even got consumption. On the other hand, I have yet to write a decent sonnet."

The Abbeys moved to Taos, New Mexico, where they loved and fought and pursued their art. "What does it mean?" asked Abbey. "What will happen to us?" Malcolm Brown wisely pointed out to Abbey, "Married couples who continually fight with each other may really need each other as desperately as those apparently desperately in love—the fighting fills an important vacuum in their otherwise empty lives."

And then in June 1953 the news came that *Jonathan Troy* had been accepted by Dodd, Mead. A check for $500 confirmed that Edward Abbey was now a writer. A ten-year dream fulfilled! But Abbey reflected,

My joy was quiet, or almost null; I knew a steady pleasure—steady for a day or two—but no exaltation, no sense of triumph or liberation. Perhaps this hour was too long, too gradual in coming; perhaps too inevitable; perhaps not fully earned.

The novel was to be released in ten months. This short schedule all but exonerated Abbey from spending any more time on *Jonathan Troy,* the hero who reflected an aspect of himself as a youth.

This sudden release sent Abbey into a spiritual doldrum. He would soon enter Yale graduate school, and not only was he planning a second novel, *The Brave Cowboy,* he still tendered the notion of pursuing musical composition as a parallel art form. Even though he had plans for the future, he was immobilized by lack of motivation; becalmed, but not at peace.

There were days when Ed and Rita would wander into the high desert simply to look out over the beauty. Rita would sketch, and Ed would record his impressions in his journal. They were especially attracted to vantage points where one could look off into the distance and see mysterious landforms like the flat-topped mesa Pedernal. Part of Abbey's mind was seduced by the mystery of the landscape. Part of him pondered the meaning of art, its purpose. He drew enormously from experience, but he was creative about it, even in his journals. The essays he eventually published were largely distillations of actual experience, and his novels, while not strictly autobiographical, reenacted episodes from his life in mythic form.

That summer in Taos and nearby Arroyo Hondo provided Abbey many hours of reflection. He thought of his friends, some of whom he now considered enemies, one for having attempted to seduce his wife, another for having accused him of perpetrating the *Thunderbird* incident of two years before to aggrandize himself.

Both of these episodes rankled. Toward the would-be seducer, Abbey reacted straightforwardly: "I'll never speak to the bastard again!" Toward the critic, his reactions were much more complicated. He felt remorse for having "fraternized" with him after the fact. He invented a character named Alexander Flack with whom he had an imaginary duel. That was not sufficient.

What I fear is laughter. Not only others', but that of my demon self:
I would look ridiculous to myself, fighting a duel over an obscure
muddy misunderstanding now nearly two years old. But nevertheless,
the conscience, the taste of guilt, spoils my pleasure. Only through an
overt act of some kind can I rectify or mollify this remorseless soul-ache.

In certain instances, Abbey could indeed be stung by criticism.

Years later Abbey would confront "Alexander Flack" in Santa Fe and speak his mind with the intent of clearing his conscience.

That September the Abbeys moved to New Haven, where Ed entered graduate school in the Yale philosophy department, a dose of heavy Ivy that lasted two weeks before Ed realized that this ivy was a trifurcated variety—poison ivy—that blistered his being. Yale made him feel like a dilettante. He was disenchanted with his professors, who in his estimation were of a stature less than Plato (whom he despised). More important, he came face-to-face with his own truth: "I can no longer play at being an academic scholar; from here on it would require intense and genuine effort, and after all, I want to be a writer, not an academician. I must choose and I have chosen." It was also expensive to go to Yale, both fiscally and spiritually. By now Abbey's soul belonged to the Southwest. He had become a westerner, a wilderness romantic who had found a landscape big enough that his libertarian spirit would not feel crowded—at least for a few more years.

Abbey wanted to write a genuine western American novel where the land-scape and environment were fundamental to the novel itself yet a universal truth could be expressed. *The Brave Cowboy,* beginning to canter through his thoughts, concerned the dilemma of the freeman in the twentieth century, the ranger who finds himself continually at odds with technology and its culture.

He longed to pursue his art in the land of space and fine light, but life wasn't so simple. Ed was married now and not free to wander. In a moment of reaction to the interminable financial crisis, he sidestepped the academic atmosphere of Yale and landed in Rochelle Park, New Jersey, "the heart of the Great American Blight," where he found employment as a blue-collar worker. He spent his days "sitting at a bench winding fiberglass around transformer coils, laminating the cores, winding coils, jig-boring in modified specs, wedging one coil inside the other, testing." (It will be recalled that Abbey had flunked handicrafts at UNM.) The other five laborers in Abbey's section were like refu-gees from a tale by Nelson Algren: "ignorant, foul-mouthed, pleasant, genial, dirty-minded, unambitious, lazy, completely uninterested in their work, concerned mainly with home, family, sex, bowling, cars, payday." One of them, whom Ed dubbed "the Slasher," threw knives at pinup girls on the walls. There they were, the Joe Six-pack sextet, whose tempos were directed by the vacuous tattoos of Muzak that was piped in and out of your mind's ear—unless you were used to Beethoven, Shostakovich, or Stravinsky, at which point the vapid melodies lingered uninvited like synthetic syrup, deadening sensitivities, edging you ever closer to mediocrity or perhaps even some form of low-level insanity.

Abbey didn't resent his fellows or dislike them, nor did he denigrate them. As a syndicalist, he was their champion. He always defended the right of the working man to dignity and adequate recompense. But his high ideals still didn't make it easy to go to work in the numbing environment of a factory when he longed for empty space and the song of a hermit thrush.

It was necessary to earn a living. "The poor are materialistic. It takes money to be romantic." He was married and in love with his wife, but he was already skewered on the horns of his personal dilemma—wilderness and solitude versus love and companionship. In his journals he tenuously began to explore an idea that was to come to fruition more than three decades later in the semiautobiographical novel *The Fool's Progress.* He gradually came to think of these written insertions as *Confessions of a Barbarian,* which he soon came to abbreviate as BARB, whose hero was himself.

He regarded his journal as a vessel of his own personal truth, and it was his hope to speak only the truth in this account of his life. But like any diarist, he either needed to be able to lock the thing shut, hide it, or neglect to mention certain inadequacies of marital fidelity, either out of fear of being found out or compassion for his wife (or both). It's a complicated thing, keeping a totally accurate, honest journal. Abbey mentioned this many times over the years. Even so, it's not impossible to read between the lines or comprehend the code.

After the Yale debacle and a year into their marriage, he and Rita had moved to the megalopolis that includes Manhattan. They loved each other but were unable to agree on where they should live. One of Abbey's regrets about Yale was that it had brought them two thousand miles east of the Pecos. He realized that Rita wanted to go to Europe and see the art treasures of Italy and France. She was, after all, an artist who took her work seriously and had a healthy longing to match her perceptions against those of the European masters.

In December 1953 Abbey received the galleys to *Jonathan Troy* to proofread. Abbey's reaction—"The book seems even worse than I thought. Very juvenile, naive, clumsy pretentious. . . . Too much self-parody—self-conscious striving for stylistic novelties." In a word, Abbey hated the book and to the end of his life wished he had never written it, genuinely hoping no one would ever read it.

Later that month, at a party in Greenwich Village, he met Norman Mailer, the celebrated author of *The Naked and the Dead*. Abbey, reticent and shy, stood on the edge of the inner circle. But self-confident Rita intervened, and soon Abbey was a part of the small group who talked about books with the young celebrity. In retrospect, Abbey was more impressed with Mailer's success than his talent. This meeting served to strengthen his own resolve to finally become a full-time writer, a resolve that would be frequently tested.

Abbey began to consider what books to write, and he committed ideas to paper. He decided to create a systematic approach to writing and not try to do everything at once. He would outline his books in advance, and then within the clarity of the construct, he would write. Frequently he resurrected the old theme of the anarchist commune. One such commune he named "Grim Prospects, New Mexico," which became the title of a novel that would never be published.

He endlessly philosophized in his journals, carrying on a monologue with himself or perhaps writing for some as yet unidentified reader. In his journals, which became rich with notes, and his *Confessions of a Barbarian,* he forever pondered the purpose of existence, the meaning of being human.

I am an animal, of course, and proud of it, and I admire and respect my body. But the mind is no alien there. It belongs, whatever its nature, be it but a phosphorescent frothing of the brain or an independent spirit making a temporary home of my hard skull. Whatever, it's mine now, and the body too, both of them, and damned if I know where the division is. I don't believe it exists at all, you know.

In January 1954 his job was terminated. He was unemployed through no fault of his own, but the job had ended a few weeks shy of his qualifying for unemployment. He was caught in the recession of the early 1950s, which the Korean War had been unable to forestall. Nothing for it but to head west, which Ed and Rita did by way of the Big Smokies, New Orleans, Big Bend, and finally back to Albuquerque. If you're gonna be broke, better be broke in a compatible environment. They moved into an old adobe mansion where they became the caretakers, rent-free. They had a splendid view of the mountains that dominate the eastern aspect of Albuquerque.

It was on a Sunday morning some two weeks after moving in that Abbey built a fire in the woodstove and managed to burn the house down. Completely. Mud rubble. "A superb, an excellent conflagration, a blazing spectacle. Sightseers came from far and wide, and the press, too." I recall Ed telling me about this glorious event many years after the fact. He was still excited by it, grinning unabashedly, gesticulating, his hands spread wide to indicate the enormity and scope of the blaze like some maddened pyromaniac confessing his magnificent act!

The Abbeys needed a place to live and moved into Malcolm Brown's studio. The Browns and the Abbeys lived under separate roofs but within the same compound. The two couples formed something of a minicommune. Everybody was chronically limited of funds, but such is the nature of *la bohème*. Malcolm painted, as did Rita. Rachel Brown was a weaver; Ed was a writer. The experiment in cooperative living was reasonably successful, especially considering the "austere, irritating bout with poverty that both families had for a spell of five or six weeks."

Abbey was arrested for reckless driving and sentenced to three days in jail by a "dapper dainty little man with the eyes and lips of an adder." Abbey regarded this stint in the Albuquerque jail as field research. He was clearly (if involuntarily) adding to his store of experience for *The Brave Cowboy*. No doubt the novel's cast of jailhouse characters was founded on his perceptions of his fellow incarcerees. He noted that the writing of this novel wasn't so much fun as the writing of *Jonathan Troy*, which had been published but was "faintly reviewed, virtually ignored, and generally unbought." C. V. Wicker, one of Abbey's former professors and to some extent the prototype for one of the novel's important characters, insisted that it was a good book. (It was Dr. Wicker who advanced the $25 necessary to rescue Abbey from "the Duke City Bastille.") Abbey, though extremely critical of the book, was still disappointed at its brisk relegation to obscurity. Besides, he needed money.

Jonathan Troy has long been out of print, and there is no doubt that the ghost of Edward Abbey wishes it to remain so. Many times when visiting Ed, I would pull it out of his bookcase and open it. Ed would inevitably look at me in a most poignant fashion and say something like, "Please don't. It's a terrible book. I'd rather you didn't read it." What Ed detested is the character of Jonathan Troy. Abbey is dead now, and I have my own copy, a great gift of Tony DelCavo. It's not the great American novel, but it's a fair novel, not without literary craftsmanship. Something that every writer knows deep in his mind and gut is that once a book is published, it is out there, irretrievably. Its message has affiliated, to some degree no matter how tiny, with the zeitgeist. Sometimes this can be a tough lesson.

In the spring of 1954 the Abbeys drove all the way back to Provincetown, where Rita could find a job. Abbey wrote, struggling with *The Brave Cowboy,* which featured Jack Burns as the cowboy, loosely modeled on Abbey's friend Ralph Newcomb, whom Abbey described as a "charming, delightful, interesting, complicated, deep . . . man of talent . . . with an honest engaging soul." The freedom-loving Burns is determined to break his friend Paul Bondi out of jail. Bondi, thinly disguised as an aspect of Abbey himself, has been incarcerated for two years for refusing to register for the draft. This notion had been a part of Abbey's consciousness since the draft card event at Indiana State Teachers College back in 1947. Even though he had long considered the plot in its various incarnations, the novel developed a course of its own, directed more by inspiration than preconception. Ed was an artist, not a scientist.

In September 1954 the Abbeys returned to Albuquerque, where they moved back into Malcolm Brown's studio and Abbey continued writing *The Brave Cowboy.* He planned to enter graduate school at the University of New Mexico to pursue his master's degree. Plunging into the study of philosophy after the hiatus in his academic career, he wrote an occasional philosophical joke: "On Plato's Republic—Trouble with perfection, it leaves no room for improvement." Indeed, Abbey became the master of the one-liner: "Sex is at least one case where you get less out of it than you put in it."

Rita took a job and the Abbeys moved into town, where the gas heat was constant and the water ran hot and cold. There was even electricity, and though Abbey missed chopping wood and building fires, it was easier to pursue life as a student when the amenities included indoor plumbing.

At UNM, Abbey was studying with Dr. Archie Bahm of the philosophy department. It was Abbey's intention to write a master's thesis titled "An Inquiry into the General Theory of Anarchism." He got along with his professor very well, at least at the outset, and regarded him as an intelligent thinker and a master of dialectic. "As a man he's quite appealing: generous, liberal, helpful, friendly to all, kind, gentle, considerate in every way, optimistic, tolerant, truly interested in others, quite unselfish. . . ." Bahm was twenty-five years Abbey's senior and a prolific writer in his own right. His best-known book is an interpretation of the *Tao Teh King*, retitled *Nature and Intelligence*.

In May 1991 Archie Bahm recalled the young man he had known more than thirty years earlier:

> I was impressed by the depth of Abbey's concern for his philosophy—for his living it as well as writing it. He was a person who was committed to living and to trying to understand living and to living life the way he thought it ought to be lived. I didn't have any doubt about that in my contacts with him, which were a bit unfortunate because he was obviously anarchistic in his own way in terms of his own conceptions. When he came to us for a master's dissertation, as academics, Hubert Alexander (then department chairman) and I were interested in knowing, "Well, if you're an anarchist, what do you mean by anarchism?" We discussed the matter and he wrote a paper for us. In it he exhibited what we regarded as ignorance of the major anarchistic doctrines that have been presented in recent history, and we were a bit appalled, but that's pure academics, you see. If you're an anarchist, you should know something about anarchism as it has been expressed by recent anarchist thinkers. That was absent from his work, so we made him read up on the anarchists. This he did, and he turned in a very acceptable dissertation. He was a little reluctant and annoyed that we made him read up on some other anarchists. He must have benefited from this in terms of learning about the documents of these particular people. They had backgrounds and biases that were different from his own. His interest in anarchism grew out of his own life, you see. His anarchism was genuine in the sense that it was his own. You have to respect him for that. As an academic thesis, we thought he ought to know a little about the traditional anarchists and so we requested that he study. And he did.

The requirements of the academy didn't suit Abbey. Possessed of a brilliant mind and avid curiosity, he wasn't one to be defeated by the challenge of difficult reading. Quite the opposite: he loved it. But he was writing a novel, and he believed he already had an understanding of anarchist thought. In addition, he enjoyed the pleasures of exploring the countryside, listening to music, and human companionship.

The more I dim my eyes over print and frazzle my brain over abstract ideas, the more I appreciate the delight of being basically an animal wrapped in a sensitive skin: sex, the resistance of rock, the taste and touch of snow, the feel of the sun, good wine and rare beefsteak and the company of friends around a fire with a guitar and lousy old cowboy songs. Despair: I'll never be a scholar, never be a decent good Christian. Just a hedonist, a pagan, a primitive romantic.

But what's an honest soul to do? I don't know. I can say: be loyal to what you love, be true to the Earth, fight your enemies with passion and laughter; but what does this mean? It's a formula too general to be useful, an intuition too personal to be generally acceptable. So there you are.

Abbey read voraciously and often included in his journals passages that he felt were particularly profound or noteworthy. He read the writing of Spanish realist Ramón José Sender, who sought a meaningful philosophical and ethical system within the human condition in spite of its horrors. Wrote Sender in his preface to *Los Siete Domingos Rojos*:

People too full of humanity dream of freedom, of the good, of justice, giving this an emotional and individualistic significance. Carrying such a load, an individual can hope for the respect and loyalty of his relations and friends, but if he should hope to influence the general social structure, he nullifies himself in heroic and sterile rebellion. No man can approach mankind giving his all and expect all in return. Societies are not based on the virtues of individuals but on a system which controls defects by limiting the freedom of everyone. Naturally the system takes a different form under feudalism, capitalism and communism.

Let anarcho-syndicalists invent their own system, and until they have attained it, go on dreaming of a strange state of society in which all men are as disinterested as St. Francis of Assisi, bold as Spartacus, and able as Newton and Hegel. But behind the dream there is a human truth of the most generous kind—sometimes, let me insist, absolutely sublime. Is not that enough?

Sender's point is one any philosophical anarchist knows to be true: Anarchism in its highest form is not achievable, since it requires that all men and women be utterly responsible in their self-direction. However, this evolved state represents an ideal toward which to aspire and from which to view one's milieu. For Abbey, the phantoms engaged in this philosophical wrestling match were personified in a military-techno-industrial system that he saw creeping ever closer to subtle technocratic totalitarianism. This system lured the entire working class into a serfdom hidden behind television, a car in the garage, refrigeration, and alienating, mechanized employment that strengthened its host, a system of corporate capitalism whose underlying principle is "growth for its own sake."

Abbey challenged his professors with his passion but had to channel into the confines of an M.A. thesis. It began, he says,

> as an ambitious project—it was going to be a general theory of anarchism. The thesis committee and professors soon condensed it to a tiny little historical study of a few 19th century anarchist writers, like Proudhon, Kropotkin and Bakunin, so it ended up, like most master's theses, being nothing but a monograph on a very limited subject—namely, the ethics and morality of violence as a political method. Everything phrased in quite a circumspect manner, bristling with footnotes, half of it consisting of bibliography and notes. And thus I became a Master of Fine Arts, a degree which means absolutely nothing.

In spite of its academic language, Abbey's thesis had some meat in it. He spoke his mind when he wrote:

Violence in itself is an evil, granted; but unless one takes up a pacifist position (which has difficulties of its own) all those who are concerned with issues of good and evil—"men of goodwill"—may someday find themselves confronted with that critical situation in which all moral alternatives have been eliminated, by circumstances, but two: passive submission to unquestioned wrong, or the exercise of violence. Even though rebellion may be doomed to failure, in the sphere of practical results, and the ideal may never be realized, it is still necessary to keep the ideal alive and to maintain and preserve that state of tension between the good and the evil, between aspiration and resignation, which is the glory, and perhaps the essence as well, of civilization in the West.

Abbey did not submit this thesis, which he titled "Anarchism and the Morality of Violence," until 1959. His life meandered considerably from the time of his return to UNM until he was finally awarded his advanced degree.

The year 1956 was of singular importance to him. His second novel, *The Brave Cowboy*, was published, and he had begun work on the outline of a third novel, called *Uranium*. The atomic age had been born in Los Alamos, New Mexico. By now Abbey's travels had taken him deep into Utah, where manic uranium miners darted over the landscape in not quite defunct surplus jeeps crammed with water cans, spare gas, beans, Vienna sausages, Spam, deviled ham, white bread, whiskey, USGS maps, compasses, Geiger counters, shovels, and picks, the assorted accoutrements of the prospector. Much of the uranium used in Los Alamos had come from mines in Utah. Abbey pondered, then disproved the necessity of donning a lead codpiece.

On April 12, 1956, an eight-pound, twelve-ounce son was born to Ed and Rita Abbey in Albuquerque. He was named Joshua Nathaniel Abbey. Ed wrote: "May he be blessed by sky and earth, Heaven and Home; may he be brave, and lucky, and good."

Abbey had to earn a living wage. He was now a father, and Rita was in no position to work. Ed applied to the National Park Service and was accepted as the back country ranger for a remote monument in eastern Utah near Moab. The monument was called Arches because of the beautiful red rock landforms. Abbey was alone there. This wasn't a place for either an infant or a nursing mother, at least from the point of view of the mother. Rita and Josh headed east to Hoboken, where Rita's family lived.

Abbey was ensconced in a drafty trailer parked near Balanced Rock. He was alone in the desert at last, cast into a weirdly beautiful landscape that caught his heart and held it forever. Abbey began to keep his desert journal, noting the natural history of the ecosystem of which he had become a part, writing his reflections, noting the lore, communicating with himself.

Abbey was a great hiker. He ranged the landscape, always looking, always exploring, called by the sirens of the canyons, yielding to their invitation to enter and experience their inner beauty. Sometimes the beauty was so intense, he could only weep and wonder, at the exquisite grace of Delicate Arch, the scent of a cliff rose, or the song of a hermit thrush. There is simply no way to express the love a man can feel for our Earth once he has surrendered to her call. It can be a raging, protective love at one extreme, or it can be exquisite and gentle, ethereal and compassionate. At night Ed would lie alone on a layer of rock still warm from the afternoon sun and gaze at the stars. "I dream of a hard and brutal mysticism in which the naked self merges with a non-human world and somehow survives still intact, individual, separate."

He would spend hours, days, weeks staring at a juniper tree and come to feel kinship with this gnarled living entity. The distinctive cry of a raven piercing the stillness of late afternoon would suggest the folly of anthropocentrism. The sound of water dripping into itself was more compelling than *The Art of the Fugue*. The graceful play of light and shadow on the canyon wall was far beyond the range of any artist's brush.

He walked across canted landforms, surefooted. He hiked animal trails, hearing the sounds of his own footfalls as the only sign of human presence in the high desert vastness. He registered the smells of bark, dust, scat, water. Abbey had an incredible nose for the smell of water, could smell it from a real distance in the driest environment and then find it. "Never turn down an offer of water."

He became fascinated with the fellow fauna, susceptible to their presence. Mice, snakes, vinegaroons, bark scorpions, lizards, ants. He took great delight in pissing into their anthills. "Little pissants." Desert centipedes, ugly and fascinating. Hawks soaring, most frequently redtails looking for food. And buzzards, or turkey vultures, gliding tirelessly through the brilliant dark blue sky. Little by little he developed a macabre image of himself as a vulture, redheaded, foul breathed, eater of carrion, maintainer of desert cleanliness, a fully grown gadfly, by gawd, easier to see, easier to shoot down.

He had duties as a backcountry ranger. He did indeed see other fellow humans, tourists whose presence he felt infringed on his own privacy. He knew that pang of subtle regret when the sound of a distant but inevitable car or truck infiltrated his field of hearing. How could he like tourists? He had to clean up after them, police their plastic effluent, or worse. Nothing quite as nasty as a pile of human shit and its attendant brown-stained Kleenex fluttering in the heart of your meditation on desert wilderness. Years later I heard Abbey tell his oldest daughter, Susie, then only eight years old, to "dig a hole two feet deep, poop in it, wipe yourself, throw the paper in the hole, light it with a match, burn it, and then bury it."

Abbey was in paradise. Alone at last in a land broad enough to accommodate the breadth of his soul. Alone? Alone. Lonely. Lonely? He missed Rita. He imagined his tiny son, Joshua, becoming a little boy. He had to admit to himself that Rita hadn't headed east only to be near her mother and a doctor. There was more to it by far. He and Rita were measuring the edges of their incompatibility. They wanted different kinds of lives. There was love between them, but their outlooks differed considerably. Few people shared Abbey's outlook on life. Few indeed in the late 1950s.

Abbey wrote in his journal and considered life as a writer. He knew his own style by now. He was committed to precision, accuracy, and hard honesty. He appreciated irony. Though his vocabulary was immense and he possessed a near photographic memory for what he had read, he wanted to write with "fidelity to common speech." A generation later, the casual reader could miss the intricacy of Abbey's writing, the symbolism, the allusion—because he wrote in the language of the common man.

Abbey questioned himself, his life, as he ranged Arches. He realized that life as a writer was difficult and utterly without security. There were times when he seriously considered pursuing a normal career as a college professor or a full-time Park Service ranger. These prospects soon paled when he actually imagined himself ensconced on a permanent basis within a bureaucracy, yet part of him longed for fidelity to one woman and a quiet family. This image would fade as he saw himself as he really was.

With only one life on this sweet earth, only one life, only one life . . .
perhaps it is unseemly, unbecoming to grasp so hard at life, to clutch at it
with all four paws like a greedy starving alley cat. . . . There is no easy
way for us. For us.

The inner conflict over Rita was splitting him, wrenching him into parts. On the one hand, he dearly wanted to be with her, to be her husband and father to their child. But Abbey also recognized that he was a satyr. He lauded the lust of the god Pan and understood it well. "Hell! look at me," wrote Abbey in his journal, "a young brown god, lusty as a goat, be-pricked like a veteran stud, and no woman within 20 miles. What a shame, what a crying shame . . . what a non-fukking shame, eh tovarish?"

Finally, Abbey was a loner, an adventurer, an idealist whose ideal was beginning to evolve beyond his fundamental anarchism. For he also loved wilderness, and he knew this wilderness was threatened by his own species. He also foresaw the advance of tourism and looked ruefully at his employer, the National Park Service, whom he considered to be commercializing wilderness preservation. Privy to Park Service scuttlebutt, he knew that Glen Canyon, that graceful meander etched by the Colorado River, was to be dammed and therefore doomed. "Glen Canyon, beautiful beyond any telling of it, to be drowned forever. Oh the filthy scheming greedy fanatical scum!"

As he wandered the backcountry of Arches through the labyrinth of his own solitude, examining his own life and motives, feeling guilty and resentful yet deeply in love in an agony of loneliness, overwhelmed by the majesty of this wilderness where he was at home, a wilderness he knew to be threatened by the enemies of Nature, all the while imagining what he wanted to write, he was too often tempted by the fatal luxury of despair.

The summer entered its waning in the late dog days of August. Abbey wrote in his desert journal frequently, outlining stories, jotting down recollections, inscribing the panoply of his emotions, writing poetry:

Black sun
Black sun
of my heart—! . . .

Abbey was imbued with the dark light of the black sun for years to come. Somehow its imagery lit the path of the anarchist (whose flag was black) to the heart of darkness.

The autumn of 1956 brought Abbey to Hoboken, New Jersey. His first season at Arches was ended, and he truly missed his wife. Both Ed and Rita were aware that their marriage rested uneasily on the sharp side of the blade.

Sobering thought: of all the world's two billion or more people, none would miss me very much if I were to die, except for my parents and possibly Rita. No one else: my own brothers would not be perturbed, nor my "friends," nor even Joshua my son. Odd that I never thought of this before. But that's why a man—an ordinary man—needs a woman: only a woman is fool enough and great enough to love a man despite his obvious worthlessness.

Hoboken and uncertain reconciliation with his family. The good news was that he could draw unemployment compensation and continue to write. He was deep into his novel *The Dark Side of the Moon,* which would never be published. (Curious to think of his preoccupation with the darker aspects of nearby heavenly bodies.)

Even though his appreciation for Rita and his delight in his young son grew, it didn't take long for "the view of Hell from the Pulaski skyway" to wear him down.

Hoboken: where the cockroaches are so big and fierce we were afraid to do anything about them. Where they miscegenate with, or even rape the mice. The rats. Worse than the flying scorpions of Utah.

Rita and Ed's needs were in conflict. She was a young mother in quest of a nest, an artist possessed of an intellect and fired by the high energy of her Jewish heritage. He was a gifted writer with an evolved mind, a desert rat in need of open country, a man who would not be dominated by anyone. Heavy chemistry.

Abbey looked hard at humanity as he walked at night through the streets of Hoboken and didn't like what he saw. He witnessed the blue flutter that issued from every living-room window: "the phantom world of TV; reality reduced to flickering shadows on an illuminated screen: every home a platonic cave; shackled by indolence, fatigue, habit."

He looked at the New York skyline across the black waters of the Hudson and saw the skyscrapers as "granite cocks—impotent phalli." He perceived the subways as meandering through the "geography of Hell." He had come to regard *The New York Times* as the "world's worst newspaper, taking current events with such loathsome seriousness." The self-importance of the *Times* represented the insidious force of the status quo, the mind-set of a society whose allegiance was to Mammon. True, it's a free country, or so it's said. But consider the degree to which each human is subject to the system of mores that holds society in place. Are we governed by an elected government, or are we governed by an economic system that controls our minds?

"We in America are being systematically robbed," Abbey wrote in his journal. "Robbed of the most elementary decencies of life—clean air, sunlight, pure unmedicated water, grass and woods to play in, silence and solitude and space, even time, even death. Instead—? Insanity. Tee Vee. Hi-fi. Super-Duper. Glittering shit. And finally, morphine."

Abbey perceived that the burgeoning human population relentlessly bludgeoned the land regardless of the soundless scream of the community of life that was eradicated to make way for more concrete, more vertical iron, more freneticism, more waste. He rued the massacre of the human spirit by the chancellors of advertising who played on the irony of dissatisfaction through acquisition. He detested the collective human weakness that allowed its spirit to be governed from without.

The spirit of resistance lay at the heart of Abbey's anarchism, and his was an anarchism especially vital in a world so overpopulated by humans. We are all beleaguered, in his view, by the spirit of growth for its own sake. This must be resisted, bitterly contested. Acquiescence is lethal.

The winter was long but not without respite. The Abbeys were somehow spiritually reunited, at least for a while. Abbey resisted sloth, continued to write his novel. Writing for its own sake is lonely business, frustrating and tiresome. If it hadn't been a passion, he wouldn't have done it.

In the spring of 1957 the Abbey family headed westward to Arches, where

Ed resumed his job as backcountry ranger. This time his solitude was tempered by Rita and Josh, now a year old. He described in his journal his experiences in the high desert. He imagined a guaranteed best-seller: "*The Jesus H. Christ Story* by Fulton Sheen, Jr., with introduction by J. Edgar Hoover & illustrations by Walt Disney." He penned a dictum: "No Automobiles in National Parks." His relationship with the park superintendent had an occasional wobble. Abbey detested bureaucracy, and the National Park Service was undoubtedly a bureaucracy. Jim Stiles, a fellow ranger at Arches, recalls Abbey's frustrations with the superintendent:

> You remember how big Ed's head was. It was size 7 & ¾. Well, when he showed up that first season, he was wearing a big black cowboy hat. Superintendent Bates Wilson did not like that black cowboy hat. They tried to order him a regular Park Service Stetson, but they didn't make them that big. They couldn't get him a hat the right size, so Bates made him wear a pith helmet, a goddamn safari helmet with a Park Service emblem on it, and Ed hated it. But it was the only compromise they could come up with.
>
> Ed told me that the second season he showed up with a beard. Bates took one look at it and totally freaked out. But Bates wasn't confrontational, so he sent Lloyd Pearson to do the dirty work, getting him to shave it off.
>
> The road building began in Arches, and Ed wanted out of there. He wanted the ranger's job down at Natural Bridges that his brother had once had. Apparently Abbey was blacklisted by then. There was a memo that came down from Regional Headquarters saying, "You may think twice about hiring this man because of his association with certain groups that are considered to be un-American." This followed the end of the McCarthy period. I don't think Abbey knew that until I told him. It really bothered him. He thought the reason he hadn't been rehired was because he had decided to grow his beard back and he was determined not to shave it off.

Abbey received a writing fellowship to attend Stanford University and study with Wallace Stegner. In October 1957 the Abbeys moved to the town of El

Granada, at the north end of Half Moon Bay. The mountains were to their backs, and the inclination was to look westward over the sea. Abbey had a circuitous drive over the mountain range to Palo Alto.

The beat scene was in full swing in San Francisco, but Stanford was far enough south of San Francisco and Berkeley to be somewhat peripheral to it. Abbey himself was peripheral to the scene, never becoming associated with the beat literary tradition.

Under the tutelage of the "baggy-eyed" Stegner, Abbey wrote and read. He read incessantly. He read works by Eliot, Crane, Rexroth, Hölderlin, Frost, Pound, Stevens, Kerouac, Traven, Miller, Freud (*Civilization and Its Discontents*), and as much of *Mansfield Park,* by Austen, as he could stand. He also read Ginsberg's *Howl,* which he regarded as the best poem written by an American "since Pearl Harbor (So far as I know.) Yes, a beautifully-shaggy little book. Wild and shaggy, and also highly accurate: 'Moloch whose heart is a cannibal dynamo,' etc. . . . Very touching. My wife hates it, of course, just as everyone I know does. They're all so superior to that kind of thing, you know."

The amount of the writing fellowship was $2,500. In order to supplement that modest income, Rita served as a substitute teacher and Abbey "swindled" the state of Utah for unemployment. Then news came that actor Kirk Douglas had purchased the film rights to *The Brave Cowboy* for the munificent sum of $7,500. Douglas would go on to produce the film, *Lonely Are the Brave.*

Abbey continued writing his *Confessions of a Barbarian* as spoken in the persona of his character Jack Tupper, so named, no doubt, because the word *tup* means a copulating ram. By now he had written over four hundred pages of an unpublished novel titled *Black Sun.* This was the first time he used the name Hayduke in a novel. It also featured characters named Kovalchick and Lightcap, names that appear in the Indiana, Pennsylvania, phone book. These were members of an anarchist commune originally named "Grim Prospects, New Mexico." The novel finally published as *Black Sun* is an entirely separate work of fiction.

He also began to conceive of a book of essays tentatively titled *Canyon Country,* which would focus on the history, the people, the future, and the strangely provocative landscape of southeastern Utah, "the heart of the wilderness."

At this time Abbey considered the novel as "only a transitional art form; or not an art form at all—a club, rather, to beat people over the head with." It was

Bertolt Brecht who said, "Art is not a mirror held up to reality, but a hammer with which to shape it." Abbey had great admiration for Leo Tolstoy "because he was able to go beyond novel writing."

The writings of Robinson Jeffers affected Abbey deeply. At this time the distinguished poet still lived in his hand-wrought tower on the craggy coast of central California. He regarded the human species with great contempt for our mindless ruination of the natural world. Wrote Jeffers, "I'd rather kill a man than a hawk." Abbey spoke many times of his great admiration for Jeffers; indeed, Jeffers was probably instrumental to one of Abbey's major insights: "To know the world outside of us, we must break through the anthropomorphic fog in which most of us pass our lives. To understand the integrity and self-ness, the existence of a tree, for example, or a wolf, or a soaring hawk."

In a sense, even though Jeffers died in 1962, he and Abbey shared a parallel course up to the idea of death. Jeffers wrote:

Our consciousness passes into the world's perhaps
but that,
Being infinite, can endure eternity.

Abbey believed also that consciousness ends at death, for "who deserves to live forever?" He was content to provide the planet with one good meal or perhaps nurture a tree or a bush and thus contribute with his own death to the continuity of life.

Poet and essayist Gary Snyder shares with Jeffers and Abbey the view of man as no more or less important than any other life-form. While Abbey and Snyder never met, they did correspond and shared mutual respect for both each other and Pyotr Kropotkin.

The Abbey family left Stanford University and Half Moon Bay in the spring of 1958 and traveled to the Gila National Forest of New Mexico, where Abbey served as a seasonal ranger at the Beaverhead Ranger Station. He continued writing fiction, but there was a hiatus in his journals, and his *Confessions of a Barbarian* was put on hold.

He was in the high country near the Plains of San Agustín, formerly an inland sea on the southern edge of which is situated Bat Cave, continuously inhabited by humans for thousands of years, and later the site of the radio telescope complex known as the Very Large Array. The country was wild, populated by a few ranchers. It wasn't canyon country. Abbey had been turned down by the southeastern Utah contingent of the National Park Service. His eyes yearned to scan the canyons, to make sense of the twisted, gnarled rock forms carved by water and wind. Instead he had to seek contentment from the ponderosa pines, hawks, golden eagles, deer, bear—and the silence.

In August 1958, after the fire season, the Abbeys moved to Santa Fe. They rented an adobe house at 802 Canyon Road. Abbey always hated Santa Fe, which he thought crawled with "promoters, creeps, thugs, vandals and parasites." He had always regarded New Mexico as "the fairest of them all," but a mosaic of bad associations was beginning to profane his vision. He considered Albuquerque, with its economic reliance on the military and weapons research, "a large dirty sinister town, subsidized by war, dedicated to death, and famed for its money, ugliness and vulgarity." He regarded Los Alamos as "an evil dirty little town." Even Taos wasn't spared; it was a "town of many hatreds."

In those days Santa Fe had yet to be discovered. Many of the streets were unpaved, and adobe houses prevailed and were inhabited in the main by a Hispanic population. The rest of the population was a mix of bohemians and state government employees. There were some bars, and an occasional gunshot split the silence of the night.

Drawing unemployment compensation, Abbey sought seasonal work with the National Park Service. He couldn't abide life in Santa Fe, so when offered a position as seasonal ranger at Casa Grande National Monument near Coolidge, Arizona, he made his decision to spend the winter in the Sonoran Desert, some five thousand feet lower than Santa Fe and considerably warmer.

Abbey was now becoming a lowlander, by desert-wilderness reckoning. The warm winter sun agreed with him, and he began the slow metamorphosis that would ultimately make him champion the Sonoran Desert.

Rita was pregnant and determined to return to Hoboken, taking Joshua with her. Their bohemian lifestyle was a test of marital endurance.

The climate was warm at Casa Grande, but the future was uncertain. By spring 1959 the season was over, and the Abbey family reunited and moved back to Albuquerque, where Ed would finally get his master's degree.

He had finished writing *Black Sun* (number 1) and sent it off to New York. It was rejected by three different publishers. Dejected, Ed felt unable to start writing a new novel. He had no job, no home. The baby was due imminently. He and Rita had "nasty grueling arguments. Hidden hates and frustrations chewing up my bowels. Premonitions of the ultimate ulcer. Bloodshot eyes. Can't hold my liquor. Little beerbelly at my bow. Can't write. Can't love or live. 'To kill love is to kill life.'"

Economics plagued Abbey. By himself, he was content to lead a gypsy life, but with a family, existence had become fraught with the endlessly nagging sense of insecurity. "Driving ourselves nuts in a half-ton Chevy truck."

Abbey came close to abandoning his writing career at this point. He took a civil service exam with the intent of becoming a career National Park Service employee. He desperately looked for the courage to continue as a writer. He restored his inner resources by reading Dante, Joyce, Mann, Proust, Huxley, Sholokov, more of Henry Miller (*Big Sur and the Oranges of Hieronymous Bosch*), more of Céline, Georges Sorel ("disappointing"), Henry James ("America's or England's most distinguished lady novelist"), Jane Austen ("ugh"), Stendhal (*Le rouge et la noire*, featuring Julian Sorel, a name that turns up as a pseudonym for a character in Abbey's last novel), Flaubert, Melville (*Pierre*), Zola (*Earth*), Rexroth (*In Defense of the Earth*), Lao-Tse (*Tao Teh King*: "Simply the world's best philosopher, that's all. As close to the whole truth as anyone's likely ever to get all by himself. A good little book"), Fitzgerald (*This Side of Paradise*: "The trouble with Fitzgerald is quite simple. He was a sycophant, an ass-kisser, who sold himself to Hollywood, Esquire Magazine, and bitchy women"). He reread B. Traven's *The Death Ship,* which he regarded as an excellent novel though he contended that it didn't hold up as well on the second reading because of the strangeness of the dialogue. Traven made Abbey's life list of favored writers along with Rabelais, Knut Hamsun, Theodore Dreiser, Céline, and Steinbeck.

Abbey was commissioned to review Beckett's *Watt* and Virginia Woolf's *Fade Out.* This boosted his morale a notch and actually gave him the courage to persist as a writer. Like a wounded wolf, he climbed out of the pit of despair and began to heal himself.

"Attention: Aaron Paul Abbey born today, the 28th of May, 1959. My second son. May he, like my first, be blessed by Heaven and Earth, grow

straight and strong in the joyous sunlight." Abbey was delighted with the birth of Aaron, his second contribution to the gene pool, even though his own future seemed ever less certain.

In June 1959 Ed and his friend Ralph Newcomb headed north with a pair of surplus rafts, paddles, food, water jugs, and their river bindles. It was their intent to run the Colorado River through the death-destined Glen Canyon.

They put in at what was then Hite's Ferry and soon found that by lashing their rafts together they could slop through the rapids with modest success and the comforting illusion of control. Once launched, there was no turning back. They did this in the spirit of true adventure, that is, they were novices and had but meager knowledge of the course of the river. It's one thing to pay hard cash to an experienced outfitter who assumes responsibility for your body and soul and paddles you forward with expertise and knowledge. It's quite another to lash your meager possessions upon which you must depend for survival into a leaky old raft and head downstream armed with only a paddle against the overwhelming current of a great and wild river, conscious of the growing roar of the unknown. While Ed and Ralph floated between rapids, gazing awestruck at the beauty of the canyon, they knew that this wilderness habitat and refuge would soon be submerged by an unnatural lake. Abbey's sensibilities were dangerously affronted. He wrote in his journal:

We cursed the engineers, the politicians who had condemned these marvels, and the wildlife sheltered by them, to death by drowning. How much dynamite, we wondered aloud to each other, would we need to destroy this dam? How delightful and just, we imagined, to have our dynamite so integrated into the dam's wiring system, that when the President, or the Secretary of the Interior and the Four Corners' Governors, together with their swarms of underlings, the Press, and the hordes of tourists had all assembled for the Grand Opening, it would be the white pudgy finger of the biggest bigshot pressing the little black button on the beflagged switchboard, that would actually blow into hell and smithereens the official himself, his guests, the tourists, the bridge and the Glen Canyon Dam. Sad and hopeless fantasy . . .

Soon, after he had returned home to his family in Albuquerque, he noted that he would one day write a book with the tentative title, *Solitude: Pages from a Desert Journal.* Or perhaps *Solitaire.* He started outlining the work, overcoming summer malaise and the chronic condition of no job, no home, no money, and no prospects. He read more of Beckett, more of Joyce (*Finnegan's Wake:* "Joyce was a great man, a prince among minds, the artist-saint . . .").

He criticized Beckett's Christianity and looked deep into his own self-ostracized state of spiritual being:

Yes, I'm atheist. Tho' earthiest might be a better term. I believe in the Earth. Let Heaven go to Hell! I am comforted in this dogmatic intuition by the everpresent recollection that two of the finest brightest cleanest civilizations yet to appear on this planet—The Greek and the old Chinese—were essentially non-theistic. Until Plato and Mao Tse-Tung came along to poison it all.

Abbey also took a critical look at his own writing. He was greatly impressed with the style of Joseph Conrad and wanted to "emulate his passion for the exact." He described his own style:

Combine intensity with (not density) but clarity. Clear and intense. Like the desert landscape, the desert light, the desert atmosphere—clear, intense, and delightfully suggestive. Hard distinctions, precise outlines— but each thing suggesting, somehow, everything else. As in truth each thing does . . . I am a desert rat! A desert rat!

In the fall of 1959 Craig Vincent, a chain-smoking, bright, curious left-winger from Taos, invited Abbey to edit his weekly newspaper, *El Crepúsculo de la Libertad,* which can be translated as either the dawn or twilight of liberty. Ed would be paid $100 a week for a modest sixty or seventy hours of work. Rita and Joshua both felt at home in Taos, although Aaron was too young to know. The die was cast at least for a while. Abbey wanted to give the job a year at the most. So in mid-November, when the light of late autumn cast shadows through leafless trees and the colors of northern New Mexico were subtle and elegant, the Abbeys headed like gypsies toward winter's haven.

Abbey immersed himself in his work—and lasted three months. Then he and Craig Vincent parted ways by mutual consent. Anarchists and communists sometimes make a bitter brew. Both were good men, but they got on each other's nerves.

One of Abbey's great friends during the second half of his life was painter John DePuy, a lifelong westerner. Born in 1927, DePuy is the grandson of Major Ozone, who trekked much of the west during the nineteenth century.

Sometime in the mid-1950s DePuy and his Swiss wife moved to Taos. The little community had become an unusual bohemian art colony.

It was the mid-fifties. Black Mountain had folded. Bob Creeley came to Taos. Peter Nabokov. Max Finstein. Jorge Fick. Malcolm Brown was there. Chris Brett. Frieda Lawrence. Mabel Luhan. Jay and Liz Walker were there. Clinton Meek who was a philosopher. It was truly a renaissance. We met nightly at the Taos Inn where we discussed poetry, philosophy.

And then finally Abbey showed up in '59. Twenty minutes after we met, we were brothers, singing Schiller's "Ode to Joy." And exchanging lies and insults.

In those days, Ed was married to Rita. It was really hard on him. I felt so sorry for the poor bastard. His first novel hadn't done well—*Jonathan Troy*. And Rita was hot. Her work went well and she was also successful as a reviewer. His marriage to Rita affected his whole life.

They moved to Taos because Abbey had become the editor of *El Crepúscolo*. Craig Vincent was the publisher. Craig and Ed were like oil and water. A devoted anarchist who wrote his master's thesis on anarchism, and a totally devoted Marxist. The whole newspaper was a madhouse. Rini Templeton was there. She was art editor. Frank Waters was some sort of roving editor. Judson Crews was printer. It was a madhouse. Marxists! Marxist-Leninists! Rakes! Mad women! Ed and I both immediately fell in love with Rini. Rini was the image of "La Pasionaria" of the Spanish Civil War, or Millet's painting of "La Revolucionaria" with her great bosoms and the flag. Oh, God!, she was the idol. We all fell in love with her. But Ed and I were the only two who had a chance because perhaps we were a little more attractive in a barbaric way. So we competed. One day I went in to see her as Ed came shuffling out the door. She was insatiable. Two men like Ed and me—we couldn't satisfy her. I was so exhausted, I couldn't walk. Well, finally I won and married her. But it was touch and go and a couple times Ed and I almost got into fights. We both had wives, of course. It was glorious. Those were the greatest days of my life.

In spite of his UNM days, I think those were formative years for Ed as well. Because of the interaction. Writers. Painters. Sculptors. Poets. We'd rave and rant and discuss life and the hereafter and anarchy and Marx. Agnes Martin was there and she was a raving maniac. The hell with the minimalism stuff. She painted these wild, red paintings. God, it was incredible. Every night we met at the Taos Inn. Ed and I were bartenders there. I had the afternoon shift and he had the evening shift. Our friends would come in and we'd pour them a glass of bourbon. The owner couldn't figure out why he had so many customers but his profits didn't go up.

Ed didn't last long at *El Crepúsculo*. He wrote an editorial about Craig. He said, "If our publisher is a communist, why doesn't he admit it? I admit I am an anarchist." Ed was fired on the spot. Then it really got tough for him. He didn't have a job. Nothing was getting published. Rita and he got along badly. It was one of the nadirs of his life.

Ed got a job for awhile as a welfare worker. It was wretched and he was depressed about his job. Then one day he was walking back to his house in Cañon and a pachuco teenager took a shot at him with a .22. That was the end. After that he was very nervous about the Hispanics. He never got over it. He would go into a bar and he would put his hand on his wallet because there were Hispanics around.

When he was down at UNM, he and a couple of his friends worked over a billboard or two. But up in Taos, ah—that was the true beginning of the "monkey wrench gang." This idiot from Las Vegas, New Mexico put up about twelve billboards north of town. Huge things. He got the commission from those assholes in the Chamber of Commerce and the rest of the conservative jerks. More and more, Taos was breeding developers and opportunists. Overnight, they had these billboards going from El Prado all the way out to where the bridge is now. So, we were sitting around—Ed, Rini, Judson Crews and I and we said,

"Enough!" We got a chain saw and a big two-man saw and we went out and knocked down every one of them. And they put them back up again. So the second time we went out, Ed, Rini and I. We were hacking away at the billboard and we heard these voices coming up the arroyo. We dove head-first into the mud and we lay there. Pretty soon, we heard this sawing just a little ways away. One billboard that we hadn't nailed. It was the town pharmacist and Spud Johnson, the poet who used to write for the paper. A whole other crew of respected citizens out there hacking them down. We went up to them and we all embraced. It was wonderful and honorable!

Then we decided to take out some of the heavy equipment that the developers were using. We'd pour sand into the crankcase. We didn't really know how to stop them in those days. But we became very interested in this new occupation. One day, Rini, Judson, Ed and I were sitting around and Ed said, "We really ought to throw a monkey wrench in it." That was the first time I ever heard him use that term. We talked about the *sabot,* the root of the word sabotage. The Luddites. Rini had some misgivings because of her Marxist orientation. But then she decided, "What the hell," and got into it.

Abbey was thirty-three years old and unemployed. He applied for sixteen Park Service and Forest Service jobs and also for a tutor's position at a prep school in Colorado where his old friend Malcolm Brown had distinguished himself by constructing a new art building. Abbey began a rewrite of the thrice-rejected earlier *Black Sun,* having received modest encouragement from McGraw-Hill.

In early February 1960 he sent an outline of the book to an agent in New York. The novel reflected the lassitude and general pessimism that Abbey was then experiencing. Although it was never published, at least three of the characters appeared in subsequent novels by Abbey and elements of it would later appear in his novel *The Fool's Progress.*

That winter Abbey read works by James, Ouspensky, Joyce, Brecht, Forster, Baudelaire, Homer, Mark Twain (autobiography), Carl Jung's *Psychology and Religion,* and the *Bhagavad-Gita.* In early March he went skiing, fell, and badly hurt his knee. The doctor in Taos prescribed rest. The knee didn't heal, and by mid-April 1960 Abbey was admitted to the Veterans Hospital in Albuquerque, where he was diagnosed as having a torn and dislocated cartilage.

Abbey was garbed in government pajamas and ensconced in an environment that depressed him. He was surrounded by the infirm and was horrified by the support systems imposed on failing human bodies. He chanced to see medical personnel "tapping an old man's anus with a tube." Abbey hastily quit the spectacle, which he was too squeamish to endure, though he regarded his squeamishness as a serious defect in someone who was a writer. He determined that he would avoid dying in a hospital.

At one point Abbey was visited arbitrarily by a Bible-waving Baptist minister who advanced the notion that Ed had better consider his possible future in hell. Abbey debated the preacher for a while until the preacher suggested that Abbey picture hell and asked him to think of bacon frying.

"Smells good," said Abbey. The preacher was not amused.

It was determined that Ed was going to have to undergo surgery on his knee. He was somewhat unsettled with the fantasy of being permanently crippled. Shortly before the surgery was to take place, Rita called him from Taos to tell him that he had been given a fire lookout position at the Grand Canyon. He was utterly disgruntled by the realization that most likely he would not be well enough to take the job.

Before the operation, his beard was shaved off (emasculation!) so that he could receive anesthesia. He was also given a spinal injection and all feeling was deadened from the waist down. "Hospital life consists chiefly of one humiliation after the other."

Ten days after Ed's admission to the hospital, the surgery was performed. Recovery was slow, and Ed was unable to bend his knee for a time. Gradually he regained use of his leg, and eventually his body was completely restored. But as he recuperated, he had time to ruminate about his life, his marriage. "The trouble is that Americans expect too much of marriage, as they expect too much of life. The only people in the world who *pursue* happiness."

Rita came down from Taos to be with him after the operation, and he was deeply moved by their love. "What a lucky man I am to have such a woman love me. Lacerated by regret, I think of the times *she* was in the hospital, and I neglected her."

Shortly before he was discharged from the hospital, the Abbeys received notice that they were being evicted from their house in Taos. Rita took the boys, boarded a plane, and flew off to New York. Abbey was utterly frustrated, and then came yet another rejection of *Black Sun* from McGraw-Hill.

By September the family was reunited in Taos. Abbey went off in search of work throughout the Southwest but to no avail. He finally secured a job at the Taos Inn as a bartender. "Wretched job, of course, but I endure. . . . Tired. Self-pity becoming my major vice."

During this bleak period an old university friend, Starr Jenkins, visited Taos in his capacity as a journalist-photographer for the U.S. Forest Service. Jenkins and Rita Abbey had both worked at the same high school in Albuquerque during the early 1950s. The Abbeys invited Jenkins to dinner, and during their conversation Abbey asked Jenkins how he could acquire a similar job. Jenkins suggested that Abbey contact the Southwestern Regional Office of the Forest Service. Of course, Abbey might have to hold his tongue concerning the Forest Service's acquiescence to special interest groups like ranchers and miners, something Abbey was not inclined to do. It wasn't Abbey's destiny to hold such a position with the Forest Service.

The winter wore on, and eventually Rita and the boys returned to Hoboken to her family, security, and an environment to which she felt better suited. Determined to remain in the Southwest, Abbey had taken work with the National Park Service as a ranger at the Painted Desert.

> *I say, this is a detestable chickenshit sort of a place. To work in, I mean. Have applied to 38 different places, including U.S. Senator Clinton P. Anderson in hope of escape.*
>
> *No word from the wife for ten days. Proceeding? Third thoughts? Give the old man another chance.*

Abbey considered the position of hydrographer at Lee's Ferry as possibly the ideal job. He imagined riding on horseback with his sons to the highway, where they could catch a school bus to Page (forty-five miles away), or Kanab (eighty miles), or even Flagstaff (only 130 miles).

He started writing a novel that he tentatively titled *Vogelin's Ranch,* which was to become *Fire on the Mountain* and dealt with the U.S. government condemning an old man's ranch so that it could be incorporated into a weapons-testing site in southern New Mexico. The story is narrated by twelve-year-old Billy Vogelin Starr (named perhaps after friend Jenkins?), who tells of that summer when his grandfather defied the government—one man against the entire bureaucracy of the U.S. Air Force with a little help from the local sheriff's office. *Fire on the Mountain* challenges America's commitment to an evolving military-industrial regime founded on economic growth and increasing power at the expense of natural habitat and individual freedom.

Said young Billy of his grandfather's ranch: "If the ranch had been mine I'd have sold the cattle and stocked the place with wild horses and buffalo, coyotes and wolves, and let the beef industry go to ruin." For many years Abbey imagined that if he were ever to get rich, he would buy an enormous ranch and stock it with appropriate wildlife.

Abbey received a copy of Dalton Trumbo's screenplay of *The Brave Cowboy,* now titled for the screen *Lonely Are the Brave.*

> *It's very good.—the dialog much livelier, heartier, wittier, than my own. More authenticity in jail scenes, truck scenes. Swift pace, no drag. Follows original in all essentials. In short, I'm delighted with the play except for change of title. Must put up a fight on that.*

The filming was shot in Albuquerque, and Abbey was given a bit part (which was cut from the film). Even so, he felt good about the movie and about Kirk Douglas, who regarded it as his favorite picture in his long and distinguished career.

Abbey received yet another rejection of *Black Sun,* which he called "the biggest publishing blunder since Simon and Schuster rejected the New Testament."

He moved back to Albuquerque in the summer and went to work for the New Mexico Welfare Department. Most of his clients were Indians and Hispanos whose main source of income was the welfare check. Abbey the altruist was confronted with human misery in its myriad forms. He was part of the bureaucracy he had always disdained. Just as his welfare cases were desperate to survive financially, Abbey was desperate to survive spiritually. He loved his wife and family in spite of his growing awareness that the abyss between him and them was widening. He remained in Albuquerque until January 1962, when, in a monumental effort to save his failing marriage, he headed east and took a position with the New York City Welfare Board, which was "truly horrible. A paper nightmare."

Yet he was, for the moment, reconciled with Rita, the future "a bright gray." Rita's father was dying in a hospital, the dread fate that Abbey could not abide. He had come to regard the hospital as a

hall of horrors. And the double-talking doctors—now promising one thing, now another, and always wrong . . . It's all like some nightmarish experiment—the mad scientist, once a creature of science fiction, now lives everywhere, and dominates our lives.

Abbey was appalled by the humiliation that life-support systems impose on the dying. Better, he thought, to leap into the Grand Canyon or drown in a rapid or even die in battle.

Abbey pondered death itself.

Annihilation . . . But not really that, a transformation rather, following decomposition. A Re-Union with the elements of Earth and sky. Certainly the consciousness is lost—how could it be otherwise. . . . The only way to overcome the fear of death is by accepting the necessity and inevitability of death. Those who cannot face and accept the eventual certainty of death are condemned to spend their lives in trembling dread, in spiritual hiding, in moral cowardice, or else to search for the comforting dream of life after death.

Ed and Rita went to see *Lonely Are the Brave.* Wrote Abbey,

Somehow an embarrassing experience, tho' it's really an honest and lucid film which follows my book quite closely. Embarrassing for Rita and me, perhaps, because it seemed so personal, intimate, revealing, almost an invasion of privacy. . . . But most of the movie reviews have been very friendly, especially those in Newsweek *and the* Herald Tribune.

The New Yorker's critic did not agree with *Newsweek* or the *Herald Tribune.*

> *Lonely Are the Brave* pretends to be a Western and has actually been hailed in some quarters as a "good" Western . . . but its screenplay, by Dalton Trumbo, struck me as a shoddy and remarkably simple-minded song of hatred for twentieth-century American society. What power the picture has springs from the irony of its starring the All-American Kirk Douglas as a natural man going down in defeat under the continual brutal assaults of the industrial-capitalistic-governmental juggernaut. The vulgarity of Mr. Trumbo's perceptions is that he has his hero, a cowboy on horseback, run down by an enormous trailer-truck filled with toilets. There may be a lot wrong with this country, but Mr. Trumbo is plainly not the man to point it out.

Said Abbey:

> *The* New Yorker *review of our movie calls it "shoddy and simple-minded, a song of hatred for 20th century American society." Exactly! Exactly what I meant the book to be. I am quite pleased by the reviewer's observation. He stated the issues clearly. The only reviewer that did so, so far as I know.*

Artistic success notwithstanding, Abbey still had to earn a living. He left his job in New York, moved with his family to Hoboken, and took a position with the Hudson County Welfare Board. He began work on a new novel, *The Good Life,* in the summer of 1962, an autobiographical work that had its genesis in *Confessions of a Barbarian* and would finally be published in 1988 as *The Fool's Progress.*

Abbey devoted his journal, in the main, to the initial outline for *The Good Life.* Another book began to take shape as the winter wore on—a book that again featured his three friends Kovalchick, Hayduke, and Lightcap. Kovalchick had been resurrected from the ashes of *Black Sun* (number 1). Lightcap was busily playing folk music, and Hayduke ultimately secured a job with a welfare department and tried desperately to keep his marriage together. This new attempt was tentatively titled *The Wooden Shoe Gang,* after the French for wooden shoes, or *sabots,* whose name lives on in the word *sabotage.* The word *hayduke* originates elsewhere. The haiduks "were a collective form of that individual peasant dissidence which . . . produced the classical bandits." The word is thought to be of Turkish or Magyar origin. During the fifteenth century Christian landlords and Turkish conquerors became ever more heavy-handed with the peasants, who were forced from their lands or who lived in perpetual serfdom. As conditions became untenable, the displaced peasants and escaped serfs sought places where they could found free communities. Fighting men emerged from this free peasantry and founded a tradition that spanned cultural boundaries, resulting in the *klepthes* of Greece, the Cossacks of Russia, the *haidamaks* of the Ukraine, and the haiduks of Hungary and the Balkan Peninsula.

Not all haiduks were of the moral caliber of Robin Hood. Some actually became "hired crossbows" for threatened Christian or Turkish nobles. Others defended their rights as freemen and became robbers by trade, avengers of the people, and perpetrators of guerrilla movements, resistance and liberation. If fortune smiled, the lifestyle of the bandit was certainly better than that of the peasant-serf. Indeed, the haiduks were brigands who haunted mountain passes and discomfited the gentry. The haiduks were insurrectionists and became a recognized social group. Their chieftains changed and their sway was held in common, their existence dependent on the collective rather than the exploits of a single individual. They were all heroes, their tales told in myriad ballads.

Abbey's novel went through various permutations, and the title changed to *Three Wizards on a Dead Limb*. He regarded this book as a paraphrase of *Black Sun* number 1, now set in New York City. He described Lightcap as

> *a sinking folksinger in a [Greenwich] Village nightclub, subsiding slowly gradually but surely into dope, boredom, despair, degradation, hopelessness—chained by inertia, losing all power of self-salvation—his home in a dismal 10th St. loft with scrawny hillbilly wife and 5 kids— his pot garden on the windowsill—straggly beard—wants to get out of the swamp but doesn't know how, has lost all power, willpower.*
>
> *Kovalchick still thinking he's Whitman . . . determined to rescue his friends tho' willing and eager to warn and arouse all to the terrible doom looming over them. His wooden shoe, sabotage, plagiarized poetry, the writing on the shithouse walls, guns, dream of the sunburnt West, his final terrible defeat, the ultimate triumph.*

*And Hayduke, not a bum but a good simple earnest young man not
in love with his job but very much in love with his wife and kinder and
tragically unable to uproot the wife (under psychiatric treatment, of
course) from her security nest of home, city, relatives, income, middle-class
standards; eager to get ahead at the Welfare Department not because he
believes in his work—he doesn't—but because he is anxious to give his
headsick wife all the luxuries she craves, requires, for her sense of security.*

By autumn Abbey was becoming embittered by the prospect of the bright
sunlight of the American Southwest, where he could work outdoors in the
clean air and raise his sons within a system of values he condoned. Instead he
donned the dread necktie and wasted his days in a stuffy office surrounded by
middle-aged women, "pushing papers and pressing dictaphone buttons."

Fire on the Mountain was published in 1962 and dedicated to Rita. Its
publication gave Abbey some sense of worth as a creative intellectual. As ever,
he sent copies to his close friends, including writer William Eastlake, a man
whose work he greatly admired.

Abbey had come to loathe New York City. He realized that it was all but
impossible to live in one of the world's greatest monuments to human domination of the natural environment and maintain any sense of the flow of Nature.
He recognized that people of true talent existed there, but he believed that
even their perceptions were warped by the conditions in which they lived. He
recognized that many escaped the megalopolis if they could afford to. He couldn't
understand why any would choose to live there.

He was horrified by the level of mental illness, the number of people who
required constant psycho-tweaking by their shrinks if they were to endure.
He noted that the people who were most in need of psychological help had
no resources to pay for it. His own job at the Welfare Department brought
him into frequent contact with many whose lives were supported entirely by
welfare checks, the size of whose incomes increased in direct proportion
to their ability to procreate. He listened to endless tales of woe describing
why the tale tellers were justified in receiving their dole. He was outraged
by the collective enslavement to the self-fulfilling prophecy of growth for
its own sake. Somewhere, at some time, growth must end because the

nonrenewable resources on which it relies will be exhausted.

Abbey's own self-esteem was falling prey to the impossible conditions of his megalopolitan lifestyle. He found no sustenance in the dreary, used-up environment of the megalopolis. He was uprooted from his energy source, the Southwest. He was ever more embittered, more hateful. As he recognized this in himself, he edged closer to a great juncture that lay ahead. In the meantime his own psyche was in trouble, and his journals reflected less and less of Abbey and more and more of the heroes of *Three Wizards on a Dead Limb*. They represented three aspects of his own being, and of the three, the voice of Kovalchick was dominant.

> *For the love of God, friend Hayduke, don't fall into that fatal habit, that*
> *fatal trap of sacrificing the present for the future which never arrives.*
> *Take the cash and let the credit go! Live for the present and the future*
> *will take care of itself. Of future future future that's all I ever hear in*
> *this bedevilled city—I say the future be fucked! What did posterity ever*
> *do for us? Run for your life! Survival of the misfittest!*
>
> *Coward! Coward am I? If you see a Tyrannosaurus Rex springing*
> *toward you, is it cowardly to run?*

To add to his woes, *Fire on the Mountain* appeared to be a flop. Don Congdon, Abbey's agent, was unable to get a paperback edition. Again Abbey considered abandoning his career as a writer. He longed to roam free in the Southwest. "There are, after all, several things more important than art. Like a pinetree on a mountainside. Like a juniper in the red desert. Like air and sunlight."

By the beginning of 1963 he had begun applying to the National Park Service for seasonal work in the Southwest. He staved off despair by listing the books he intended to write, including *Solitaire in the Desert* and *The Wooden Shoe Gang* or *The Monkey Wrench Mob*. He had begun making notes for a novel titled *Don Coyote* and continued amassing material for his "fat masterpiece."

Abbey took solace in writing. He had discovered, as many writers have, that by focusing his attention on the act of writing, giving his imagination free rein in his fiction or his journal, he could release some of the stress from the unsolvable problems that threatened to engulf him. When he wrote, his head literally sweated with the passion of it.

He began to have forbidden affairs of the heart when he was conducting "fieldwork" for the Welfare Department. "How can I be faithful to one woman without being unfaithful to all the others?" Old Scottish proverb: "The standing cock has no conscience."

By the spring of 1963 he had secured a job as backcountry ranger for the National Park Service at Sunset Crater, near Flagstaff. Even though he had longed for the West, the transition from the mega-dense human population of the New York metropolis to the outback solitude of the American Southwest always took getting used to. His neighbors were extinct volcanoes, hawks, coyotes, the wind. But the feel of the wind against his face cleared his sight as always and blew out the heavy cobwebs that strangled his mind. Conditions weren't good between Rita and Abbey, and he experienced great anguish that two people who have loved each other deeply could find themselves embittered, caught in festering hatreds. "I am bitter, even though I understand that this weary game is partly my own fault . . . and there's nothing I can do but endure it and hope for eventual good luck."

That summer Abbey began to contemplate *The Wooden Shoe Gang* with renewed vigor. It would feature Kovalchick, Hayduke, and Lightcap in their late middle age. "Three men and a girl— . . ." and the arsenal of the anarchist as they pursue "their greatest project . . . the attempted destruction of the Glen Canyon Dam. As the book progresses, the movement spreads: other Manos Negroes, spontaneously. . . ."

What had begun as an expression of resistance years earlier when he was an undergraduate at the University of New Mexico with his program of cutting down or firing up the unsightly billboards that blighted Route 66 was evolving into a new form. Abbey was beginning to apply his anarchism to defense of the natural environment. A whole new and complex point of view was churning in his psyche. He was about to found a new revolutionary movement. Soon, but not quite yet. For the time being, he was content "to be an inspector of volcanoes."

When the season ended, Abbey returned to Hoboken, anticipating a reunion with his family but dreading another winter in the city. He was able to get his old Welfare Department job back, a job that, in theory, was an ethical redistribution of wealth but actually, to the horror of his egalitarian sensibilities, pushed myriad recipients of welfare checks beyond the reach of self-sufficiency, self-esteem, and responsibility to the community. He was disgusted at the lying and cheating of many whose entire lifetimes were funded by welfare, and he detested becoming a petty bureaucrat, convinced that it was but a small step above being a welfare recipient. His sense of Kropotkinian ethics, of mutual aid, was eroded by the reality of the deteriorating urban human condition. But this was work required of him if he was to continue his marriage, remain with his family.

He completed and submitted two novels, both of which were rejected. Even so, he spied a glimmer of hope, both in his marriage and in his writing. He had been given solid advice by his agent, Don Congdon: "Write about that which you love!" He loved the wilderness. He hated New York. He couldn't escape the fact of growing human presence in the wilderness, and he began making drawings of bridges and compiling lists of materiel necessary to blow them away. Bridges across canyons lead into wilderness, and when humans enter the wilderness, they destroy it in the name of progress.

Thanks to Stewart Udall, then Secretary of the Interior, a wilderness bill was before the Congress of the United States, which, if passed, would go a long way toward wilderness preservation. Abbey watched the progress of the bill closely, but he had little faith in the political process.

Even though he was plodding through forty hours a week as a welfare caseworker in Hoboken, even though he complained to himself in his journals, a new fire was singeing Abbey's edges. He felt that Rita was trying very hard to save the marriage, and they had agreed to try to move to San Diego, where Abbey's old friend Al Sarvis lived. This move would be a compromise between Moab and Hoboken. Still, there was a restlessness. It was like a new scent in the air, and Abbey was extending to his full height, thrusting his head above the crowd, sniffing out the flavor of it, elusive as it was like the waft of the cliff rose or the poignant springtime scent of Russian olives along the banks of a western river.

Even so, he sought favor with women other than his wife. Occasionally he got drunk, alcohol being his opiate of choice, and he listened to music and read. He thought of his friends in the Southwest—John DePuy, Malcolm Brown, William Eastlake, Bill Letcher (a fellow flute player), Max Finstein (a poet)—that collection of bohemians whose company he deeply missed as he shuffled papers on behalf of the bereft on the dreary banks of the Hudson.

Abbey became immersed in his reading and even returned to *Leaves of Grass,* by "Uncle Walt," who wrote:

> This is what you shall do: Love the earth and sun and the animals, despise riches, give alms to all that ask, stand up for the stupid and crazy, hate tyrants, argue not concerning God, devote your income and labor to others, take off your hat to nothing known or unknown or any man or any number of men, go with powerful uneducated persons and the mothers of children, re-examine all you have been taught in church or school or in books and reject whatever insults your soul . . . and your very flesh shall become a great poem.

Abbey listed Whitman as one of about a hundred great souls thus far produced by humankind and was greatly influenced by him throughout his life. He included other poets in his "great" list, such as Lao-Tse, Lucretius, and Robinson Jeffers—who wrote of "the immense vulgarities of misapplied science and decaying christianity."

He was eventually fired from the Welfare Department. But fortune favored him with a contract from McGraw-Hill for two separate books: *A Desert Journal* and *American Lives,* a study of welfare clientele and their actual way of life. He was wildly enthusiastic about the first book and utterly disinterested in the second. He was an altruist to the end, but he was also a realist. And what he saw of welfare clientele biased him enormously. In years to come, Abbey would be heartily criticized for his position concerning "minorities," but his opinions were based on years of firsthand experience as a caseworker. Besides, he regarded himself as a minority of one.

He signed on to go on a river trip in May 1965. This triggered a series of quarrels with his wife, which finally poised him to commit the unthinkable. On Bastille Day, the day of liberation celebrated by the French nation, Edward Abbey "bolted. Left wife and kids and job [newly acquired in Las Vegas, Nevada] for exile in the desert." Staggered with grief over the abandonment of his children, he was determined to survive on his own, free to pursue the greatest love of his life—deep wilderness as far beyond the pale of men as he could abide.

Ed, ca. 1929.

Summer 1945, Ft. Mc Clellen, Alabama.

1946. Ed captioned this "a picture of a military p-p-policeman and his Neapolitan . . . godmother."

William Eastlake, Military Policeman, ca. 1945, in England.

Editor, UNM Thunderbird, 1951.

At UNM, 1951.

Ed and Jean S. 1951.

At home in Albuquerque, 1954.
Photo by Malcolm Brown.

At White Sands, 1952.

With Homer at Rough Rock, Arizona, on the Navajo Reservation.

At Arches, Utah, 1957.

Ed, Rita, and Josh at Arches, 1957.

The Abbey Family, ca. 1957. Back row: Paul, Ed, Bill, Mildred (holding Josh), John, Howard. Seated: Rita (Ed's wife), Iva (Howard's wife), Nancy.

Poster, Lonely Are the Brave, 1962.

Ed, Rita, Aaron, and Josh, Taos, 1959. Photo by Mildred Tolbert.

Ed and Judy, Organ Pipe Cactus National Monument, April 1968.

(for the Indians ~~██████~~ / Any Indians) Anywhere: Moab or Madras —

A private anthology: ("Private Stock")

— Lao-Tse & Chuang-Tse ; Epic of Gilgamesh ; myths of the Navajo ; from the Bible: Song of Songs, Job, Ecclesiastes, Genesis, Ruth, St. Matthew, John, Revelation ; Anacreon ; Euripides ; fragments from Homer ; Lucretius ; Catullus ; songs of the goliards ; Villon ; Rabelais ; old Eng. ballads of Anon.; frags from Chaucer, Shakespeare, Marlowe & Malory ; Cervantes ; Rochester (Wilmot); Burns ; Blake ; Keats, Shelley etc ; Heinrich Heine ; Whitman ; Thoreau ; Tolstoy, Chekov ; Sterne ; Smollet ; [None & nothing from any other Eng. novelists,]; Melville ; Twain ; Bierce ; J.W. Powell - cowboy songs ; mt. songs & Baptist hymns ; frags from Proudhon, Bakunin, Marx, Kropotkin ; Spinoza ; Giordano Bruno ; Montaigne ; Schopenhauer, Nietzsche, & frags from Goethe ; and so on into the 20th — Joyce, Mann, Yeats, Vachel Lindsay, Pound, Jeffers, Doc Williams, Dylan Thomas, Housman, ██ Dreiser, B. Traven, Sholokoff, Tom Wolfe, Hemingway, Algren, Neruda, Beckett, Brecht, Conrad, Chief Joseph, ? egg Hood etc

██████ ——→ but these ? quien sabe ?
Aeschylus Sophocles Homer Bible Confucius Upanishads the Mythology Plato Plotinus
Aquinas Rig-Veda Nibelungenlied Cicero Horace ██████ (Shakespeare?) Spenser

A composition from Ed's journal, Sept. 13, 1966: "For the Indians, Any Indians, Anywhere: Moab or Madras."

Standing: Ed, Alvin Josephy, Jack Loeffler, John Kimmey, Karl Kernberger, Richard Klemmer.
Seated: Katherine Loeffler, North Rim of Grand Canyon, 1971.

Reneé, Ed, Reneé's mother and brother,
and Susie Abbey, ca. 1976.

Facing page photos:
Ed, Aztec Peak, Arizona, ca.
1978. Photo by Buddy Mays.

From left: Dave Foreman, Coconino County Deputy Sheriff, Ed holding Jim Stiles's rendering of the Glen Canyon Dam, two unidentified people, March 21, 1981, near Glen Canyon Dam.

Ed and Susie, Utah, 1982. Photo by Bill Hunter.

Susie Abbey, Ed, Clarke, Organ Pipe Cactus National Monument, 1981. Photo by Jack Loeffler.

Facing page: Earth First! meeting, Granite Creek, Wyoming, 1982. Photo by Pete Dustrud.

Abbey in Desolation Canyon, Green River, Utah, 1982. Photo by Bill Hunter.

Clarke, Rebecca, and Ed, 1984. Photo by Jay Dusard.

chapter 4

Abbey headed for the red rock country, the home country near Arches. He was amazed at his behavior and thought that perhaps he had gone mad. But he had done what he needed to do, to break with his wife of nearly thirteen years in order to find the meaning of his own life. He bitterly rued abandoning his sons, whom he loved deeply. And now he had lost them.

He hiked through the high desert, inhaling the perfume of juniper, feeling the clean hot wind against his face. He watched the circling buzzards and wondered if he should surrender, lie down and die, to provide them with one good meal. Or hike down into the maze and disappear into the ghostly silence. Or relinquish himself to a magnificent rapid in Cataract Canyon. He was frightened by the sound of his own breathing in the vast emptiness where he must keep his own company or lose control.

There is little solace to be found in failed matrimony. It's like joining the fellowship of the damned. But little by little, the high desert reclaimed him, and he felt the presence of the Earth like a balm, soothing and healing. The relative permanence of the landforms and their familiarity grounded Abbey, and he yielded to the magic. Few of us have ever experienced true solitude in the wilderness, the extraordinary transformation that occurs when one hikes day after day over unpeopled terrain. It's not for everyone. But for those who have breathed that free air and have had to rely on their wits to endure the desert, who have lost count of nights spent alone beneath the dark firmament, with songs of owls and coyotes their only company, there is a bond, not just between themselves, but with the planet, the mother Earth. That bond becomes the most powerful force in their lives. With that bond comes the realization that the planet is indeed a living entity and we and all the other species are complex parts of the greater organism. Our planet is our support system and is far more sacred than any anthropocentric projection, and must not be profaned by human folly.

Abbey absorbed this knowledge, and his mind turned to his book, for which he had settled on the name *Desert Solitaire.*

In early September 1965 Edward Abbey and his friend Bob Waterman descended into the Maze, a labyrinth of rock and canyon where for five days they explored terra incognita. The Maze befuddles the human eye, which can make little sense of the random mass of formations that constitute that part of Utah. Abbey faithfully registered his impressions of that adventure in his journal and later transformed this narrative into a compelling chapter for his new book.

By early autumn he was divorced, truly an outlaw now, by his own reckoning. As he wandered the canyon country, he looked at every spring as a possible roost, a potential hiding place. The anarchist in him was also undergoing a major transformation. He was trekking beyond anarchist tradition by perceiving that the land itself was bound by the long arm of centralized government and had therefore lost its freedom to exist as wildlife habitat. He imagined a greater form of revolution that freed the land from any governing body. He recognized that the human species had as much right to exist as any other species, but *not more right by virtue of being human.* He began to imagine individual watersheds as being self-governed by their own distinct ecologies and inhabited by *optimum* populations of appropriate biota—including humans. The key is optimum, not maximum. This thinking began to edge into his writing.

Abbey had read *Anarchism,* by George Woodcock, a good overall history of the subject, similar to the book he himself had wanted to write as his master's thesis. Now he was extending the scope of anarchism and by so doing was unconsciously carving his own niche in the distinguished heritage of anarchist thinkers.

Before leaving the East, Abbey had met and fallen in love with a young woman named Judy Pepper. It was the vision of love and its promise that had given him hope. By late September Abbey headed east to Judy. She was living in New York City, but the prospects, for once, filled him with enthusiasm. He was happy. They were married on October 16, 1965. He had been a bachelor for forty-six whole days.

Abbey applied for several seasonal ranger's positions and accepted a job in the Everglades of Florida. He was fascinated by the density of it and by the relative strangeness of the biota. "Fireflies in January." It was a good way to honeymoon. In retrospect, he was glad that he had spent a season in the Everglades but found that he needn't return.

Ed and Judy Abbey moved to a fire lookout atop Mount Harkness in Lassen Volcanic National Park in northern California. He had written 194 pages of *Desert Solitaire,* two-thirds finished. The book on welfare, which Abbey referred to as *Scum of the Earth,* had dissolved in his mind, but he was obsessed with the fact that he owed $2,500 to the publisher for work unwritten.

He had come to regard a fire lookout job as perfect for a writer, especially if he shared it with a compatible, companionable, beautiful woman with whom he was in love. Life atop an eight-thousand-foot peak with Judy delighted Abbey. The problems that drive the mass of men into "lives of quiet desperation" seemed trivial from his lofty vantage. He was secure in the moment, which for Abbey was quite enough.

In September 1966 Ed drove Judy to the bus station in Reno. She boarded a Greyhound bound for Death Valley, where she had accepted a job as a teacher at the Death Valley Elementary School. Abbey would join her there at the end of the fire season. He was alone again on top of a mountain, looking at a ten-thousand-foot-high neighboring volcano and eighty-mile distant Mount Shasta, which he likened to Mount Fuji.

Two weeks earlier he had finished the first draft of *Desert Solitaire* and shipped it off to his agent. Abbey felt good about the book and regarded it as his best book yet. It would be his first published book of nonfiction, his first one-on-one expression of ideas. *Harper's* magazine intended to publish a chapter later that autumn. He pondered the next book. Would it be *The Good Life? Don Coyote? The Iron Gates?*

Other issues commanded a great deal of his attention, namely achieving some sort of accommodation with Rita so that he could visit his sons regularly and often. He missed them deeply and even made preliminary designs for a desert home where each of them had a bedroom with a window looking out over the vast desert landscape. This dream never came to be, and Abbey's relationship with his two sons grew more remote.

He became disoriented on his fire lookout. He was west of the West he loved—New Mexico, Utah, Arizona—and west of his lookout lay the great cities of San Francisco and Seattle, which seemed more easterly in their white man's tradition. He was anxious to leave and as ever was pining for his sweetheart. He began to reminisce in his journal.

> *Say! Remember that afternoon on Malcolm's lawn, boiling thunder-storm overhead, Debris and Malcolm watching, I teased, shocked and exasperated poor Judaeo-Catholic Bob Granat by pointing an iron crowbar at the sky and challenging God to strike me dead? A childish stunt of course—and yet how pleasing! Almost as good as that evening at Dead Horse Point when I hurled the flaming spear-and-flag off the brink to the immense delight of John DePuy and the horror of my father—he thought I'd get killed.*

As Abbey paced the floor of his tiny lookout, staring out over the expanse of forest over which he presided as protector, he ever fantasized on the female form and even penned a provocative essay titled, "On the Biological Basis of Female Beauty." He became convinced that monogamy was the result of a Judaeo-Christian snow job that relegated the fundamental nature of *Homo sapiens* to a forbidden zone defined by the dictates of an invented god. Who the fuck was Moses to tell Abbey not to commit adultery? No more guilt! Abbey imagined a free society where love was given freely by both sexes and the offspring were freely parented by the collective. Sounded great to Ed, although it would be impossible to achieve and could become a petri dish of identical cousins.

Finally the fire season ended, and Abbey was exonerated from further responsibility to that particular forest. It could burn in good conscience now that Park Service bureaucracy was appeased. Actually, it would be good for the forest's health to burn a bit, but it would look bad on the records. He left the mountain peak with his gear, climbed into his white Chevy Greenbriar cab-over-engine panel, and drove southeast to Death Valley and his wife. He got a job driving a school bus for the same school where Judy was a teacher. He spent his days cruising the low desert and contemplating his novel.

On October 22, 1966, Ed Abbey took a trip on the "Good Ship LSD." It was his one and only voyage on the psychedelic sea, and perhaps fear of foundering plus the cap being a light dose resulted in a mild bad trip.

What am I afraid of? Physical pain? No; going out of my mind and never
getting back? Not really—altho' the faint possibility cannot be ignored.
Losing control of my own ego, shattering the hard-built facade? Yes, I
suppose that's the main thing—but compensated by the hope of gaining a
newer, stronger sense of the whole self. And the possibility of spiritual
growth—a breakthrough. And most of all, an escape from this Sargasso
Sea of sloth, lassitude, inertia, enervation, dull despair in which I am
presently trapped—becalmed.

Abbey ingested the blue capsule on an empty stomach lined with the con-
tents of a bottle of beer and a mind laced with a few tokes of reefer. In the
main, the trip made him nervous and irritable, his body uncomfortable. In a
word, he felt drugged. His friend who had supplied the acid decided that it was
time to drop a second cap, which he did. Abbey refused, by now feeling that
above all, he wanted out. No more. He had a few flashes but few, if any, insights. Judy had refrained but was monitoring in case of freak-out. Little by
little, the high subsided. His friend plunged deep into it, having taken a total
of seven hundred micrograms. Finally Ed and Judy loaded their nirvana-bound
companion into the Chevy and went home.

In retrospect, Abbey was disappointed. Not for a second did he believe that
enlightenment comes in capsule form. But he had hoped for that sense of the
mystical that sometimes accompanies psychotropia. Although he rarely mentioned this in his writings, he had a yearning to experience that realm which
lies beyond the five senses. He glimpsed it infrequently, as all solitary wilderness wanderers must. But he never became submersed in it. He experimented
with marijuana a few times, but it hurt his throat. He tentatively concluded
that "grass is a gas, but likker is quicker."

It seems that God is making a comeback in certain circles—Mailer, the
LSD hippies, etc.; but me, I'll stick with Democritus, Lucretius, Occam,
Sartre & Company: "He Dead."
The world of the living contains enough marvels and mysteries as it is;
marvels and mysteries acting upon our intelligence and emotions in ways
so inexplicable that it would almost justify the conception of life as an
enchanted state. No, I am too firm in my consciousness of the marvelous

to be ever fascinated by the mere supernatural, which (take it any way you
like) is but a manufactured article, the fabrication of minds insensitive
to the intimate delicacies of our relation to the dead and to the living,
in their countless multitudes; a desecration of our tenderest memories;
an outrage of our dignity.

Throughout his life, Abbey was subject to periods of deep melancholy. The acid trip did little to alleviate his spiritual lassitude. Creative writing seemed the only real solace. Not even Judy (or any of his lovers) could more than momentarily relieve his misery.

I am resolved therefore to continue on my present course: to compose
somehow the one good novel; to try to be good to my wife; to run Cataract
Canyon in a kayak; to raze more billboards; to build that solid house of
rock and wood far out somewhere where my sons and grandsons can find
at least a temporary refuge from the nightmare world of 2000 A.D.; and to
be ready, with rifle or rood, for the apocalyptic showdown which may yet
come—I hope—in our lifetimes. . . .

That winter he wrote fifty pages of the second draft of *Desert Solitaire* and a couple of articles. He drove his school bus scores of miles daily through Death Valley, "the true test of the desert rat." People actually died of exposure in this cleft in the Mojave, the most formidable patch of sparsely vegetated desert in North America. He considered summer in February "an ominous portent."

The essay that had been printed in *Harper's* was reprinted in *Reader's Digest,* which he regarded as a literary disgrace. But he accepted the check for $1,000—"the lures of Mammon." It seemed that little by little, he was becoming recognized as a writer in spite of what he regarded as his creative lethargy.

When the school year ended, the Abbeys quit the fiery sands of Death Valley and Ed procured yet another seasonal job as the river ranger at Lee's Ferry, the dividing line between the fifteen-mile-long remnant of Glen Canyon and Marble Canyon between the upper and lower basins of the Colorado River.

Abbey was issued a motorboat and a badge, and he patrolled twenty-three miles of the Colorado River daily. Every time he rounded that northerly bend and saw the Glen Canyon Dam, bile rose in his craw and bitter anger all but overwhelmed him. The sight of that concrete monstrosity that rises seven hundred feet above the surface of the river inspires dire thoughts in the mind of *any* halfway sensitive and sensible human being.

Judy had gone east to visit her family in New Jersey, and Abbey's old billboard-razing university chum Al Sarvis came to visit, bringing with him a sexy wench clad in a tiny bikini. The three of them piled in Ed's Park Service motorboat, well-heeled with an ample supply of bourbon, and up the river they went. The feckless river ranger took his eyes off the lovely form before him only long enough to gaze skyward as he tilted the bourbon gulletward, and thus he ripped the propeller off the shank of the motor, thwarting their forward momentum. Even so, they glimpsed the Glen Canyon Dam, and the two billboard saboteurs of yore imagined the collapse of the Glen Canyon Dam by the hand of man.

In October, after he had turned in his badge for the season, Abbey went down the Grand Canyon all the way to Temple Bar. It was a glorious adventure where he worked as "the number 2 nigger." He vowed to go down again and explore the myriad side canyons. After the river runners took out, Abbey, refreshed in spirit, headed west to San Francisco.

Gawd, what a sweet town. The first time I think I ever loved a city. A city. I, Edward Abbey, hater of cities, have fallen in love with a city. . . . City of light, of pastel fogs, of silvery smog, city of hills—like the hanging gardens of Babylon!—and city of love.

He visited his sister, Nancy, and her three "golden children, Bill, Abigail, and Kelly." Abbey thought his sister beautiful. "How that Seneca [Indian] strain reveals itself in her—the dark chestnut hair, the dark brown eyes, the big cheekbones, the slender limbs, the dark skin. An Indian maid if I ever saw one. . . ." Abbey had begun to consider that one-sixteenth of his blood was of Seneca provenance. He talked about this from time to time but rarely wrote about it.

By November 1967 the Abbeys were living in Tucson, where Judy was pursuing her master's degree and Ed was ruminating on *Desert Solitaire,* which had almost been

cted by the Book-of-the-fucking-Month-Club. Almost. Too bad
ut them. Well, what would I do with another 20–30 thousand
dollars anyway? Get fat and insolent, prob'ly. The book, incidentally
looks OK. A solid, handsome little book—I'm pleased with it. It should
last for many years. (For a century at least.) . . . I'm glad I did it. I'm
satisfied. . . . What more is required?

Agent Don Congdon called Abbey to announce that there was a $15,000 advance to write *The Good Life,* his masterpiece. That meant he was actually going to have to write it. He signed the contract on March 17, 1968, at Organ Pipe National Monument in the heart of the Sonoran Desert, where he had recently become a backcountry ranger. He was also writing *The Iron Gates,* which he regarded as an excellent little novel. This novel would be published as *Black Sun.* It would remain one of Abbey's favorite pieces of his own work.

That winter in the Sonoran Desert captivated Abbey. He was a scant seventy or so air miles from beloved Baboquivari, and the lush columnar cacti of the upper Sonoran caught the light of a full moon and cast shadows across the floor of the desert to the sound of elf owls and coyotes. DePuy had come to visit him. "Mad Debris. A good man, a good comrade, and an *artist.* Has only one vice: Garlic."

While he was at Organ Pipe, Abbey made two close friends, Jim Carrico, the chief ranger, and Bill Hoy, the Park Service interpreter. Sometimes Abbey and his friends would go adventuring in the Sonoran Desert wilderness. Bill Hoy recalls his friend Abbey:

One day several of us had gone into a restaurant to have lunch. DePuy was there and six or seven others. When no-one was looking, Ed quietly got up and went over and paid the bill. He didn't have to. He didn't say anything. He just did it. For his friends.

Judy spent much of her time at the University of Arizona, where she eventually received her master's degree. While she was gone, Abbey couldn't resist the life of a randy philanderer. Judy slowly became aware of her husband's infidelities, and their marriage suffered.

The final night at Organ Pipe, Abbey ruminated on his existence while listening to *La Bohème* on the radio. Judy slept in the next room. In Abbey's mind, so much remained to accomplish.

Judy headed east and Abbey went to Denver, ostensibly selling a book but in reality partying hard in the big city, drinking too much, undoubtedly womanizing.

By mid-May 1968 he was once again ensconced on a fire lookout, this time atop Atascosa Peak in the Coronado National Forest.

The lookout merely a flimsy old frame shack perched like an eagle's
nest on this pinnacle of rock 6235 feet high. Built in the '30s by the
C.C.C. of course. Held together by paint and wire and nuts and bolts.
Shudders in the wind.

He was lonely there, pining for Judy, ever ruing his inability to remain faithful to his wife. He suffered a strange portent of impending disaster and was unable to identify its source. But it was a time of disaster in America.

On June 5, Robert Kennedy was shot and died the next day. "If it's not a conspiracy, it sure as hell follows a pattern. Every time a leader for change appears, somebody shoots him down. How can we be *sure* it's *not* the C.I.A.?"

Abbey's thoughts hovered around death, even his own. The day Robert Kennedy died, he wrote:

Last Will and Testament:
In the event of my premature death, of which I have all too many
premonitions, I hereby direct that any and all income and/or monies from
my literary properties be divided equally between my wife Judy and my
former wife Rita, for the care and education of my children.

Being of sound mind and body I do subscribe hereunto my signature, etc.

[his mark, which looked like a star] Edward Abbey [signature]
Atascosa L.O.
June 6, 1968
Witness Gawd

On August 8, 1968, Judy gave birth to Susannah Mildred Abbey. She weighed seven and a half pounds, was blond. And beautiful! And spirited! The Abbey strain ran strong in her veins.

It was during this period that Abbey found a beautiful rock-hewn house with a wood-paneled interior in Sabino Canyon, east of Tucson. He made a down payment and for the first time had his own house to live in when he wasn't doing seasonal work for the Park or Forest Service. He loved this house, which backed up against a high scarp topped by a serrated ridgeline.

Abbey's pal Al Sarvis talked him into accepting a job teaching at "Redneck U" in Cullowhee, North Carolina. The Abbeys were reunited after Susie's birth, and Ed taught, hating every minute of it.

How I despise it. How I loathe it. . . . All them unspeakable truly hideous little bluebook themes . . . And the hours and hours of preparation, reading filthy garbage like Homer and Aeschylus and Shithead Plato and Dante and that ancient archaic bore Wm. Shakespeare. . . .

Abbey sank into another melancholy phase. He lasted a single quarter and resigned.

He returned to Organ Pipe National Monument, where he could wander the backcountry, explore the Ajo Range, trek down Kuakatch Wash, watch desert pupfish at Quitobaquito, and otherwise bask in the warmth of the Sonoran Desert. He contemplated American culture and realized that for the last five millennia, humanity had been enslaved (or enserfed) by the state— a phenomenon he attributed to the domestication of animals and the rise of agriculture, which tolled the knell for the nomadic hunter-gatherer. He realized that "society is like a stew. Keep it stirred up or you get a lot of *scum* on top."

Abbey had an altercation about a woman with Al Sarvis, whom he mortally insulted. Sarvis now hated Abbey's guts. Their friendship was dead. Abbey carried this in his heart for years to come, and it no doubt affected him as he began to conceive his best-known novel, *The Monkey Wrench Gang,* one of whose heroes was named Doc Sarvis.

As the winter season at Organ Pipe National Monument ended, Abbey was able to acquire the job of fire lookout on the north rim of the Grand Canyon. He had established a pattern of moving from one seasonal job to the next. The pay was modest, but the lifestyle allowed him the time to write. After *Desert Solitaire* was released, his reputation as a writer was established and his list of published articles grew.

Look magazine interviewed him, and he was immortalized in a photograph where he appeared tiny against the magnificent background of red rock country. *Life* magazine commissioned him to write an article about mountain lions. "Anything that eats sheep can't be all bad." He attacked mountain lion hunters.

As his reputation as a writer and gadfly grew, so did his insatiable desire for sex.

I believe in marriage. I love my wife. And yet I can't bear monogamy. That's the rub—for me it's unnatural. Cruel. Painful. Unbearable. I like girls: can't seem to get over it, or outgrow it, or sublimate it—in fact the more active and creative I am, the happier I am, the more I crave sexual excitement. Which means for me, a new girl now and then, in bed. Is there something wrong with me? Am I sick? Am I truly a satyrmaniac as Judy thinks? Do I really need a shrink? Or just a good deep fuck now and then with some fresh young thing out of the blue. . . . Sex is one of the few outlets we have these days for a man's inherent lust for adventure. The only frontier—besides science, and maybe revolution, and maybe (doubtful) art.

Abbey abandoned the reins on personal monogamy. He simply couldn't handle it. He concluded that this was the way men were supposed to be, and that women had to figure out how they were supposed to be, and that the way they were frequently supposed to be together was making love. Simplistic? Maybe. But that was how Abbey felt about it.

Female rumps: I know why I like them but I don't know why I like them so much. The ass-man cometh.

In the autumn Abbey returned to Pennsylvania to spend time with his family and to work on his novel *The Good Life*. Judy left him and said she'd never come back. Ed and his brother Johnny had a fight over the Vietnam War during Thanksgiving dinner. Ed fell in love with a woman named Bonnie, whose first name lingers on in *The Monkey Wrench Gang*. Jack Macrae from E. P. Dutton called Abbey with a proposal to write a twenty-thousand-word essay for the Eliot Porter book on Appalachia. He received various commissions to write book reviews for different magazines. He was asked to review *The Bamboo Bed*, by his friend William Eastlake, whom he regarded as the "best living U.S. novelist with this qualification: my own best books have not been published, yet. Have not, as a matter of fact, been written yet."

He kept his inherent melancholia at bay but admitted that he was "half in love with easeful death. To disappear, to vanish, to float away (down the river) into the wonderland of death, out back of beyond . . . the allure of the hermit thrush."

He went back to Organ Pipe for yet another winter season and worked on the Appalachia manuscript and discovered that he was now being invited to deliver lectures at universities. On Earth Day 1970 he gave a speech at a teach-in at the University of Utah, which was regarded as a great success.

Later that spring Judy fell ill. Even though their marriage had fallen apart, largely due to Abbey's philandering nature, they still were in love with each other. Abbey had taken his old lookout at North Rim for the summer but had to go east in June because it was apparent that Judy was dying of leukemia.

This was perhaps the most difficult time in Abbey's life, as he went daily to the hospital to watch his wife, the mother of their daughter, Susie, waste away from a dread disease, the pain of which even morphine couldn't entirely allay. Abbey witnessed the morass of medical accoutrements that Judy was condemned to abide as her hours grew short. He agonized with her and felt a tremendous mantle of guilt enshroud him for not having told her the truth, that she was indeed dying, her condition hopeless. Early on in their marriage they had agreed that one would not let the other die in the hospital. But the doctors told Abbey that perhaps she could go into remission and drugs could miraculously appear that might even yet save her.

Malcolm Brown was living in Manhattan at that time, having broken up with his wife, Rachel. Malcolm went to visit Judy several times and knew that her days were numbered. He also knew that Judy wasn't aware that she was soon going to die. Ed and Malcolm talked about this, and Abbey said that he simply didn't have it in him to tell her the truth.

On July 4, 1970, Judy Pepper Abbey passed from this Earth in Mount Sinai

Hospital while fireworks celebrated the 194th anniversary of the birth of the United States of America. Judy was dead, and Abbey was totally devastated. He was forty-three years old, his twenty-seven-year-old wife was dead, and his twenty-two-month-old daughter would never know her mother again.

> *Judy. Her death. Just too goddamned cruel and unjust and absurd and unnecessary to be borne. . . . Two and a half weeks now. Every now and then it hits me like a blow in the soul, and all I can do is weep.*
>
> *The novel* Black Sun *(which is dedicated to the memory of Judy), which I never clearly understood altho' I wrote it, now has meaning for me: it is a novel about death—which, in the case of one you love, is an inexplicable vanishing—an unaccountable deprivation—an opaque void—a hopeless disappearance . . . A meditation upon death.*

PART II

Integrity is wholeness, the greatest beauty is

Organic wholeness, the wholeness of life and things, the

beauty of the universe. Love that, not man

Apart from that, or else you will share man's pitiful confusions,

or drown in despair when his days darken.

—*Robinson Jeffers / 1887–1962*

chapter 5

The year 1970. The genesis of a decade of infamy for the landscape of the American Southwest. Actually, the infamy had already begun with that concrete-and-steel monument to Mammon, overindulgence, and heresy against the flow of Nature, the Glen Canyon Dam.

In order to understand what fired the passion of Edward Abbey during the final decades of his life, I must tell something of its story.

The Glen Canyon Dam stoppers the mighty Colorado River just upstream from Lee's Ferry, that arbitrary line of demarcation that divides the upper basin of the Colorado River drainage from the lower basin. The Colorado River is 1,440 miles long, draining a watershed that spans 244,000 square miles and includes parts of seven states: Colorado, Wyoming, Utah, New Mexico, Nevada, Arizona, and California. For seventeen miles it separates the United States and Mexico; it thereafter flows another eighty miles until it drains into the Sea of Cortez, one of the world's most beautiful seas.

"The Colorado River is a unique river system," according to the *Encyclopaedia Britannica.* "No other stream in the world has cut such a remarkable series of extremely deep trenches, with the Grand Canyon the deepest and most spectacular. The river drains the most arid sector of the North American continent; and because of its intensive development, it is called the 'Lifeline of the Southwest.'"

In the last third of the nineteenth century, a one-armed veteran of the Civil War, John Wesley Powell, and his men ran the Colorado River through the Grand Canyon in wooden dories, charting its course for the U.S. Geological Survey and having the adventure of a lifetime. In 1878 Powell published his *Report on the Arid Regions of the United States,* a milestone in conservation literature, written at the time of the taming of the West by the white man, a time of infamy from the point of view of the Indians, a time of land grabbing by cattle barons, a time of realization that the West is drier than a dead man's sense of humor. It wasn't long before everyone was making plans for the water in the Colorado, with no compunctions about rearranging the watershed and its adjacent ecosystems.

In 1922, when future U.S. president Herbert Hoover was Secretary of Commerce, the Colorado River Compact was designed by representatives of the seven western states constituting the drainage area. It was decided that Lee's Ferry, downstream from Glen Canyon and upstream from Marble Canyon in northern Arizona, would mark the boundary separating the Upper Colorado River Basin from the lower. Colorado, Wyoming, Utah, and New Mexico were included in the upper basin and California, Arizona, and Nevada were in the lower basin. It was erroneously determined that seventeen million acre-feet of water courses down the Colorado in an average year. (It's more like 15 million acre-feet per year.) The upper and lower basins would equally split fifteen million acre-feet a year. An acre-foot is an acre of water one foot deep. Three acre-feet comes to roughly a million gallons.

It took another twenty-two years to establish what share of this water would be reserved for Mexico. And no one thought to ask the Sea of Cortez how much it needed for the maintenance of its biotic community.

In 1928 the Congress of the United States authorized construction of Boulder Dam (now Hoover Dam). It was completed in 1936 and resulted in Lake Mead. This dam, supervised by the U.S. Bureau of Reclamation, established the hegemony of Washington, D.C., over the fate of water in the West. Shortly after Hoover Dam was constructed, a second dam was built—Parker Dam, which created Lake Havasu. It is from Lake Havasu that one billion gallons are pumped westward every day, supplying Los Angeles and San Diego with the lion's share of their water.

After the apparent successes of these dams, the federal government started eyeing the Colorado River with more dams in mind. Some even seriously considered building dams in the Grand Canyon! In 1956 the Colorado River Storage Project Act authorized construction of yet another dam just upstream of Lee's Ferry: the Glen Canyon Dam.

Of all the places in the world to build a dam, why there? Why stopper the river there and flood what was truly one of the most beautiful places on Earth? It has made grown men weep. It makes me weep as I write. If there was ever a monument to the technomaniacal mind of man, it is the Glen Canyon Dam.

In the early 1960s the Glen Canyon Dam was completed, plugging the

Colorado River and filling Glen Canyon with water, turning it into Lake Powell, named after John Wesley Powell, who spins in his grave.

For many years the idea of the Central Arizona Project had been fomenting, conceived by Arizona politicians who relentlessly cursed California for claiming the largest single entitlement to the Colorado River. "We want our share! We want! We want!" Phoenix needed water. Tucson needed water. Early on, Arizona senator Carl Hayden pushed for the Central Arizona Project, as did his political descendants. California kept shouting it down. In 1952 Arizona filed a lawsuit to get rights to a major portion of the Colorado River. In 1963 the U.S. Supreme Court decided in favor of Arizona with the result that Arizona would receive 2.8 million acre-feet per year plus the flow of its own in-state tributaries to the Colorado. But problems remained. How would the water get across the desert from the river to Phoenix and Tucson? There was an enormous coal deposit in northern Arizona that could fire a power plant or two to generate the juice to pump the water to Phoenix. "Great idea. Too bad the coal is under Indian land." "That's okay. We'll screw the Indians. Been doin' it fer years. Why stop now?"

Peabody Coal Company, from East St. Louis, got the contract at a ridiculously low price thanks to John Boyden, a Salt Lake City attorney who was counsel for the Hopi Tribal Council and through a masterful weave of conflict of interests also worked for the Peabody Coal Company. The coal would be shipped via railroad across the Kaibito Plateau to the shores of Lake Powell, where the Navajo Generating Station was to be constructed. Power lines would radiate in great webs borne by gigantic metal structures that looked like japes of the local deities. Electricity would be carried by these power lines to Lake Havasu to run enormous pumps to pump water out of the lake into canals that would channel the water all the way to Phoenix and finally to Tucson.

Another power plant would be constructed near Laughlin, Nevada, fed by coal from the same source—Black Mesa, the female mountain sacred to both traditional Navajos and Hopis. After the coal had been crushed into small particles of under an inch in diameter, the coal particles would be slurried for 273 miles in water pumped at the rate of two thousand gallons per minute from the ancient aquifer underlying Black Mesa, an aquifer that had provided water to Hopi springs for centuries.

An entire power grid was being blocked out over the fragile landscape of the American Southwest. It had begun with the Four Corners Generating

Station near Farmington, New Mexico. The plume of smoke from the Four Corners Generating Station was said to be the only human artifact visible to the men who went to the moon.

The Southwest was being raped by developers and mining companies. The land was being pillaged, the waters fouled, the air smoke-dimmed, traditional cultures left bereft. Power lines marched across the land like electric kachinas.

Traditional Hopi and Navajo Indians were utterly dismayed that their sacred mountain was to be strip-mined for its coal. The Hopis were aghast that the ancient aquifer that had replenished their springs for centuries was to be tapped at the rate of over two thousand gallons per minute. Much of the electricity generated there was to be used for glitzy lighting arrangements along the avenues of Las Vegas. The Navajos learned belatedly that over thirty thousand acre-feet of their water entitlement was to be extracted from Lake Powell every year to supply water for the cooling towers of the Navajo Generating Station, which would in turn generate electricity to power the Central Arizona Project. That is the equivalent of a minimum of fifteen gallons of precious water every day for every member of the Navajo Nation. For a people accustomed to hauling water in thirty-gallon containers from well to hogan, that's a lot of water—more than most Navajos even use in the course of a day!

Consciously or unconsciously, the U.S. government and the current coterie of extractors, power magnates, and developers were hornswoggling the Indians yet again. The effects of the Central Arizona Project on natural and cultural environments were uniquely devastating. Never before had such an enormous area been so affected by a single project.

It was into this milieu that Edward Abbey gazed as the despair wrought by the death of his wife was shorn away by the healing desert wind. He had returned to his lookout at the North Rim of Grand Canyon. He looked out over the Colorado Plateau and grappled with his reaction to the Glen Canyon Dam, the projected coal-fired generating stations and accompanying strip mine. His anarchist inclinations surfaced, and he reflected on "the morality of political violence," the subject of his master's thesis. He was by now anarchist, outlaw, widower, and father. Distraught as he was, the spirit of revolt that fired his soul never wavered. The current of anarchism that coursed through his being had focused on humankind's pillaging of the planet. When Abbey was born, the human population of the planet had yet to reach two billion. By the time of the Judy's death in 1970, the population had more than doubled. For the rest of his life Ed's prevailing passion was the defense of the natural environment against his own species. He was haunted by the Glen Canyon Dam, that symbol of the prevailing cultural paradigm of turning habitat into money.

At times Abbey wandered off by himself to ruminate on the nature of reality. He headed east to Muley Point, where he could look out over ten thousand square miles of the Colorado Plateau. He wandered Black Mesa, where he schemed on every conceivable means of liberating the land from the avarice of man. He pored over *The Anarchist Cookbook,* the saboteur's version of the *Whole Earth Catalog.* Only on occasion would he inflict damage on an earthmoving machine. He watched as just such a machine dozed away the hogan of an elderly Navajo woman who had lived there all her life, whose dreams and prayers were swept away in a single swipe of this monster that had invaded her homeland. He watched as the Navajo woman fell to her knees, weeping, then fainted dead away. He crawled on his belly and looked at corrals of equipment hauled in over the new roads that scored the desert. He peered at the Four Corners Generating Station and wondered if it were true that an armor-piercing missile fired from a high-powered rifle could actually cause the station's flywheel to begin to wobble itself to death. (The revenge of the Wobblies!) As time wore on, he tried unsuccessfully to procure a bazooka, deeming it a superb anti-Earth-terrorist tool. He hauled around a gunnysack full of splitting wedges that he intended to piggyback and affix to the tracks of the Black Mesa Railway, which hauls coal across the Kaibito Plateau to the Navajo Generating Station. The notion was that maybe the wedges might overturn the unmanned train. However, there was always someone on board when he scouted, and his first rule was, "Cause harm to no human!" He paid special heed to the conveyor belt that transported coal from the strip mine to the loading silo for the coal-bearing train. It looked particularly susceptible to ecotage. He followed many miles of the slurry line that extends from Black Mesa to Bullhead City, considering blowing away a section of it, which would, of course, result in a small stockpile of coal for any indigenous people who might live in the immediate area. He formed a plan to take a tape-demagnetizing device, or degausser, into the master computer room at Laughlin, Nevada, in the hope that a few minutes of high-level magnetization might cause the computer to commit suicide through some accident of binary ethics and thereafter leave the Southwest in peace. He salted roadways with nails and other sharp objects to slow down the endless trucks. He pulled up surveyors' stakes, experimented with the effect on motors of Karo syrup, sand, graphite, and various other substances; he thought about demolishing the Glen Canyon Dam, thus effectively shutting down the entire catastrophe. Without Lake Powell, the Central Arizona Project could not happen.

These eco-shenanigans became the basis for a research project that was to result in Abbey's best-known and most beloved novel, *The Monkey Wrench Gang*. It features the adventures of an unlikely foursome: Doc Sarvis, an M.D. from Albuquerque whose avocation is the razing of billboards; Seldom Seen Smith, jack-Mormon white-water outfitter who hates the Glen Canyon Damn and whose true home now lies beneath the waters of Lake Powell; George Washington Hayduke, a violent Vietnam War veteran who is a relentless self-appointed destroyer of the tools of terrorism; and Bonnie Abbzug, Doc's nurse and paramour, who titillates the fancy of the three male members of the gang. With this novel Abbey established himself as a master of humor and poignancy and joined the thin ranks of original American philosophers by melding anarchism and environmentalism.

The Monkey Wrench Gang was difficult for Abbey to write. For a year and a half he suffered writer's block, during which time he had an affair with a lady from the Bronx named Ingrid. Abbey thought highly of her for the rest of his life and mentioned her frequently in conversation.

The Defenders of Wildlife hired Ed as manager of a wildlife refuge in Aravaipa Canyon, in southern Arizona in the northern reaches of the Sonoran Desert. Doug Peacock worked there part of the time. He and Abbey had met at the home of writer William Eastlake and gradually came to influence each other's lives. Peacock's personality traits influenced *The Monkey Wrench Gang*'s George Washington Hayduke, just as Utah-born Ken Sleight was to influence the character of Seldom Seen Smith and Ingrid was critical to the original character of Bonnie Abbzug. Doc Sarvis was a bit more complex. He took his name and part of his manner from Al Sarvis, part from a doctor friend, Brendan Phibbs, part from other friends.

In 1973 as he sat at his large wooden desk in his Aravaipa refuge, his manuscript piling ever higher, his old manual Royal typewriter leering at him balefully, Abbey worried over this novel and urged it to come to life:

No, I don't love every comma. Having trouble as usual with people: character. How to create personality in the novel. Tough to do. All my characters—Doc, Bonnie, Hayduke, Capt. Smith—seem thin, superficial, one dimensional. Worse, they tend to get blurred, to sound alike. Worse yet, they all tend to talk like me. Or like I think. Hardest of all, the girl, Bonnie Abbzug, half-Scot, half-Serb, with Bronx background, NYC accent. Doesn't seem sufficient somehow merely to toss in a Yiddish word now and then. Not good enough. And Doc tends to sound like a sententious prig. Maybe he is. And Joe Smith a moron. Only Hayduke seems real—but he is crude, ugly, brutish, hardly a sympathetic character. And I want the reader to like these people—nay, to love them. Otherwise the whole novel will fall on its face. On its bazoonga. On its premises. They've got to be lovable—even heroic—perhaps tragic. How? O Muse of Novelists, bring me thy wit and wisdom, thine grace and understanding! QWIK!

In truth, they are all Abbey, or almost all. At one juncture in the novel, the Monkey Wrench Gang stands atop a knoll, looking out over the Black Mesa strip mine. Abbey writes:

Their view from the knoll would be difficult to describe in any known terrestrial language. Bonnie thought of something like a Martian invasion, the War of the Worlds. Captain Smith was reminded of Kennecott's open-pit mine (world's largest) near Magna, Utah. Dr. Sarvis thought of the plain of fire and of the oligarchs and oligopoly beyond: Peabody Coal only one arm of Kennecott Copper; Kennecott only a limb of United States Steel; U.S. Steel intertwined in incestuous embrace with the Pentagon, TVA, Standard Oil, General Dynamics, Dutch Shell, I. G. Farben-industrie; the whole conglomerated cartel spread out upon half the planet Earth like a global kraken, its brain a bank of computer data centers, its blood the flow of money, its heart a radio-active dynamo, its language the technetronic monologue of numbers imprinted on magnetic tape.

But George Washington Hayduke, his thought was the clearest and simplest: Hayduke thought of Vietnam.

Compare this with a letter Abbey wrote on May 5, 1973, to *The Arizona Republic*. It was rejected.

> Dear Sir:
>
> I hear the Forest Service wants to name a mountain after our late senator, Carl Hayden. I got a molehill in my backyard they can have. . . . Hayden is the man primarily responsible for the Central Arizona Project and Glen Canyon Dam, two of the worst atrocities ever committed against the people of Arizona and the United States by the United States Government. Until those structures disappear, as they surely will, let us remember Carl Hayden as one who idolized the false gods of greed, growth, industrialism—not a benefactor, but a destroyer of all that makes Arizona precious.
>
> Yrs., Edward Abbey

In 1970 we stood on the bridge that spans the canyon immediately south of Glen Canyon Dam.

"Are you a praying man, Loeffler?"

"Not particularly."

"Are you willing to join me in a prayer?"

"What prayer?"

"For an earthquake to shake that fucking dam loose once and for all."

"I'll pray for that."

Abbey and I got down on our knees and prayed as hard as we could to the local deities to stir up an earthquake. Ed prayed aloud while I chanted. We gave it our best shot. But we were either out of practice or the gods of Mammon had finally come to prevail. After several minutes we gave it up. We discovered that our fellow tourists were giving us a wide berth, either because they thought we might be insane or because they rightfully assumed that if our prayers were successful, the bridge would also be shaken loose. In either event, we were definitely regarded as pariahs. So with that in mind, we headed a few miles north and set up camp in Paria Canyon.

chapter 6

(one)

Aravaipa Canyon is a beautiful ecosystem where mountain lions, Mexican black hawks, and javelinas roam the country. Abbey lived there as caretaker for nearly two years. It was there that he wrote much of *The Monkey Wrench Gang*. While he lived there, Abbey fell in love with Renée, a beautiful seventeen-year-old girl. Indeed, Renée was beautiful and intelligent, a gentle lady who cast light with her glance.

Abbey's spirits soared. On the thirty-second anniversary of the bombing of Pearl Harbor, Abbey noted:

Cold rainy day at Aravaipa. The heartbreaking loveliness of this bloody, incomprehensible world. Cardinals and thrashers, woodpeckers and wrens and gilded flickers, cowbirds and doves in the air. And I, lord of it all, custodian and janitor of a 70,000 acre wildlife preserve. With a fine novel to finish and a sweet young absolutely delightful girl to love and a bright jewel of a daughter and the body in firm fettle and what is there to despair about, anymore? Except despair? I have been and am a very lucky man. And I have earned and deserve every fucking bit of it.

And I rejoice.
And I am exceedingly glad.
And I shall piss and whine no more, nay nor moan and bitch, nor take the name of My Lord in vain, for he has been exceedingly good to me and lo! his servant Abbey waxeth fat, and prosperous, and curseth not so much as formerly, nor shaketh fist at old, heartbreaking, wild and iron sky which seals and shelters us from (peace!) that which lies beyond. I am blessed. Amen.

Art and Bess Pepper, the grandparents of Ed's daughter Susie, had moved to Tucson from New Jersey, so Susie divided her time between the Pepper household and Aravaipa. Susie and Renée got along well. Abbey's demeanor grew downright cheerful. He hiked miles daily, exploring the beautiful canyon. He found a *tinaja* filled with water that was so deep, he couldn't plunge to the bottom of it. He spent hours strolling naked in the sun, wearing only the jungle combat boots he favored.

He kept a horse that he rode, ranging the hundred square miles of his domain, looking for signs of human interlopers. "Fun and games in the old wildlife preserve. Hunters cutting chains, pulling guns, getting drunk, trespassing all over the place." He took his job as caretaker seriously and would put himself on the line before a cadre of drunken hunters and kick them off the preserve.

Life at Aravaipa afforded Abbey the time and space for the reflection that comes in the middle of a man's life:

> *What was it we dreamed of, imagined, in those infinite summer days, gazing off far away not merely into space but into time, into some fantastic visionary future, if not toward this very moment? So that, as it were, so to speak, looking back, from here to that idyll—that strange, obscure, mysterious idyll of boyhood—I find myself looking into the eyes of myself—and the boy I was (if time is real and all the past not simply a haunting dream) gazes "forward," outward, into my eyes, and so, thus linked by this simple image, we are one, the boy and I, we are the same, we both exist, neither one more real than the other? At this moment?— A momentary hallucination, perhaps. Do I really believe this? Do I even understand what I am trying to say? Do the words come even near the idea, the feeling, the vision that preceded them?*

Aravaipa was an enchanted land for Abbey. Finally spared the desperation that comes with financial worry, lost love, and hiatus in creativity, he now had the time and freedom to speculate, to wander, to be in love, to write without having to worry all the time.

Abbey had been gaining success as a writer of magazine articles, which would prove useful since he could select from these essays to fill future books. He finished writing original text for *Cactus Country*, a book about the Sonoran Desert for Time-Life Books, which was released in 1973. Time-Life then asked him to write a book on the Sierra Madre of western Mexico. "Truth is I don't actually want to write words for *any* more goldarned travel books, but *must* out of greed, necessity and old debts coming back to haunt me."

Abbey never wrote the book on the Sierra Madre, but he did go on an expedition into the compelling landscape. He and Renée hired the services of pilot Ike Russell and flew with their gear from Arizona to the heart of the Sierra Madre Occidental, homeland of the Tarajumara Indians. They landed in Creel, a town almost equidistant between Chihuahua Ciudad and Los Mochis, and stayed at the Hotel Nuevo, a timeless hotel, handcrafted and filled with old curios. They could imagine that B. Traven might have stayed there decades earlier, smoking a Faro and tossing back a *tasa* of *tesguino*. In the streets of Creel they saw mestizos and *indios* shod in *huaraches* soled with treaded tire. Wearing these sandals, the Tarajumaras could walk or run endless miles up or down canyon trails.

Before Abbey and Renée left Tucson, Abbey invited Bill and Marina Hoy to join them for the adventure into the Barranca del Cobre. Ed didn't speak Spanish very well, and he needed somebody who could translate. Bill Hoy remembers the adventure, one that Abbey recalls in *Abbey's Road.*

We went out to Ryan Field out west of town. We had all this camping gear and food. The plane was loaded with barely enough space to sit. Marina started to cry. And for good reason. The plane was overloaded. Ed and Renée flew on down in the plane with Ike Russell, the legendary bush pilot. Marina and I went over to Nogales, took a bus to Los Mochis, and from there we took the *ferrocarril,* or railroad, to Creel in the Barranca del Cobre.

We got to the Hotel Nuevo in the town of Creel. Ed and Renée didn't know where we were and we didn't know where they were. So Marina and I went into this wonderful old, creaky hotel with sagging beds and huge piles of blankets and went to bed. The next morning I was about to go out and look for Ed and Renée. Then I heard this monster walking across the floor and I knew that couldn't be a Mexican. I opened the door and there was Ed just outside. He had a big old shit-eating smirk on his face. We shook hands. We found the hotel owner, Ricardo Domingo, who had a carryall. We told him we wanted to go to a wilderness area for three days. Domingo dropped us off at a side canyon and we started packing. It turned out that Renée was a very strong girl.

We finally found a place to camp down in the boulders. Ed had built a campfire and there he sat, bare-ass naked. Marina, my wife, was a little bit offended by that but she didn't say anything. We sat around the fire and had some good talks.

On the last day, Ed and I decided to walk to the Río Urique. We walked and we walked. There was bend after bend. The boulders were all trailer sized. And we couldn't see all that far ahead. We got to worrying about our wives alone back there in camp. We never did get all the way to the river. Ed was stronger than I was. I could hardly keep up with his bounding gait going through and over these big boulders. It was a great thing being there in total wilderness. There were Tarajumara Indians on the trail. We saw caves with pots in them. That was a great trip. Ed was a great companion. Totally comfortable. Things always went smooth and easy.

As he looked out over the "cowburnt" landscape of the northern Sonoran, Abbey's thinking turned more and more to preservation of habitat and wildlife. He had come to love the ugly javelinas, the wild desert pigs that hunters shot for sport. He loved their smell, javelina musk, and their explosive nature. At the approach of man, they scatter like billiard balls cracked by the cue. Javelinas ranged the Aravaipa country, and Abbey came to regard them as distant kindred. He wrote an article titled "Merry Christmas, Pigs!" that was originally published in the magazine section of the *Tucson Daily Citizen* and later included in *Abbey's Road*. Abbey admitted that if he were hungry, he would hunt the javelina for food. When one is hungry and the family must be fed, he said, hunting is an honorable act. This conclusion led Abbey to one of his fundamental tenets:

> *I believe that humanity made a serious mistake when we gave up the traditional hunting and gathering way of life in favor of settling down to agriculture. Someone said that the plough may have done more damage to human life on the planet than the sword. . . . So it began. We enslaved the horse; we created the mule; made slaves of dogs. Soon afterwards we learned to enslave human beings. Now, today, our technological-industrial social machine is trying to enslave the whole of Nature—put everything to work*

for the sake of human greed and human power. That, I think, is the great
evil, the ultimate evil, of the modern age. By "modern" I mean of course the
last 5,000 years, when the nightmare of human history began.

This sort of thinking dominated the mind of Doc Sarvis of *The Monkey*
Wrench Gang. It dominated Abbey's own mind as he ranged his domain when
he wasn't sitting at his typewriter. He took his job as caretaker seriously, so
seriously that he was fired almost exactly two years after having signed on to
defend wildlife for Defenders of Wildlife. At first he was puzzled. But he told
me that shortly before he was fired, he had tangled with some politicos who
wanted to shoot javelinas and that possibly their leverage with the powers that
be was stronger than his own.

By early 1974 Ed and Renée were married. He was nearly finished writing
The Monkey Wrench Gang. He sold the Sabino Canyon house and bought an
old wood frame house in Moab, Utah, where he and Renée set up housekeep-
ing. *The Monkey Wrench Gang* topped out at 740 pages. It was turned down by
Knopf and Random House. His agent sold it to Lippincott in September 1974
for $37,500. Little by little, Abbey was "creeping up to the bottom of the pov-
erty level." He was actually making a living as a full-time writer. He rued the
end of his career as caretaker of Aravaipa, but he was at home near the heart of
red rock country, and he was in love with his wife.

In 1974 Abbey applied for a Guggenheim fellowship to write *The Good Life,*
which he had conceived years before and which was to have taken place back
on the farm in Pennsylvania. He received the grant, as did his friend Edward
Hoagland, with whom he had begun a lively correspondence that would last
many years. Abbey never wrote *The Good Life,* although there are shadows of it
in what was to be his "fat masterpiece" in its final form, *The Fool's Progress.*
Instead Abbey wrote myriad articles for magazines. Having written the text for
three large-format books of photographs—*Appalachia,* with Eliot Porter, and
Cactus Country and *Slickrock* with Philip Hyde—he was becoming regarded as
a major essayist. Many people also thought of him as a naturalist.

I am not a naturalist. I never was a naturalist. I never will be a naturalist.
I do not want to be a naturalist. I have never written a naturalist's book.
I don't give a shit about natural history.

(t w o)

In 1974 I took my parents on a tour of the American Southwest, to them an alien landscape since they had spent their lives east of the hundredth meridian. Five or six days out, we pulled into Moab, Utah, where we intended to spend the night. After dinner I excused myself, saying that I wanted to call an old friend. My parents were content to go to bed early.

I dialed Ed's unlisted number in Moab, and he answered the phone.

"Abbey here."

"Loeffler here."

"Where are you?"

"Moab."

"Why?"

"To destroy your serenity and peace of mind. Would you care to partake of some of that vile, green liquid that passes for beer in this culturally strange but otherwise beautiful land?"

"I'll check with Renée."

"You've been tamed by feminine beauty and elegance, you poor hillbilly."

"I'm in love."

"Is it true? Are you really older than your father-in-law?"

"It is true, you miserable bastard. I'll meet you at the La Vida bar in fifteen minutes."

I left my parents in their room and went off into a different world. I parked in the parking lot at the tavern. There were many cars but no sign of Ed's old carryall. I exited my Nazi-bus and stood waiting beneath the rich and velvety night sky.

"Attack! Surrender!! *Kamerad!!!*"

I was hoisted aloft from behind, a pair of long arms wrapped around my trunk, hands locked on wrists above my breastbone. Helpless.

"I gotcha . . . you trivial excuse for humanity!" He dropped me. I landed on my feet and spun to face the grinning, glaring countenance of Abbey.

"You didn't have the courage to attack me from the fore, you coward!"

"Ha! You're dead, Loeffler. You owe me at least two beers. I stand here ready to collect. Don't forfeit what little honor you possess, you puny pissant."

We staggered around the parking lot, laughing and gasping. So much for decorum. In we went, charming the waitress into giving us a table near the window, overlooking the lights of Moab below. The beers came, two bottles each, the first for gulping, the second for sipping.

"Boy, you'd sure have to drink a lot of this to get a buzz," says I.

"Yeah. If I'd known you were coming, I'd have asked you to bring in a couple of cases of real beer. This stuff's only three point two," says Ed.

"I guess I'm lucky I have a couple of cases of real beer in my van for *me* to drink while I drive my folks through Utah."

A pause. Ed's face grew serious. "Your folks are here? In Moab? I'd like to meet 'em."

"You just want my beer."

He cocked his head slightly and sighted down his nose at me. "Seriously. I've never met your folks."

"Well, we'll be here tomorrow and probably leave the day after that. How about you and Renée meeting us at the motel for breakfast?"

"Why don't you bring your folks by our house for breakfast?"

"I don't want to do that to Renée, Ed. It ain't fair. This way she can have some fun, too."

"Okay by me."

We drank a few more of the disgusting pseudobeers and decided to call it a night.

The next morning the Abbeys showed up and we had breakfast. My parents were pleased to discover that I had friends who didn't appear to be criminals, who wore clean clothes, and who spoke with some modicum of intelligence. It was decided that Ed and I would chauffeur my mother on a ride through the La Sals, that beautiful mountain range that dominates the eastern skyline beyond Moab. My father wanted to take a day off from sitting in the bus and opted to watch a ball game on the motel TV.

The trip began in dignity, Ed and I on our best behavior in the presence of my mother. We headed up and out of Moab past Pack Creek Ranch and onto the dirt road that leads through the La Sals. My mother was sitting in the rear seat, while Ed and I sat in front, I driving, Ed navigating.

"'Tis a long, dusty road, brother Jack."

"'Tis indeed, brother Ed."

"'Twas it my understanding that you carry real beer in your ice chest, brother Jack?"

"'Twas indeed, brother Ed."

"'Twill it bother your good mother if we sip of the beer, brother Jack?"

"'Twon't, brother Ed."

"Terrific. Stop the bus, brother Jack, and I shall fetch the brew." Which he did.

We explained to my mother that it was our old custom and fraternal rite to sip beer as we wandered down life's highway. Indeed, we measured the miles in terms of six-packs. For example, in those days of our autumnal youth, we considered the trip from Santa Fe to Albuquerque a one six-pack trip, Tucson to Phoenix a two six-pack trip, Santa Fe to Los Angeles a fifteen six-pack trip, and so on. One multiplied by the number of travelers. We had just embarked on a four six-pack trip through the La Sals and environs, multiplied by two (Ed and me), meaning eight six-packs, or two cases of cold beer, which is exactly what I had on ice in my cooler. Plan ahead, Abbey.

Curiously, we didn't get drunk. We talked, laughed, told jokes that didn't offend but only delighted my mother, sang anarchist songs and Christmas carols—my mother joining in on the carols. She was intermittently laughing, exclaiming in awe of the landscape, or nearly swooning of vertigo at the narrowness of the mountain road and the sheerness of the side of the mountain. It was a great day for all three of us—and a day that wound down gently as my mother and I dropped Ed off at his home.

My mother was enchanted by the tall, handsome man who was the great friend of her only offspring. "Ed is a gentleman," she said to my father.

The next morning my folks and I sat eating breakfast at the motel restaurant. Ed loomed through the door and came over to the table. We invited him to sit. He sat and maintained that reserve he wore most of the time. He looked me square in the eye.

"Jack, I'm going up to the Piceance Basin for ten days to do research for an article. Why don't you come along with me?"

"When?"

"Now."

"Jesus," was all I could say. There I was with my folks in Moab, Utah. My wife, whom I hadn't seen for a week, was at home in Santa Fe. Ed peered down his beak at me, his arms crossed across his chest, his earnest face deadpan.

Silence.

Finally broken by my father. "Go ahead, Jack. Your mother and I can catch a plane back home."

"Where could you catch a plane around here?" I asked, off guard.

"Grand Junction," said Abbey.

Disbelief flickered across my father's face. But he rallied quickly.

"Can we make connections to Denver, Ed?" he asked.

"Yes," said Ed, who returned his noncommittal green-eyed gaze to me.

"Ed, I don't know. I'd have to check with Kath and . . ."

"Aha!" said Ed, his face suddenly alive, fire in his eyes, a challenging, tooth-bearing grin transforming him. His look bore volumes of unspoken words to me, revenge and retaliation almost within grasp for my comments to him about his asking his wife's permission two evenings before.

"But I'll call her and tell her to expect me home in less than two weeks," said I, accepting his challenge. Ed continued to grin at me; my folks looked at each other nervously. This was not the way responsible people comported themselves.

I excused myself and made my way to the telephone. I called my wife, Kath. She didn't exactly bestow her blessings on this adventure, but she indicated that she might still live at home in Santa Fe when I got there, if I got there.

I returned to the table.

I sat down.

My parents looked at me anxiously.

Ed transfixed me with his grin of wicked mischief.

"I'm ready," said I.

Ed blinked, but the grin remained. "Touché, *compañero*," he muttered, but I heard him say it.

My father laughed in genuine enjoyment. My mother looked stunned. "C'mon, Lou. Let's get packed. These boys have to get going."

These boys? Ed was forty-seven, and I was thirty-eight. Just a couple of kids.

In those days Ed had an old Dodge carryall. We drove in random tandem to Crescent Junction, then east to Grand Junction. After my folks made sure they could get a flight out the next day, they took a room at the Holiday Inn, where there were no surprises. We bade each other hearty farewell, with good humor but no tears. They had taken it well, for which I salute them.

In the parking lot Ed and I came face to face.

"Did you bring your piece in case we need to shoot our way out?" says Ed.

"Yeah. Did you?"

"Yeah. We probably won't need 'em, but I'm glad we have 'em."

"*Tambièn,*" says I.

It should be understood that both Ed and I were fundamentally paranoid adventurers born at least half a century too late. We always camped with our pieces at hand, not to protect ourselves from wildlife, but rather from wackos not unlike ourselves. We were part of a coterie of misfits, all of whom went heavily armed to bed. There's a message here somewhere.

"Let's buy our food and drink here, then head up toward Rifle." We spread a map over the hood of Ed's carryall.

The Piceance (pronounced pee-aunce) Basin is in the northwest corner of Colorado. A vast deposit of oil-bearing shale is buried in this basin, and the energy mongers were scheming to A-bomb the oil out of the shale. Ed was to write an article that would expose the sinister stupidity of this concept.

Over the next ten days our trail would wind throughout the basin and we would become familiar with Piceance Creek, White River, the Danforth Hills, Dinosaur National Monument, Cathedral Bluffs, Book Plateau, Twin Buttes, and myriad unnamed landmarks in between.

Many are the miles that Ed and I trailed one behind the other in our respective vehicles. We ate a lot of each other's dust over the decades. But it tasted great, that gypsy dust—the taste of freedom, the smell of adventure, the feel of the endless dirt road, windows wide open, the better to hear the song of the meadowlark or catch a whiff of the wild cliff rose. Too easy to drive into a rut while watching a falcon stoop, then both of us spending hours dislodging a truck stuck in sand or high grounded or, tougher yet, digging out of ice-slick mud or quicksand, jacking up a wheel to free it and filling in with brush and branches to get a better bite, then sinking that wheel twice as deep as before so that we became inventive with the omnipresent come-along in air blue with our invective, finally to get free at last, thence to savor the satisfaction over two cold beers in the shade of a pungent juniper tree, one or both of us spotting a rock formation or canyon entrance a mile or two distant and hiking over there to explore its secrets. Someone has to do it. Might as well be us. We *need* to do it, otherwise we'll miss yet another opportunity to live as hard as we can this phenomenon of existence, whose mysteries are legion. Nothing—not one thing—is better than being lodged in a healthy body with a curious mind and propelling oneself far and away to a beautiful landscape heretofore unknown, potentially unknowable, with a true friend whom you trust implicitly who understands well your own need for solitude. That's the best of it, the finest aspect human existence has to offer. Or so I believe.

Ed and I headed north out of Rifle well stocked with supplies and gasoline. Soon we were driving on a dirt road generally north, looking out over country neither of us had seen before. It had a big sky, this landscape, and wasn't heavily vegetated. We found a campsite on a high knoll where the ground was level and the view expansive.

After parking our vehicles, we went about the business of making camp. We put on our elk hide gloves and gathered firewood, mostly dead juniper, and dragged it back to camp. Juniper burns clean, smells fine, and leaves a swell bed of coals, the better to cook over. We built our fire in a circle of stones and affixed ourselves to the place. Ed loved each place for its own sake and refused to assign any human overtones that might smack of the anthropomorphic. I, on the other hand, always felt some inner need to make peace with the local deity, the spirit of place. We were different that way.

It was always our practice the first night out to cook the best meat we had brought. As the days wore on and the ice in our coolers melted, our meals became simpler. But first night was celebratory. We were exonerated from any responsibility except to ourselves. There was an eternity before us. Time is relative. A week can seem eternity or pass with the exhalation of a breath.

Tonight we cook the favored meal—grilled pork chops and potatoes—each of us performing tacitly assigned tasks, at ease with each other and with the place. We don't talk much. Don't need to. Every now and then one or the other of us will look to the distant horizon. Why is the air slightly opaque? Dust? Don't recall there having been much wind. Moisture? Been drier than devil's breath for weeks. Smog? No. Couldn't be—could it?

The chops smell great cooking as they do on a grill over red-hot coals beneath which roast the potatoes packed in mud. The beer is cold. The appetites are honed.

"Let's eat."

"You're not supposed to eat rare pork." Abbey, a man of infinite patience, a man to savor the moment in anticipation, a man to avoid trichinosis.

"They look done to me. Do you suppose the potatoes are done?"

"Dunno. Let's find out."

We lift the chops off the grill, remove the grill, scrape away the coals, and dig for the spuds. There they are. Four spuds wrapped in dehydrated mud packs. I jam my knife into one of them.

"Feels tender to me."

We fish out the hot spuds and start to crack off the mud.

"I usually wrap potatoes in aluminum foil," says Ed.

"So do I."

"The modern age has destroyed more than a few good men."

"Who says we're good men."

"The real question is, have we destroyed these perfectly fine potatoes," says Ed.

We clean off the mud. We cut them open. They are hot, done right. We serve up our chops. We eat. Life is good.

That night, restless after we had cleaned our utensils, we looked out across the land, now lighted by the near full moon.

"Let's go for a walk."

We strapped on our pieces, took up our walking staves, and set out down the twin tracks of the jeep trail we had been following earlier that day. For a while we walked in silence. There was ever silence to our conversation.

"I like it here," says I.

"So do I. It's not spectacular like parts of Utah, but it's good enough."

"It's good enough for me. I sure hope they don't destroy it going after the oil shale."

"It's too expensive to extract the oil from the shale," says Ed. "It would cost a barrel of oil to make a barrel of oil."

"Do you really think that would stop them? Money's money from their point of view. If they can turn oil into money, do you think they care how costly it is to this basin?"

"Hard to say."

We walked on in silence, easily having found our stride.

"I hope I die out in the open," says Ed.

"What brought that on?"

"Oh, sometimes I get to thinking how grotesque it would be to die in a hospital, with tubes sticking in you in places where tubes don't belong. I can't think of anything more grisly. Did you ever see anyone die?" asks Ed.

"Yeah."

"Tell me about it."

"Well, I had stopped at the bank to cash a check. In that bank there's a foyer between the outside doors to the street and the inner doors, which open into the bank. As I was leaving the bank, I got to that foyer and there was an old man lying on his back, breathing hard and turning blue. I knelt down beside him and I could see he was dying. I took his hand and looked into his eyes. I felt his hand squeeze mine. I said something dumb like, 'Concentrate on the light,' as if I knew what the hell I was talking about. He looked me right in the eyes, and little by little I could see life passing out of him. He inhaled one last time. It was a terrible sound. I guess that's what they call the death rattle. Finally I was looking into a pair of dead eyes that were looking back at me. I let go of his hand and closed his eyes. That's what you're supposed to do, isn't it? And I looked up to see Don Van Soelen, the vice president of the bank, looking on pretty anxiously. 'He's dead. Do you have a blanket handy?' Don found a blanket, and we covered the body. An ambulance came and took the body away. That was it."

"Jesus," says Ed. "What did you feel like?"

"I felt strange, aware of my mortality. 'Do not ask for whom the bell tolls. It tolls for thee.' I hoped that I could pick a better place to die than the foyer of a bank. But I also realized that this old guy had no choice. His heart gave out and that was that. *No más. Es finito.*"

"I suppose we don't really have any choice, do we? Pretty hard to maintain your dignity. Maybe if we can see it coming early on, we can prepare for it. Gotta think about that." Ed became silent.

We walked on into the night, listening to a chorus of distant coyotes. The moon was rising higher in the heavens and we could see our shadows preceding us down the road, Ed on the left, me on the right, as we ever walked through our friendship. The southpaw with his piece on his left hip, the northpaw with his piece on his right hip. Romulus and Remus suckled on the teats of a lone wolf, or so we liked to think of ourselves.

"How do you imagine your own death, Jack?" Ed always asked questions that I always tried to answer. That's how I knew he was smarter than me.

"Making love with a beautiful lady when the sun goes nova." We both laughed, and Abbey pushed me off the road.

"That's what I like about you, Loeffler. You're too goddamn serious." A pause. "Well, how *do* you imagine your own death?" he asked.

"Alone, I hope. I don't want anyone to watch me die. I've always hoped that I could see it coming well enough in advance to be able to get myself out in the desert somewhere where there's some kind of shade and I have water and maybe morphine or opium to ease the pain."

"And then what?"

"Coyotes. Buzzards. If I'm fit to eat, that is."

"Don't you want a marked grave?"

"Why bother?" I said. "Why not be content with anonymous demolecularization? Seems to me that when you're dead, you're dead. You no longer make a difference, especially to yourself."

We walked on in silence for a little while, still heading away from camp, which was perhaps two miles behind us by now.

"How do you imagine your death, Ed?"

"Aha. Thought you'd never ask."

Silence except for the crunch of our boots in the desert.

"Well?" I was truly curious.

"I'm thinking about it. Maybe an accident while mountain climbing. One last wonderful downward flight into freedom. My last free act. Maybe my only free act. One accomplishment that is totally of my own free will. Or maybe a bullet in the brain. Or why not fall out of a rubber raft in the canyons of the Colorado. Or fill up a boat with dynamite and go out in a moment of splendid glory taking that fucking Glen Canyon Dam with me. Maybe build an adobe houseboat so that it would sink more easily down closer to the base of the dam. And then blow everything to smithereens.

"I sure as hell don't want to die in a hospital. In the end, a man has only his dignity. His accomplishments are behind him. There's little dignity to be found in a hospital amidst the stink of other deaths, other sicknesses. Give me a death outside that I can call my own, for chrissake. A death on my own terms."

Silence, the night our witness.

"Jack."

"Ed."

"Whaddya say that whoever of us goes first, the other will make
doesn't die in a hospital. Rather die outside in a proper sort of a death."

"Well, it would work for one of us. You're older than me, so chances favor
me doing all the work while you gaze off into the sunset."

"True enough," said Ed, grinning. "But you might die first. I'd be willing to
make absolutely sure that if there were some choice or chance, you would die
where you wanted to die and your carcass hauled off to where you wanted it to
be hauled off."

A pause.

"I'd agree to that," I said. We had stopped walking. We were facing each other.

"Do you solemnly vow that if I am about to die, you will make sure that
I will not die in a hospital and that you will take me out into the desert to a
place of my choosing if I am capable of choice, or a place of your choosing if
I am not, and will support me while I die and will bury me in my sleeping
bag with the full understanding that I will do exactly the same for you if you
are about to die?"

"I solemnly make that vow to you, Ed."

"I solemnly make that vow to you, Jack."

We looked each other in the eye and shook hands. The moment was too
charged with energy.

"Does this mean we're married?" I asked.

Ed let out a great guffaw. "You bastard, Loeffler." We gave each other a
violent shove that set us both on our asses in the dust. We laughed long. But we
had made a solemn vow to each other. And we both knew it.

"Let's go back to camp and drink some of that beer," says Abbey.

(t h r e e)

In May 1975 Abbey turned down a fire lookout at Jacob Lake in the Kaibab
National Forest of northern Arizona because the Forest Service provided no
accommodation for his wife, Renée. He rued this decision because he knew
full well that they could have comfortably camped out in the back of their

truck in the woods. He did accept a fire lookout atop Numa Ridge in Glacier National Park, Montana, and by early July, Ed and Renée were lodged in a square wooden shack on a rocky peak seven thousand feet above sea level. They were in grizzly country, and Abbey remembered Doug Peacock ruminating on what it feels like *not* to be at the top of the food chain! Alert to the noises behind you, to your side. Alert to the whiff of *Ursus horribilus,* scariest bear in the lower forty-eight. Reflections on a pile of bear shit—is this to be Abbey's fate?

A month passed, and Abbey grew to respect his young wife as well as to delight in her company. Sharing life on a fire lookout isn't for everyone. However, in early August Renée received word that her grandfather had died, and she went to Washington State to attend the funeral. Abbey was left alone atop the mountain, staring into his solitude.

Abbey was a list maker. His books reflect this. His journals reflect this. He listed the names of all the women with whom he made love. He listed the names of southwestern landmarks, animal species, plant species, friends, enemies, sums earned from his writings, camping equipment, books recently read. While on Numa Ridge, he made one of his many lists of good, bad, and indifferent writers.

The writers he regarded as bad: Racine, Molière, Corneille, Dante, Sophocles, Aeschylus, Proust, Lawrence, G. Eliot, James, Gogol, Nabokov, Hesse, Balzac, Austen, Cooper, Howells, Fitzgerald, Hawthorne, and Virgil.

The writers who fell beneath the "?": Homer, Milton, Goethe, Shakespeare, Smollett, Joyce, Dickens, Turgenev, Sterne, Defoe, Fielding, Miller, Hardy, Hugo.

The good writers: Cervantes, Rabelais, Marlowe, Euripedes, Mann, Tolstoy, Twain, Whitman, Dostoyevsky, Céline, Zola, Wells, Dreiser, Wolfe, Faulkner, Hemingway, Melville, Beckett, Traven, Poe, Hamsun.

Of Shakespeare, Abbey noted:

Certainly a master poet—but his plays are archaic bores: the childish humor of his comedies; the farcical nonsense of his tragedies; the tedious sycophancy of his histories. One of the many things I dislike is the total absence of any real, free, independent men in his world. All we have are masters and slaves, bosses and the bossed, and the prevailing slime of servility by which the hierarchical machinery is lubricated; in short, no men. Therefore, no heroes. No tragedy. Shakespeare, the immortal bard—

vastly overrated. Really belongs to the company of other distinguished hacks, such as S. N. Behrman, J. T. Racine, Ben Jonson, J. M. Barrie, Gilbert & Sullivan, etc. The characters I admire most in Shakespeare are his villains: Jack Cade, Caliban, Edmund the Bastard, Macbeth, Iago, that chap who married Hamlet's mother—what's his name, etc. In all of Shakespeare there is no Spartacus—not a single one. Ah, you say, but such a figure could not have been regarded as heroic in Shakespeare's time, and Shakespeare was very much a product of his time. To which I reply, "Precisely." I think it's unbecoming of a writer to submit, supinely, to evil institutions, merely because they constitute the prevailing order of things. Raleigh serves as an example of a man who was capable, unlike Shakespeare, to rise above and see beyond the narrow limitations of his own time. Marlowe another.

Abbey's criticism of Shakespeare and other literary figures occurs throughout his journals. He was as well read as anyone of his time, and he was decidedly a discerning reader. He believed that it was not just his right, but his very calling to challenge every hierarchy, every institution, everything ponderous that threatened the soul of man, the spirit of the land. This was his lifelong commitment.

By mid-decade the power combine had had its way in spite of the pitiful efforts of a few radical environmentalists. The Peabody Coal Company was gouging away at the heart of Black Mesa. The Navajo Generating Station loomed like an ominous deity of death whose breath filled the once crystalline skies with yellow-brown poison. The land bore the weight of endless transmission line towers. The spirit of the time had been mortally wounded by men who schemed for profit and growth. And now their intended pièce de résistance, a series of power plants designed to generate up to ten thousand megawatts, five times the size of the Navajo Generating Station, to be situated the scant breadth of Lake Powell away, atop the wonderful wilderness of the Kaiparowits Plateau, where coal could be easily stripped.

A haggard handful of environmental diehards had fought for years to stop the rape of the Southwest. David Brower, founder of Friends of the Earth; Brant Calkin, director of the Central Clearing House and national president of the Sierra Club; Bill Brown of the National Park Service; the environmental anarchists of the Black Mesa Defense Fund; Dave Foreman of the Wilderness Society; Joe Brescher, Bruce Green, and John Echohawk of the Native American Rights Fund; Richard Klemmer, anthropologist; Hopi traditionalists David Menongye and Thomas Banyacya; the great Navajo lady Ninebah Hufford; Tom Turner, editor of *Not Man Apart;* Alvin Josephy, editor in chief of *American Heritage;* photographers Dan Budnik and Marc Gaede; author and designer Jerry Mander; ethnomusicologist Bob Black; attorney Richard Hughes; Harvey Mudd; Melissa Savage; Pennfield Jensen; David Padwa; Gary Snyder; Drummond Hadley; Robert Redford; John DePuy; Edward Abbey. With the threat of the rape of Kaiparowits, the members of America's environmental movement rallied yet again, each in his or her own way. John DePuy recalls a foray that he and Abbey made:

> We were fighting Kaiparowits on the basis of court action, legal action, fighting it with propaganda. We had had enough and we said the hell with this. We went in a rented 4-wheel drive, courtesy of *National Geographic.* It had a winch. We had to take direct action. We stayed out there for a week and pulled up miles of sensors. Luckily, we had some industrial garnet and we did in a couple of drills. Then we camped somewhere else. We went back a week later and discovered that they had replaced the sensors. So we pulled them all out again and threw them over the side of the plateau. Apparently, their insurance rates went up so high that it helped cripple the company.

With the publication of *The Monkey Wrench Gang,* Ed Abbey had become recognized as the leader of the radical environmental movement. He was invited to speak before student bodies on college and university campuses. In 1975 he addressed the student body at St. John's College in Santa Fe. Greeted with great applause and enthusiasm, he rallied the audience to the defense of the Kaiparowits Plateau. During the course of his speech, he lapsed into an uncharacteristic public speculation on the meaning of reality:

> One reason for saving the wilderness is very simple even if it's philosophically impossible to substantiate, I suppose, and that is that

wilderness is worth saving for its own sake. *Not* for human benefit or pleasure, but simply for its own existence. In other words, I'm saying that wild things and wild places have a right to exist and continue existing with no relation to human wishes. I say that bees, birds, animals, snakes, buzzards, bugs, whatever, have a legal and moral right to continue. Even rocks have the moral right to continue being rocks. The Book of Genesis was *wrong*. Man was not put here to have dominion over all things. That's Woman's function. The Earth was here first, and all these living things before us. *We* are the newcomers, the late arrivals in the evolutionary pageant. Of course, we, too, are products of the process. We also belong on this planet no matter how alien we may sometimes feel or often behave. We too have a right to exist here. *But* there's not enough evidence to support the common and prevailing human belief that we have a right to expand our numbers indefinitely and to exploit the Earth indefinitely for our own purposes alone, at the expense of other living things and non-living things. How about this? Rocks have rights, I've said. Is it not possible that rocks, hills and mountains, and the great physical body of the Earth itself may enjoy a sentience, a form of consciousness which we humans cannot perceive only because of the vastly different time scales involved? For example, the mind of a mountain may be as powerful and profound as that of Buddha, Plato, Spinoza, Whitehead and Einstein. Say that a mountain takes 5,000,000 of our human or solar years to produce a single thought. But what a grand thought that single thought must be. If only we could tune in on it. The classic philosophers of both east and west have tried for 5,000 years more or less to convince us that *Mind* is the basic reality, maybe the only reality and that our bodies, the Earth and the entire universe is no more than a thought in the mind of God. But consider an alternative hypothesis. That Buddha, Plato, Einstein and we are thoughts in the minds of mountains, or that all humanity is a long, long thought in the mind of the Earth. That we are the means by which the Earth, and perhaps the universe becomes conscious of itself. I tell you that God, if there is a god, may be the end, not the origin of this process. If so, then our relationship to Earth is something like that of our minds to our bodies. They are interdependent. We cannot exploit or abuse our bodies without peril to our mental health and our survival. We have definitely seen some mindless bodies dancing around us, but we have yet to observe a disembodied mind. At least I haven't seen any. And as mind is to body, so is humanity to Earth. We cannot dishonor one without dishonoring and destroying ourselves.

Abbey perceived centralization of the American economy as a negative force of enormous proportions. He regarded defense of wilderness as a necessary step toward decentralization. By defending a given region against governmental and private development, one was actually affiliating with the land. One was defending the ecosystem against the geopolitical system. To protect the wilderness for the sake of wilderness rather than for future economic gain was to shed a dangerous part of our culture.

Decentralization could lead to a more balanced communal way of life with minimal impact on the environment, especially if human population were gradually reduced through natural attrition to an optimum rather than maximum level. In this way, the human community could evolve socially and economically to accommodate the needs of the land and the larger biotic community. Abbey contended that humanity had as much right to existence as any other species but certainly no greater right. Indeed, with our evolved intellect and capacity for science and attendant technology, we have a responsibility to our planet to practice forbearance rather than growth for the sake of growth. As the present dominant species, it is our primary obligation to maintain the health of the ecosystem in pursuit of the greatest good for the greatest number of species. In no way does this attitude detract from the destiny of our own species. It only enhances our existence!

In January 1976 a meeting of leading western environmentalists convened at the Wahweap Lodge in Page, Arizona. The purpose of the meeting was to stop the development of the intended Kaiparowits power plant. David Brower, John MacComb from the Sierra Club, Brant Calkin, Alvin Josephy, Edward Abbey, David Menongye, and other notables assembled to represent the voice of sanity and reason. Malcolm Brown, Dennis Hopper, artist Sam Scott, photographer Karl Kernberger, my wife, Katherine, and I assembled to express passion on behalf of the land. A group of locals—coal miners, power plant mechanics, and folks who needed jobs to survive—assembled to demonstrate against the environmentalists. Their position could be understood by any good anarchist who had fought injustice. They needed work, and Ed Abbey, who regarded himself as a Joe Six-pack, knew that the basic problem did not lie with the Joe Six-packs.

I've been a Joe Six-pack for much of my life—had to work various
jobs, most of them rather tedious, simply to get by, make a living. No,
I certainly don't blame working people. They're more victimized by this
process than the rest of us. Most of them have their lives and their health
threatened more directly and more constantly, simply by the work they do,
than we lucky ones who escaped that trap.

I recall seeing the look of torment on Ed's face as he watched the laborers carrying their placards that admonished environmentalists for threatening a possible source of jobs. When David Brower stood to speak, the laborers sent up a howl that shook the building. Somehow peace was restored.

Later that evening, a gang of us had assembled around a big table to have dinner together. Dennis Hopper sat there in blue jeans, wearing his cowboy hat with a big eagle feather lodged in the brim. Two FBI agents came up to our table and busted Dennis for his eagle feather, thus establishing a bad relationship between the FBI and environmentalists that has only grown worse over the years. Dennis had been given the eagle feather by a Native American friend as a blessing. By law, Native Americans are allowed to possess raptor feathers for religious purposes. One could imagine that the FBI viewed arresting Dennis for possession of the eagle feather as a means of weakening the environmentalist position.

Ultimately, the plan for Kaiparowits was put on hold, even to the time of this writing, thanks to the staying power of many stalwart environmentalists, including members of the Southern Utah Wilderness Alliance.

In 1976 Abbey received a commission to travel to Australia and write about it. He devoted sixty-five pages and four essays to Australia in his book *Abbey's Road,* which wasn't published until 1979. Abbey told me that he loved Australia. It wasn't as grand as the American Southwest—what could be? But it possessed desert and many forms of wilderness. He liked the backcountry people and considered them straight shooters. He had rented a car and driven it relentlessly to the edge of its current assemblage. He had become fascinated with the bushrangers, Australia's outlaws. Time to revive an honorable tradition.

In late July 1976 Ed and Renée embarked on a trip down the Colorado River in wooden dories in the spiritual wake of John Wesley Powell. John Blaustein photographed the expedition and the extraordinary beauty of the Grand Canyon. The river ran cold downstream from the Glen Canyon dam at a maximum of forty-five thousand cubic feet per second. In the days before the dam, the river ran as high as three hundred thousand and more if heavy rain clouds had dumped upstream.

The dories ran high and dry for the first few days as the river runners settled in. In the evenings Abbey would hike about, exploring side canyons, dislodging an occasional boulder to watch it crash over edges and carve its own trail with gravity as its guide.

Several days and nights out, some of them sleepless because of insects or the thought of pending storms, the party stopped at Phantom Ranch, where fifteen passengers departed and fourteen new passengers joined the party. The boatmen were uneasy.

Much talk about the Greta Wave at Horn Creek. Instruction to new passengers about what to do if boat flips. That freight-train roar down-canyon. The river appears to disappear. Drop-off so abrupt cannot even see waves or jets of water rising; barely a faint mist rising. We all stow hats away in forward hatch, everything else that's loose. Buckle up. Trim boat (bigger passengers in bow). Hang on.

Over the edge on the oily bronze tongue, between the heave of oil surging over two boulders. Into the maelstrom. Giant brown waves and yawning holes. Blindness as waves crash over us. One, two—"one more," says Rich the boatman—"hold on!" Into a hole we hadn't even seen before. The Great Wave looms above. We climb toward it. Chaos. Under water, I feel the boat careen to the right, on my side. Turns completely over. Under water, free of the boat. Up to the surface. I grab lifeline on overturned boat—me, Jenny, Renée, Rich on upstream side, Jane (the

*cook) downstream. Boat carried toward canyon wall. Rich climbs on
bottom, pulls up Jane, who is in danger of being crushed between boat
and rock. Boat crunches into rock. I am carried under again. Instinctively
(I guess) I get out from underneath, clear of boat and come up in eddy
beside tail of rapids. Renée also castaway. Rich and Jane still on boat,
pulling up Jenny. Carried past us. Renée warned away from current by
Jane. Renée calling me. Each of us scared for the other. I try to grab a hold
of slick polished rock—impossible. Then discover I can swim downstream
to pile of rocks at foot of wall. Renée joins me there. Stranded, we wait for
next boat—Blaustein. He rescues us, rows hard after Rich. John, Rich,
Jane and I get Rich's boat (Celilo Falls) righted. Start bailing. Empty
forward hatch, bail it out. At last I begin to feel cold, the deep chill of my
immersion in that 40 degree water. Remove life jacket and shirt. Hot
wind warms bones. Gliding onward through incredible beauty. Feelings
of relief, of triumph (we survived), of peace. But Rich appears despon-
dent—his boat badly fractured at stern, leaking into center hatches. All
other boats make it safely through Horn. All stopped to look except for
John in his Peace River who'd hurried after us. "Afraid to look."*

    *Primary sensations: need for air; swallowing water; waves over my
head; lack of confidence in life jacket (which probably saved my life);
momentary despair at being left behind, to revolve forever, round and
round in eddy; concern for Renée; fear for her until I found her down below.*

Days later they ran the great rapid at Lava Falls. Blaustein took a magnificent photograph of a dory approaching Badger Rapids, but this was a mere
shadow of the rapid at Lava Falls. Abbey's text and Blaustein's photographs
were published in *The Hidden Canyon* in 1977. It was a great adventure, that
river trip, one that Abbey savored for the rest of his life.

On January 29, 1977, Edward Abbey celebrated his fiftieth birthday. Renée
baked him a cake and decorated it with fifty candles. They had a regular party,
which included their friends from Moab. Abbey lost thirteen bucks in a poker
game. In my experience, Abbey was a rotten poker player.

*Fifty years old! Haven't I done most everything I ever wanted to do?
Enjoyed the friendship of a few good men, the love of several fine women.*

Fathered three sound, superior children (superior to their father). Wrote a couple of novels I'm not ashamed of, and some other books. Enjoyed a modicum of fame and glory, sudden money and easy living. Been fairly good to my parents, fairly generous to my friends and lovers and wives. Seen a bit of history in action. Seen some of the world's most beautiful places—Capri and Amalfi, Florence, Toledo, the Great Barrier Reef, Sydney Harbor, the Sea of Cortez, a desert isle called Angel de la Guarda, Mount Hood and Mount Rainier, Glacier, all the wonders of the Great American Desert. Camped in solitude on the rim of a high plateau, overlooking eternity. And so on. And yet—and yet—of course, I am not satisfied. There must be something more. Something more I wanted to do . . . or be. What is it?

The Edward Abbey of my books is largely a fictional creation: the true adventures of an imaginary person. The real Edward Abbey? I think I hardly know him. A shy, retiring, very timid fellow, obviously. Somewhat of a recluse, emerging rarely from his fictional den only when lured by money, vice, the prospect of applause.

It is true that Abbey was very shy. He was uneasy around groups of people, especially strangers. For all his brilliance with the written word, Abbey was frequently at a loss for words in conversation. Many people found it painful to talk with him on the telephone. There was a lot of dead air at his end of the line. Many's the time the phone would ring and I would hear, "Jack, it's Ed." Then nothing for many seconds. Then, "Whaddya say we go camping." It was disconcerting the first few times until I became used to Abbey's manner. We became adept at sharing silence, even over the phone.

(f o u r)

Northwestern New Mexico delights the eye with peaks that extend over thirteen thousand feet skyward, vast forests of ponderosa pine, great swaths of piñon-juniper woodland, riparian areas along both the Rio Grande and the Rio Chama, and high desert that smells of sage and promises mystery before the far distant horizon can be reached by foot, horseback, wagon, or pickup. Ed and I leaned against the windowsill in my living room in Santa Fe Canyon, staring at a peak 108 miles to the west. We would soon go northward to Bluff, where Ed had left his pickup parked under a tree. We said, "So long," to Kath, and left.

We headed out of Santa Fe and said little all the way to Española, twenty-five miles to the north. There the road divided and forked left toward Chama. Soon we were on a two laner that passed through the Hispanic village of Medanales, past the turnoff to El Rito, thence to Abiquiu, where artist Georgia O'Keeffe still lived.

We turned west just north of Abiquiu and looked out over the valley of the Rio Chama, so beautiful with vermilion and buff cliffs surrounding part of the sage plain, now violated by a lake that appeared with the advent of the Abiquiu Dam.

"Look at that pitiful, fucking puddle," said Ed, mournfully staring at the lake. "This used to be one of the most beautiful places in New Mexico. Remember that little ranch we thought about buying west of the Rio Chama?"

"Yeah. I also remember how we were going to pipe water out of the river straight up for a thousand feet or so."

"Details. Just details. Geniuses like you and especially me could figure out the details. By now we could be sitting on our own land as gentlemen of leisure, figuring out the details."

We drove past the Abiquiu Dam, and I stopped the truck in the middle of the road.

"Whaddya think it would take to remove this stinking dam?" says Ed.

"Perseverance and attention to details," says I.

"What kind of details?"

"The flood would probably take out Española."

"Too bad," says Abbey. "It would have been nice to free the Chama River."

We got back into the pickup and drove off toward Cuba, New Mexico, forty-six miles away. We stopped a couple of times to admire the lay of the land with an eye to buying the right to live unmolested on some acreage if we could only agree on which acreage.

As we drove along the Continental Divide, Ed said, "Eastlake used to live near here. On his ranch. But he sold it and moved south."

"I know. It gets really cold here in midwinter. Now he lives in southern

Arizona near you. You lowlanders have thin blood."

"You know, Bill Eastlake wrote three fine novels when he lived in New Mexico. *Go in Beauty, The Bronc People,* and *Portrait of an Artist with Twenty-six Horses.* He's been a friend for a long time. I haven't seen him for a while. I talk to him on the phone every now and then. I used to visit him when he lived here. Too bad he moved. New Mexico was good for his writing. Let's stop for a minute and go for a walk. For old times' sake with Eastlake."

William Eastlake had purchased a 1,280-acre ranch near Cuba in northwestern New Mexico in 1956, where he ran cattle and kept horses for thirteen years. It was here that he wrote his New Mexico trilogy, which stands today as a classic in the annals of southwestern literature. Abbey and Eastlake remained good friends for three decades. Eastlake recalled when they met:

Ed was tending bar at the Taos Inn when he and I first met. He had recently been the editor of that newspaper, *El Crepúscolo.* He called me on the telephone one day and asked if he could come over and visit. He was writing, but he wasn't doing very well. He had read some of my work. I invited him on over. Among other things, I remember that he brought me his recipe for making beer. He also tried to get me to buy the ranch next to the D. H. Lawrence ranch north of Taos.

Ed told me that while he was tending bar at the Taos Inn, Lawrence's friend Lady Brett came in carrying her ear trumpet, sat down at the bar, and ordered some exotic drink, a Grasshopper. Ed said, "I never heard of such a drink." Lady Brett got so mad, she complained to the owner and got Ed fired.

One time he came to see me and my cows were just coming down off the mountain and the weather had turned bad with a light snow blowing up. I wanted to go up and see the cows coming down. I was trespassing the forest, actually, because they didn't fix their fences. So Ed and I went up on my little mesa and we still couldn't see them. I said, "I'm going to get a horse." Ed said, "Get a horse for me." As I recall, there was only one horse in my local pasture. The other horses were down in my cross-fencing. I said, "There's only one horse. You can take it. Just go up and ride back with the cows and open the gate for them." So he got on the horse. It must have been about two or three o'clock in the afternoon. I waited and waited for him and it started to get dark and I got worried about him. Finally it got black. I said, "How the hell is Ed going to get back?" So about nine o'clock, I went down to the cross-fencing and caught a horse and started up one of the arroyos where I had told Ed to go. It was too dark to track him. I couldn't see very well. I rode maybe three or four miles up one of the arroyos and by God, I saw a light up there. I thought, there's no house up there. I got up out of the arroyo and went toward that light. It was precipitous. I finally got all the way up and there was a cave there. And in the cave was Ed, sitting at a fire. He said, "I got lost. I didn't know where I was. But you shouldn't worry about me. I'm having a great time."

I helped Ed get Don Congdon for his agent. Ed asked me if I would speak to Don, and of course I did. But Ed didn't do too well. Soon he told me he was leaving Don and going with a woman agent. Sometime later, maybe a year or two, he called me and asked me if I would contact Don and ask him to take Ed back again. So I did and Ed stayed with Congdon for the rest of his life.

Sometimes we talked about having been in the military. Ed told me that he had been an MP in Italy and had ridden a motorcycle. I told him that I had been an MP and had also ridden a motorcycle. So that became a bond between us. Ed would sometimes talk about the horror of the poverty of Naples and the ladies of Naples and some adventures that he had had there. It was interesting that we rarely talked about writing. It was my impression that at that time, Ed was more interested in what books were about than about how they were written. I don't think he was too much a student of style as distinct from myself. For me, it's not what a book is about but rather how it is written. Ed very gradually came around to how they were written.

Ed was a true outdoorsman. He wasn't a faker. He had enormous energy. And an enormous ego. He did everything he said he did. He was very competent. He could cope. Nothing bothered him. He was a genuine outdoorsman who had a right to make fun of Thoreau. "Henry" he called him.

I thought that Ed's writing was uneven. I preferred his nonfiction. One time we were discussing books that had become best-sellers. Ed thought that something got lost when a book became a best-seller. I told him, "Better read than dead!" Ed laughed at that.

Ed told me stories that mitigated against himself, that made him look bad. How he got out of a fight. Things like that. In other words, Ed was an honest man.

Ed and I hiked around for a while through a landscape that Eastlake had immortalized in his New Mexico trilogy.

"I used to help Eastlake chase down his cows," said Ed. "We'd saddle up and ride all over this range. It's not beautiful like Utah, though."

"Maybe not. But it's a hell of a lot more interesting culturally," I said.

"Tell me why you think so."

"Well, there are a lot of Navajos, Puebloans, Apaches, and Hispanos within a fifty-mile radius of right here as the crow flies. At least they're still in touch with the spirit of the land. Utah's too white for me. I don't much like missionaries of any persuasion. When I lived in that old forked-stick hogan at Navajo Mountain, a Mormon missionary would come by once a month and try to convert me to his faith. He regarded Indians as descendants from a dark side of the Bible. I hate missionaries. They try to lure real people away from their own traditions, their own cultural realities. I tried offering him coffee, tobacco, a beer in hopes that he'd take the hint. Finally I had to ask him to leave. Next came a pair of Catholic missionaries. They were easier to deal with. They took me up on the beer. I still have a bone to pick with that villainous Mormon lawyer John Boyden, who ostensibly represented the Hopi Indians as their legal counsel while he worked for the Peabody Coal Company at the same time. The progressive Hopis paid him a million bucks for screwing them. Traditional Hopis like my friends David Menongye and Mina Lansa knew he'd sold them out. Now the Peabody Coal Company's ripping coal out of the heart of their sacred mountain. Black Mesa's sacred to the Navajos, too. It's the body of their female mountain." I was getting worked up.

"Jesus, Loeffler, and you call me a bigot? The Navajos may be in touch with the spirit of the land, but their endlessly copulating sheep and goats have ruined northern Arizona. That reservation of theirs is one of the most overgrazed places I've ever seen. It's a disgrace. And not only that, they're all on welfare. They live in a welfare state just because they're Indians. The Navajo Welfare

Nation. Goddammit! I don't understand why you idealize these people." Ed's life as a welfare caseworker had profoundly affected his egalitarian sensibilities.

"Look, Ed, after your hero Kit Carson, who was working for the federal government, either murdered them or ran them off to Bosque Redondo in the 1860s, where they actually fed them coffee beans and did their best to starve them, demoralize them, and otherwise break them all the way down, they marched them hundreds of miles back, gave them back a few scraggly sheep and goats and threw in a few tools, and told them, Raise sheep from now on. No more raiding or we'll finish you off permanently. So they became full-time sheepherders, which they've been now for enough generations that it's their tradition. That's the way they measure their wealth."

"Jack, do you condone what their livestock does to the land?"

"No," I said begrudgingly. "How can anyone condone a disaster like that? But can you condone a government that treats human beings like we've treated the American Indians? A government that all but annihilates them and then tries to reeducate a rich, diverse culture like the Navajos and Apaches to become a part of a leaden, spiritually bereft culture like our own?"

"As you well know, I don't condone any government any more than you do. But I sure as hell don't idealize the noble savage, either. They collect their welfare checks and go get drunk in Gallup. I'm buying those bastards their beer, and I resent it!"

"You buy your beer with your fucking unemployment check and you make value judgments about where they get their beer? Bullshit, Abbey!"

We stood facing each other, glaring at each other in a Mexican standoff. We both started to grin and shoved each other around a little.

"C'mon, Loeffler. I'll buy *you* a beer with *my* unemployment check. Didn't you ever collect unemployment?"

"Yes. And I am filled with shame," I said.

"Now, that is a goddamn lie!! You are the most shameless bastard I ever knew."

"I, a liar? I, shameless? I am wounded too deep to bear."

"There's only one thing that's too deep around here. And not only that, I haven't collected unemployment since *you failed* to go in with *me* on that fire lookout job. Christ, we had it made. Each of us could have been on the lookout for three weeks and then off the fire lookout for three weeks. And we could have both collected unemployment. I face financial ruin and it's all because of you, you fucking beatnik."

"I thought you said you were going to buy me a beer."

"Go to hell. Or better yet, let's go to Cuba and we'll get a coupla six-packs."

An hour later we were cruising northwest on Highway 44 toward Bloomfield. Our thirsts were quenched and our tempers cooled. I was driving, contemplating the moonscape southeast of Dzilthna-o-dith-le, which is known by the Hispanos as Huerfano Grande. Barren country dotted with gas wells and occasionally splashed by the colorful blouse of a Navajo woman herding her sheep through the gray-green sagebrush. Beautiful country that didn't fit the white man's concept of livable. Great country as far as I was concerned. Abbey preferred a more colorful land. He hunkered in the passenger seat, reading.

"Listen to this," says Abbey. "'In the girl nature has had in view what could in theatrical terms be called stage effect: it has provided her with super-abundant beauty and charm for a few years at the expense of the whole remainder of her life, so that during these years she may so capture the imagination of a man that he is carried away into undertaking to support her honourably in some form or another for the rest of her life, a step he would seem hardly likely to take for purely rational considerations.'"

"Jesus," says I. "Who wrote that?"

"Schopenhauer," says Ed.

"Aha! The master misogynist," says I.

Ed continued to read: "'Thus nature has equipped women, as it has all its creatures, with the tools and weapons she needs for securing her existence, and at just the time she needs them; in doing which Nature has acted with its usual economy. For just as the female ant loses its wings after mating, since they are then superfluous, indeed harmful to the business of raising a family, so the woman usually loses her beauty after one or two childbeds, and probably for the same reason.'"

"I wonder if he ever fell in love," says I.

"Pretty harsh, isn't he? But he makes some sense."

"Do you agree with him?"

"Not really. But I think there's a lot more to biology than many women *and* men are willing to admit. For example, I don't think monogamy is natural for men. I think we're compelled by some biological law to pursue women whom we find attractive. I also think that a wife should always respond to her husband's sexual needs unless she's sick. Otherwise she'll lose her husband. A man needs sex. Conversely, a man should try to satisfy his wife's needs and do his best not to hurt her. I couldn't stand to hurt Renée. Jesus, Jack, we're all cowards on some level when it comes to women."

"Can you imagine living alone? Not having a wife?"

"I try to imagine that. It's hard. But I could foresee a time when I get so old and crotchety that Renée kicks me out. And I can imagine Kath kicking you out, too. Face it, Jack. We're two old farts used to having our own way. We could easily be displaced by two young bucks a hell of a lot more lively than we are."

"I give our wives a hell of a lot more credit than that. Christ. The fourth time's the charm. Ed, you're extremely lucky to have a wife like Renée."

"I know. But is it fair to her to be married to some morose old bastard like me when she could be with someone her own age?"

"She made her own choice, Ed. You'd have to look long and hard to find a better woman than Renée. Of course I suppose she could have found a better man. Would you please open me a beer?"

"Seriously, Jack. Suppose we both get kicked out. We should buy some land somewhere and you live on one end and I'll live on the other. We'll build a couple of hogans or cabins. Take lots of walks."

"What are you going to do when you get horny? Not many women roamin' them thar hills."

"Ah. There's always masturbation. And what I like best about masturbation is you don't have to talk afterwards."

We both laughed and quaffed some beer.

I glanced over at Ed. "Whaddya say we buy a couple of Airstream trailers and camp out on public land. Move around when the rangers kick us out. Be real nomads like the Navajos and Apaches. Raid the rich and distribute to the poor like you and me. Attack land developers and mineral extractors. Commit a few final desperate acts of heroism. Become a geriatric kamikaze unit. Robin Hood and Little John. Don Quixote and Sancho Panza. The Lone Ranger and Tonto. We could spend our declining years as desperadoes."

"Whaddya mean we, Kemosabe? I may be Tonto, but I ain't stupid."

Near Shiprock, Ed and I stood on the banks of the San Juan, pissing out beer into the river, looking back to the southeast at the Four Corners Power Plant, which converts coal strip-mined from the land into two thousand megawatts of electricity to help energize Los Angeles. The noxious plume that emanates from the great smokestacks spews tons of sulfur dioxide, nitrous oxide, and particulate matter into the once clear air.

"I actually hate that power plant," I said. "It may seem irrational to hate a nonliving form, but I hate it anyway."

"I hate the swine who own it, who conceived it and built it. They deserve to spend eternity suspended by their balls immediately above those smokestacks."

"Remember when Shiprock was the prevailing characteristic of this landscape?"

"Yeah. Let's get outta here, Jack. It's too depressing."

We climbed back into my pickup and began our ascent out of the San Juan Basin, once a glorious desert habitat for the wild and free, now glutted with a panoply of gas and oil drilling rigs, gas wells, oil wells, two strip mines, and two monstrous power plants.

We drove past Shiprock, that beautifully be-spired volcanic plug that shoots up out of the desert and assumes a mythically provocative posture that is embedded in the psyche of every Navajo as the site where Nayanezhganíí, one of the Twin War Gods, slew the monster eagle who jeopardized the lives of the Diné, the People.

"You know, Dave Brower was the first known white man to climb Shiprock," I told Ed. "He did it back in the 1930s. One night he and I and a few others camped beside it and he told me the story of his climb."

"What route did he take?"

"He went thataway."

"It must have been exciting for him. I admire Brower. He's done as much as anybody to preserve the environment," said Ed. "I've only met him a few times. I'd like to get to know him better."

Years later, after Ed's death, Dave Brower and I were driving through southern Arizona. We had both gone to Prescott to provide spiritual support for the first day of the trial of our mutual friend Dave Foreman, a founder of Earth First! who had been arrested by the FBI for conspiracy to commit sabotage, a charge of which he was innocent. Brower and I weren't allowed in the courtroom. Later Brower started reminiscing about Edward Abbey.

I never had any private moments with Ed Abbey. My first reaction when I read *Desert Solitaire* was not that there weren't good things in the book, but that he was paraphrasing Robinson Jeffers and others whom I had been quoting and he wouldn't give the origin of what he was saying. Then I read some more of his work. He was very kind. He inscribed a book to me where he called me one of his heroes. He certainly became one of mine.

On one particular occasion, I was to deliver a lecture on wilderness to young wilderness users at Timberline Lodge at Mount Hood. They were very uncomfortable about all the restrictions they were running into. When I arrived, I came down with some sort of intestinal problem, and in the next twenty-four hours I lost eleven pounds. And the day I was to speak, I didn't have any voice. I had already written out my speech. Abbey was there, and he read it for me and probably gave it a much better presentation than I would have. That's one of the things he was good at. He would read his stuff and milk it for all of the laughs he could get. One of the things the young people were bitching at was that there wasn't enough wilderness. Well, instead of complaining about it, they should go out and claim more wilderness.

Another time I was visiting San Diego and Ed was giving a lecture. During the question-and-answer period I asked how you sign up for the Monkey Wrench Gang. He answered, "You don't sign up. You just follow your conscience." The audience loved that. I wish I'd had more contact with him. I was very fond of his perspective. He seemed outrageous. But he really wasn't outrageous. What he was complaining about was outrageous. I remember reading an article he wrote for a magazine where people were complaining about him throwing beer cans out of the car and he said, "It's not the beer cans that are the insult. It's the highway that's the insult."

Ed and I followed the highway past the northern aspect of the Carrizo Mountains at Teec Nos Pos and the turnoff to Four Corners Monument. We finally reached Mexican Water and turned north. We were in country whose basic hue was red. Ed was perking up, having put Schopenhauer away. Ed loved this country in spite of the Navajos and their flocks of sheep and goats. To our west was Nokaito Bench, which is Navajo for Mexican Water Bench. We gradually descended into the San Juan River valley, crossed the river, and turned back east to Bluff, where Ed's truck was parked. We had loaded up with food and beer in Farmington, knowing that once inside Utah, beer was only three point two and twice as expensive.

Ed and I were set. We drove straight to his truck. He quickly hopped out of mine and into his and started the motor. We both peeled out back west to a dirt road that leads to a paradise created by the flow of Nature. Soon we were headed north just east of Comb Ridge, a geological phenomenon that resembles a plumed serpent frozen in motion. Or perhaps we're simply moving too fast in this human form to understand motion within the parameters of geological time.

After several days and nights in this country, we were enveloped in that state of grace where one melds with the flow of Nature. Having once tasted it, one craves that state like water . . . or one scurries back to what passes for civilization. The rocks and ridges and labialike crevasses had beckoned and irresistibly drawn us in to reveal formations extending heavenward in phallic majesty, or exquisite and delicate biotic communities consisting of elements that have somehow produced life. Just add water, heat, and bingo! Another miracle—no theology required. It happens on its own, satisfying some urge to which the planet is currently in a position to respond.

We were in a canyon that bifurcated. We agreed that each would follow his own trail and either meet farther on or have returned to camp by sundown. Ed took the left branch and I took the right, both of us happy to quit each other's company for a spell.

May in canyon country is sometimes gnat fraught, hot, and presided over by relative silence. The silence seems to await the raucous *auk!* of the raven that echoes against the walls, or the mellifluous glissando of the canyon wren, or the hum of insects, or the sound of your own boots plodding in sand and scuffing rocks, or even your own breath measuring the intensity of your labor as you climb into a fern-filled grotto, cool in the shadows of an overhang that hides and protects a tiny spring. What a haven to shade one's ever aging hide and bones against the stern blast of the midday sun. Why not hunker into the comfort afforded by soft sand, cool to the touch, and snooze a mite?

The shadows had assumed different patterns by the time I awoke. I could always head back to camp, that virgin spring of cold beer, and tell Ed that I had wandered into a *rincón* all too soon. But that would be fibbing. And so I continued my trek up canyon, climbing ledges, striding across vast rocky reaches that frequently ended abruptly above the eternal abyss. Looking. Endlessly questing, examining the lay of it, strangely moved by clusters of potsherds blazing a trail from human antiquity.

Juniper, ubiquitous on the Colorado Plateau, twisted tree of infinite shapes, blueberried and beautiful, sometimes slapped me with a branch bountiful with pollen and set me to sneezing and laughing at my clumsiness along the trail. I climbed higher until the round swell of a fin of the comb dominated the horizon forward and above. I could feel my heart thudding in my chest, heard the rasp of breath in my throat, and felt the trickle of sweat coursing through my beard. Slow down and take a breather. Lean on that old maple walking stick, friend of a thousand trodden miles. Cough out a hawker of gritty phlegm and feed it to the soil. Lighten the canteen by half of its warm, delicious water. And head up that long, dusty trail again, the strains of "Round Midnight" coursing like a stuck record through my mind's ear.

Finally I topped out onto a ridgeline extending between two of the great fins that characterize Comb Ridge. I stood a few feet east of the lip of the rim that dropped straight down for hundreds of feet along its western aspect to bottom out in Comb Wash, which drains into the San Juan River, miles to the south. Westward was an expanse of tortuous terrain that included the mass of Cedar Mesa and myriad canyons such as Mule Canyon, Owl Creek, fish Creek, and Lime Creek, all of which end in Comb Wash. The sun was lowering. I caught the scent of the cliff rose and was spellbound in the silence and incredible beauty of the moment.

"Reach for the sky, mother-sticker. This is a fuckup!"

Startled almost witless, I spun around and saw the seated figure of Abbey leaning against a rock not more than forty feet away.

"Jesus!" I exclaimed. "What are you doing here?"

"Just sitting here contemplating my novel," said Ed, grinning.

"Well, you got me that time."

"I know. It wasn't all that hard. You sounded like a tired old mule wheezing and farting along the borax trail."

We both laughed, and I walked over and sat down near Ed. We gazed out to the west, tacitly enjoying the magic light of late afternoon. Twenty-five miles more or less to the northwest we could see the twin pinnacles of the Bear's Ears marking a trail we had traveled before and would travel again. Many more miles to the southwest, well beyond Muley Point, the swell of Navajo Mountain marked the farthest visible formation. For our friend DePuy, Navajo Mountain remains the omphalos of the universe.

The late afternoon was mostly still, an occasional breeze stirring juniper branches and the tips of yucca spines. For the moment, at least, we had fused with that spot on the planet, and we took our ease.

From somewhere deep within the bottom end of my range of hearing, I thought I heard a grinding sound. I listened for a few moments.

"What's that?"

"What's what?" Ed replied.

"Do you hear that low rumble?"

Ed concentrated. "Can't say as I do." Like his father, Ed was losing his hearing.

We were both quiet for a few moments. Then Ed said, "Yeah. I can hear something. It sounds like machinery."

We edged closer to the cliff and looked out over a few hundred square miles of empty landscape. Nothing moved. But the sound of rumbling machinery slowly became louder.

"There. I see 'em. The swine." Ed pointed to the northwest.

"Where?" I tried to discern motion in the distant stillness.

Ed turned and looked at me. "Jesus, Magoo. You're blind and I'm deaf. That's a hell of a note for a couple of youngsters like us."

"Yes. But we're both brilliant and beloved of all women." I strained to see the source of the sound and lo, I caught the motion of aliens out there where I knew Route 95 to be. "What the hell are those?"

Ed squinted. "Looks like uranium trucks."

"Where do you suppose they're coming from?"

"Can't say. Remember that old uranium mine up on Elk Ridge near where we camped that time?"

"Yeah. But that seemed pretty well closed down."

"Remember all those mining claim stakes we addressed south of there?"

"You don't suppose. . . ."

"Could be." Ed looked morose. As usual. Ed had spent many years looking out over once empty country and watching it be eaten away by mankind. He had a right to look morose. "Debris probably knows all about it. I suppose we could go ask him. If we could find him. If he wanted to be found."

"I thought the atomic age was supposed to be over," said I, lying to myself.

"It comes and goes. Comes and goes. Looks like now it's coming again instead of going." Ed's perpetual frown was deepening. "Oh, the swine. The dirty, rotten swine."

"Which swine are you referring to? The truck drivers? The scientists?"

"Not the truck drivers, poor bastards. They have to earn a buck just to stay alive. Their jobs are more dangerous, and they get less pay. They sit with their backs to radioactive dirt when they're working. And the same for the miners. They figure they have to eat and this is the work that's available. They'd find work elsewhere if they could."

"Do you know that for sure? That they'd work at other jobs if they could?"

"No. I don't know that for sure," said Ed. "But I know I've had to work at jobs I hated because there was nothing else available."

"I think truck drivers are just as culpable as anybody else," I said.

"Hell, Jack. They're slaves to the system. In a sense, we're all slaves to the system. If we don't abide by the rules of the system, the system will spit us out . . . and we'll starve."

"I'll tell you, Ed. I used to think Joe Six-pack was a hero just because he was Joe Six-pack. He wears a collar that's blue. He earns his bread by the labors of his body. In theory, he's one with the universe. But if his work serves a purpose that's fundamentally wrong and he does it anyway, don't you think he deserves to share the blame?"

"Goddammit, man! Are you trying to make me think? We're not here to think. We're here to not think. That's why we hiked all the way to the top of this ridge. To not think!"

"For this you became a Master of Philosophy."

"A pointless endeavor."

We watched the distant uranium haulers pass from sight, but their sound continued as a low throb that threatened the stillness.

"That highway should never have been built," said Ed. "Just once, you and I should do something significant."

"Like what?"

"Like blow up one of those goddamn bridges near Hite," said Ed. "Wouldn't that make a glorious sight?"

"Yeah. It sure would. And they'd never in a million years figure out who did it."

"We could establish perfect alibis." Ed was serious. "We could research the technical end. We could get what we need from different sources. And then on some dark night, after having established our alibis, we could blow that bridge right out of its moorings and watch it fall into the water. If we did that just one time and did it well, we would die honorable men when our time came. Whaddya say?"

"We should have tried harder to keep the highway from having been built in the first place."

"Yes. But we didn't."

"That's true."

"Think about it, Jack."

"I thought we were here to not think," said I.

We both laughed, but there was between us a vision of a bridge careering into the river as the result of our collaborative efforts.

The rumble of the trucks finally subsided. The sun was close to the horizon, and we had a three-mile hike back to camp. The moon wouldn't be up for at least two hours, so we turned and began the trek back. Ed wanted to follow the branch I had taken to see what it was like. Going down was easier than climbing up, and it took us just over an hour to find our two old pickup trucks well separated by a stone hearth we had built our first night out. There was still beer enough for a few more days. Tonight would be the last of the fresh meat.

Beyond our campsite, a few hundred yards east of Comb Ridge, was a grove of juniper that we had been raiding for the dead standing firewood. Of all firewood, that's my favorite, although Ed favored Sonoran mesquite. It's hard to say which is meaner, juniper or mesquite. One spits at you from the fire, the other stabs you on the way to the fire. Probably every organism resists transformation by fire. But who wants to eat his pork chops raw? Life is a series of value judgments and problems to solve. Ed and I solved our cooking problem by each dragging four or five loads of dry, rich-smelling juniper to camp. We busted it into smaller firewood-size pieces. At one point I stood on one end of a dead branch and pulled back on the other in a effort to snap it. My foot slipped, the branch sprang about, and I landed in the dust. Ed walked over, picked up the branch, adjusted himself to it, pulled back, and snapped it in two.

He looked at me and grinned like a wolf. "Anybody can bust up firewood . . . if he's man enough."

I jumped to my feet and took out after him, chasing him through the sagebrush for fifty yards or so. Finally we gave it up and, panting and laughing, returned to camp.

"I want a beer!"

"Me too!"

"Great," said I, reaching into the cooler and pulling out two frosty Michelobs. We unscrewed the bottles and banged them against each other in a toast. *"Salud!"*

"Salud!"

"Jesus, that tastes good," said Ed, a look of triumph emanating from his great countenance. "The first swallow of cold beer after a long, hot hike is one of life's two greatest sensations."

"Three, if you count taking a good crap." We drained our bottles. Ed looked at his empty bottle, then at me.

"I wouldn't mind a second beer, *frijol viejo,*" said Ed.

"Nor would I, old bean." Ed got up and went to the cooler while I started breaking up twigs for kindling. It was late dusk, and in the distance I caught the occasional ripping sound of a nighthawk braking fast flight. Ed came over and handed me a beer. I lighted a match and set the curled juniper bark to burning. We watched the flames grow, one or the other of us feeding ever larger pieces of wood to the fire until a merry blaze spit back at us or launched a funnel of sparks toward the sky.

We cooked our pork chops over juniper embers and heated up the beans. We also had some hard rolls. Satisfying. The perfect meal, at least to a pair of hillbillies transplanted, thank God, to the Southwest. Ed also liked turnips. He liked them better than potatoes, or so he said. Not I. I may be from West Virginia and have been known to eat snake, but I have my limits.

After dinner Ed pulled the old, blackened bucket out of the back of his truck, poured some water in it, added a little dish-washing soap, and snuggled it into embers on one side of the fire. We wiped off our utensils and put them into the bucket to soak. After a while they came clean, me washing, Ed rinsing.

Our bellies were full. The moon was up. A breeze danced through our camp.

"C'mon, Loeffler. Let's go for a walk."

I grabbed my old maple stick, Ed his bamboo rod. We walked out to the dirt road east of the main arroyo and headed south, knowing that the nearest pavement in that direction was many miles away.

"Ed, you didn't answer my question." We walked along avoiding rocks and ruts.

"What question?"

"Do you blame science for the presence of those uranium trucks we saw this afternoon?"

Ed was silent for a few moments. He was generally careful to think before he spoke. "I think scientists have to share the responsibility for their discoveries. Human curiosity is powerful and can't be denied. The growth of science is a natural extension of that curiosity. And those of us who become scientists are responding to a need to satisfy that curiosity scientifically, not metaphysically. For some people, faith isn't enough. Hard evidence is the path to truth."

"I agree," I said. "But science doesn't stop with pure research. It usually leads to some sort of application. Some kind of invention. Take the atomic bomb, for example. I've watched atomic bombs be detonated from seven miles away and have been mightily impressed by the quality of light and color, by their immense capacity for nonselective destruction of life."

"Science leads to technology," said Ed, "and industry. And industrialism. Science itself isn't bad. It's what it can lead to that could be bad. Take industrialism, for example. Normal men who should be out hunting for a living find themselves working in factories or building skyscrapers or doing some kind of work for hire to make somebody else . . . not themselves . . . rich. Human population tends to gather in cities, and soon enough, the country is forgotten. Along with the sense of self-sufficiency that is every man's and every woman's birthright. No, science itself is not bad. And scientists are not necessarily any worse than anyone else. But they should assume some responsibility for the application of their discoveries."

"Like nuclear power plants."

"Yeah. Like nuclear power plants. As Garrett Hardin says, we have to consider the ramifications of what we do. That isn't easy. Who could have predicted that we would become a race of energy junkies? Or that growth for the sake of growth would have become the central theme of western culture, so called? In a situation like that you have science, technology, and industry all feeding each other until they collectively predominate in a state of technocracy to the extent that other values are hidden or lost to most of us. And it takes virtually everybody adjusting to this system to make it work. Very few of us are willing to admit that the system can't go on forever. Things begin to go wrong and scientists are called in to think up remedies. More and more, the system comes to rely on remedial tinkering and becomes ever more centralized until utter collapse is inevitable. The sooner the better, by gawd! Then maybe we can stamp out this blight, this cancer of modern industrialism."

"I've had this terrible thought lately," I said.

"What's that?"

"Suppose all of the nuclear waste that's being stored near the world's coastlines was suddenly deposited by an earthquake or other act of Nature in the nearest ocean. We'd be in hot water!"

"Oh, Christ."

"What life-forms could withstand it?"

"I don't know. I don't know whether there's enough radioactive waste to destroy the seas or not. I wonder if anybody knows. And what could be done about it, anyway?"

"Well, in America there's WIPP, where they plan to ship radioactive waste to New Mexico and bury it near Carlsbad, where they're deluded into thinking that it'll be safe for two hundred and fifty thousand years, which is about twenty-five times the length of recorded human history."

Ed ruminated for a bit. "That's what I mean. Science is misapplied or, at best, applied without regard to ramifications until it's too late. The scientific process itself can't be thought of as culpable. But scientists are if they don't assume responsibility for their discoveries. Yet you can't blame cancer researchers who want to find a cure for cancer knowing full well that human population growth will be less curtailed if they do. It's a real dilemma."

"No," I said. "I don't think you can blame scientists any more than anybody else. I think everyone is to blame. I guess it's a matter of degree. Consider the scientist who is working on human birth control. Can he be regarded in the same light as the scientist who's perfecting a superweapon? If one accepts the premise that human overpopulation is the fundamental problem, then either or both of those scientists could be regarded as heroes. The end result of both areas of research is fewer humans."

"So much for ethics," said Ed. "There's a qualitative difference there. You could argue that a good method of birth control results in collective ecstasy while a superweapon results in collective misery. They may both result in fewer humans, but the difference lies in quality of intent."

We walked down the road in silence for a while, occasionally hearing the plaintive call of a great horned owl.

"These are tough questions, Jack. Who can say where the blame really lies? To my way of thinking, it lies with anyone who can clearly see what we're doing to this poor, defenseless planet in the name of profit and greed and then doesn't do anything about it. That's the real crime. You and I talk about this all the time. But what the hell do we do about it? I sit at a typewriter all day and hack away. I never have figured out what the hell you do. But except for pulling up a few survey stakes or venting anger on an occasional piece of heavy equipment, what have you or I really done? Not a goddamned thing. Even worse, we contribute to the general malaise. We both drive pickup trucks that burn gasoline. We both own refrigerators and stereo sets and hot water heaters and God knows what other appliances. What the hell is an appliance, anyway? It's an application of energy designed to make human life more luxurious and the manufacturer richer. It's also a human artifact that somehow lessens the chances of survival for the rest of the biotic community and denigrates the human user by weakening his own ability to be self-sufficient.

"Science should be used to aid us in our quest for understanding the meaning of existence, if indeed there is any meaning to existence. Instead we largely misuse this ability to be scientific. We use it to enhance our proclivity to consume more and more and more. Mankind is insatiable."

Swirls of dust began to be lifted in a gradually increasing wind. The moon had edged westward. We tacitly agreed to turn about and head back to camp. Ed walked off into the bushes to relieve himself. I heard him say, "I shall piss this way but once. Henceforth, I shall aim downwind."

(f i v e)

By late winter of 1977 Abbey was beginning to realize his marriage was soon to be challenged by the fact that Renée was maturing and discovering that she had a destiny of her own. She was gradually becoming interested in living in a larger community near a university.

Abbey, on the other hand, couldn't deny his need to spend as much time in the backcountry as he could. He applied for and acquired the job of fire lookout on top of Aztec Peak in the Tonto National Forest of south-central Arizona. Surrounded by yellow pine, aspen, and spruce atop the eight-thousand-foot peak, he could see Roosevelt Lake, the Superstition Mountains, the Mogollon Rim, and parts of the Salt River Canyon. He was alone with Ellie, his black part-Labrador mutt.

His fifty–foot-high fire tower, built in 1960, was modern by Forest Service standards, equipped with a solid Osborne fire finder mounted in the center of the square live-in cubicle. There was a propane stove, though Abbey much preferred the scent from a wood-burning stove to the stench of gas fumes. His water was collected in a cistern. Once he had to fish out a dead rat and boil the tainted water.

He missed Renée but luxuriated in his solitude. Even so, he was mindful of possible disaster.

Gotta be good to my wife. I mean better. For I'll never find another woman better than Renée. And I know it. And yet I keep making these careless, thoughtless, mindless gestures toward breakup and disaster. Out of sheer sloth! stupidity!, some atavistic blind urge to self-destruction. As if I wanted to be lonely and miserable again. As if my present contentment and happiness were not tolerable. As if dejection were my natural norm. As if I hated my good fortune in marrying a girl as pretty, sweet, clever, intelligent, and loving as Renée. As if I wanted, once again, to sink into despair, touch rock bottom of the soul one more time. Why?

Is happiness a bore?

God, the absurd pain we inflict not only on one another but also on ourselves!

Abbey was visited only rarely at the fire lookout. Renée spent some time there, but in the main, Abbey was alone. By mid-July he had finished reading Proust's *Remembrance of Things Past* ("the greatest mama's boy in all literature, this Marcel"). He continued working on *Good News*, which he regarded as the world's first futuristic western. And he made some insightful observations about some fellow writers:

B. Traven, Dreiser, James Jones, et al.—their prose is so bad, so crude, so stupid that it's painful to read. And yet these lads often wrote better books than such master stylists as Henry James, Joyce, Nabokov, Proust. Why? Perhaps there's something in great verbal felicity that misleads the writer, that betrays him into technique for the sake of technique; while the simple-minded prose writers, free of such allurements, are able to keep their attention fixed on the subject of their interest—the real life of actual human beings. Thus, their work, while repellent in style and detail, achieves great cumulative power through its steadfast devotion to fact, which equals and in the long run is equivalent to, the supreme poetry of truth. The greatest writers were those, are those, capable of both powers: i.e., Tolstoy, Conrad, Chekhov, Hemingway, Cervantes, Steinbeck, and so on.

Whom then, shall we praise? Why, Cervantes, Rabelais, Villon, Melville, Twain, Dreiser, Traven, Hemingway, Wolfe, Conrad (my sole readable Victorian), Tolstoy, Chekhov, Camus, Flaubert, Mann and Heine and Brecht, Whitman and Thoreau, Becket and O'Casey, and Shaw and Dylan Thomas, Knut Hamsun, Jack London, John Steinbeck, Robinson Jeffers. A hundred or so others, I suppose. E.g., Sartre, Russell, Andreyev, Gorky? No, I think not. . . . Shakespeare was a good poet but had the soul of a sycophant, the heart of a toady. That servile streak that poisons English literature begins with him.

Neglected writers: Berry, Eastlake, Alan Harrington, Algren, Traven, Van Tilburg Clark, Wolfe (the real one—the author), Steinbeck, Mumford.

Stuffed mediocrities: Bellow, Updike, Mailer, Gardner. Soreheads and sour grapejuice (I really envy Pynchon, Coover, McGuane), am tired of being the famous unknown "underground" author.

McPhee: can't get through his books, exasperated by his constant temporizing; Alaska book (tho' highly praised by the NY school of literary fish) the most disappointing of all.

In late November 1977 *The Hidden Canyon* was published. In spite of his successes, Abbey was edging closer to the dark side again. Renée was soon to leave for Tucson. Ed and his daughter, Susie, would spend a lonesome period together in Moab. Abbey recognized that he was becoming ever more irritable and reticent.

His journals reflect a growing disdain for the work of John McPhee, who was a friend of Edward Hoagland. Abbey and Hoagland had carried on a correspondence for some time, and Abbey sensed that his own dislike of McPhee, "the Thoreau of New Jersey," might well be affecting Hoagland's attitude toward Abbey himself. This uncomfortable side to their relationship persisted for some time. Abbey felt he was alienating all but a very few friends.

William Eastlake said that Ed "was upset with me because I hadn't supported him on his stand against illegal immigration from Mexico. The City of Tucson wanted to give the Edward Abbey Award to a Mexican-American who had done something outstanding. The fellow turned it down because it was named after Edward Abbey."

While Abbey, along with Garrett Hardin, opposed illegal immigration into the United States, he contributed to the Sanctuary movement initiated by Reverend John Fife, the Presbyterian minister who was arrested for smuggling political refugees across the border and harboring them in his church in South Tucson. However, Abbey thought that each illegal alien should be given a supply of food and water and an up-to-date firearm with ample ammunition and released back across the border to help solve the problems in his own country.

Abbey's opinions were strong. There is little point in having weak ones.

In early 1978 Abbey sold his Moab house and some land in Utah and bought a house on four and a half acres of Sonoran desert west of Tucson. He went deep into debt to buy this house so that Renée could go to the University of Arizona.

Abbey returned to the Aztec Peak fire lookout that summer.

One day in July my wife, Kath, and I had an extraordinary experience while visiting Abbey on his lookout. We had brought the sheet music for a trio by Vivaldi and two wooden alto recorders. Abbey pulled out his flute, and we laid the music across the top of the Osborne fire finder that dominated the center of the tiny room atop the tower. We started playing the trio, Abbey sight-reading the music. We were about halfway through the first movement when Kath stopped playing.

"Look!" she said.

Just outside the window was a peregrine falcon, holding a small rodent in its talons. It was eating as it hovered, apparently listening to our music at the same time. We watched for several minutes until it finished eating. A small kettle of turkey vultures had entered the territory about a hundred yards down mountain. The peregrine wheeled and stooped, plummeting toward the vultures. It hit one in the middle of the back with enough force that a small cloud of feathers and dust flew up and the vulture soared limpingly away.

We visited Abbey a few times over the years that he held the lookout at Aztec. In the main he was by himself, although Renée was there once when we visited. I recall that at a certain time of year, thousands of ladybugs would cluster around the bases of the agaves. On one such visit when the ladybugs dominated the top of the mountain, I had brought my trumpet. I was still a performing musician in those days, and I had to practice every day to keep in shape for a forthcoming concert. I was going to hike off into the woods to practice.

"C'mon, Loeffler," said Abbey. "You don't get off the hook that easily. Play me a tune."

I played a few long tones to warm up, and then I commenced to struggle through the Haydn Trumpet Concerto in E-flat Major, unaccompanied. It was one of life's more surreal moments. Abbey stood on the walkway atop the tower, stark naked except for a wide-brimmed cowboy hat. Kath was off staring at agave, utterly engrossed in watching thousands of ladybugs. I was blatting away at Papa Haydn while my wolf-dog, Shadow, and Ed's dog, Ellie, howled at the high notes. The version I played has a cadenza with a high F above the staff, high enough to cause an aneurysm. After I finished, Ed started clapping and howling along with the canines. He danced around the top of the fire lookout, his cock flopping around in the sunshine.

"It's pretty out today, so I decided to leave it out," he declared.

Abbey spent much of that summer and the following summer alone at Aztec Peak. While he relished the solitude on one level, he realized that too much solitude leads to madness.

One entry in his journal reads:

*A pretty good day. Left a neat coil of shit under a rock in the woods,
jerked off, earned (as it were) my $25 as fire lookout, wrote 3,000 words,
and this evening walked five miles—down through the woods and back
up the road; and now I'm going to toodle my flute. Why can't I do as
much every day? Why don't I?*

Ed and Renée were having difficulties, and he feared for their marriage. He
loved her deeply, but he had to follow his own trail, as did she. By mid-autumn
Abbey returned to his Tucson house. He could barely tolerate being there,
and his fantasies turned to moving onto a houseboat and living with Susie.
He had enough money in the bank to buy beans and rice to last for twenty-
five years. He imagined hiding out in various canyons, hunting game to fill
out the rest of his diet.

His writing had temporarily come to a standstill. He had written nothing
on *Good News* or *Confessions of a Barbarian* for weeks. He did finish *Abbey's
Road,* which was due out in the spring of the following year.

*Why write? Among many other reasons, to defend the honesty of man
against the lies and lying institutions of caste and hierarchy and power,
of church and state, of technology and war, the heavy machinery of
domination that has been attempting for five thousand years to enslave us
all, now, once and for good and forever. . . . To unfold the folded lie.
To record the truth of our time, to witness what is. . . .*

Somehow the Abbeys survived the winter, and in April 1979 Abbey immersed himself in the writing of his "fat masterpiece," which he would finally
call *The Fool's Progress.*

By May he was back up on Aztec Peak. The winds were cold, and he was
sobered by solitude. He was well over fifty and still randy. For decades he had
advocated the legalization of prostitution so that men could act out their sexual
fantasies in a clean environment. In Abbey's opinion, this was far superior to
sneaking around behind the wife's back in a liaison that could only end in pain.

Later that month Renée visited Abbey at the lookout and told him she wanted a divorce. Abbey went through several mood changes from resentment to despair. But he was certainly able to admit to himself that he had not been the perfect husband.

Renée had come to realize that she had been far too young to marry Ed, who was nearly three decades her senior. Now he was in late middle age and Renée was just coming to consciousness of herself, involved in her own pursuits. Their points of view no longer coincided. There was still love, but there was also an abyss. Still, they remained married, at least for a while.

There is nothing I hate more than cruelty. And yet I have been cruel. Many times. Mental cruelty to others. Especially to my wives. And no form of suffering is more real than the anguish caused by doubt, uncertainty, the loss of love, the fear of loss. . . .

What to do about Renée? I am sick at heart thinking of her. Has our life together really run its course? So soon? And I had really hoped, at one time, that I'd spend the rest of my life with her. Now I seldom ever see her. Weekends, about all. And me bound for Utah next month, New York and Home in November, two weeks at Verde Valley in December . . . The same old part-time marriage we've always had. She is very unhappy. And my Susie living with Grandma. The sweetest years of my little girl's life, and I am failing to share them with her.

Abbey left the lookout that autumn of 1979 and journeyed east. Renée went with him to New York, but they were unable to do much together. Afterward Abbey made a trip to Home, Pennsylvania. He was appalled at the bitterness that had come to exist between his parents. He remained only a few days, then headed west to Tucson.

On New Year's Day, 1980, Renée left Ed. Their time together had come to an end.

Ed and Jack Loeffler digging up cabrito in Jack's Santa Fe backyard, June 9, 1985. Photo by Jeff Loeffler (Jack's father).

Ed and his parents, ca. 1986.

Ed and John DePuy, ca. 1986.

In writing cabin west of Tucson, ca. 1986.

In writing cabin, ca. 1984. Photo by Jay Dusard.

Cabeza Prieta Wildlife Refuge and Bombing Range, 1987. Photo by Jack Loeffler.

*Ken Sleight, unidentified friend of Sleight, and Ed, May, 1988.
Photo by Mark Klett.*

Near Tuscon, 1988. Photo by Jack Dykinga.

10 March 1987

Irving Howe, Chairman
Awards Committee
American Academy of Arts & Letters
New York

Dear Mr Howe:

Thank you for your letter of March 4th
informing me that I am to receive an award
from the American Academy. I appreciate
the intended honor but will not be able to
attend the awards ceremony on May 20th;
I'm figuring on going down a river in
Idaho that week. Besides, to tell the
truth, I think that such prizes are for
little boys. You can give my $5000 to
somebody else. I dont need it and I
dont want it. Thanks anyhow.

Edward Abbey
Oracle, Arizona

American Academy and Institute of Arts and Letters

633 WEST 155 STREET · NEW YORK · N.Y. 10032-7599 *Tel.* (212) 368-5900

March 4, 1987

Dear Mr. Abbey:

It gives me great pleasure to inform you that you
have been chosen by the American Academy and Institute
of Arts and Letters to receive one of eight $5,000 awards
to honor and encourage writers in their creative work.

After I've published 15 books!

This award will be presented to you at our annual
induction and award ceremony on Wednesday afternoon, May
20, 1987, at three o'clock.

The award ceremony is preceded by a luncheon at
noon, to which you may bring a guest. The officers and
members of the Academy-Institute would greatly appreciate
your attendance at these functions.

In other words, I have to go to stinking NYC to pick up their stinking check.

Please keep this information confidential until it
is released to the press at the end of March.

We would appreciate your acceptance of this award
by return mail.

Sincerely yours,

Irving Howe, Chairman
Awards Committee for Literature

Mr. Edward Abbey
3757 El Moraga
Tucson, AZ 85745

IH/ep

10 May '87

Dear Jack —

You'll enjoy this brief correspondence between one Irving Howe and one E. Abbey. I'm sure you'll understand my reason for declining the prize, too: simple animal pride. Tell our friend Horgan about this: he'll be amused.

Best

Ed

PS:

How's it going anyhow? Been to Central America yet? Terry Moore just back from Baja, says he had a "great time." We hope to be trailing north to Moab about the middle of June. I'm going down the Yampa in early July as a guest of a commercial outfit. Maybe you could tag-along. Anyway, let's do something great this summer. Run a river! climb a mt! Discover a new arch!

"After I've published 15 books," Ed commented apropos of Irving Howe's letter, to which this was his reply.

Fort Llatikcuf
Arizona

July 17, 1988

Dear Jack —

Just because I demanded that you write a letter didn't mean you had to do it, damn it. Now I'm morally obliged to respond and I'm not sure I'm up to the task. Anyhow, yours is a jolly & delightful letter and I thank you for your wit (?) and wisdom (?). Whuffo' you do dat to me, monkey - fuck'?

Especially love your comments to the grants panel. ("One man can be pretty dumb, but for true stupidity there's nothing like a committee.") We just belong to wrong minority, Jack — we ain't female, Negro, homo, Meskin, 1/16 Chippewa, Ivy League, eastern, southren, or even crippled except in the head and that don't show. Well, on you it does.

So whuffo' next'? I like your feral fantasy best and someday by Gawd when it's probly too phukkin' late well do it. And whuffo' I tryin' write dis here bukke so far'? (104 pp already, man! — only 296 to go!) 'Cause so I can quit quicker and go a-floatin some fukkin' river this fall with my ole buddy Jackson. Love to y'all. Ed

A politically incorrect missive from Ed.

With Becky, August, 1988. Photo by Jack Dykinga.

With Ben, August, 1988. Photo by Jack Dykinga.

Last known photo of Ed, March 4, 1989. Photo by Charles A. Hedgcock.

Jack Loeffler, Terry Moore, and John DePuy at Abbey's wake, March 22, 1989.

Memorial for Ed at Arches National Park, May 1989. Photo by Marc Gaede.

chapter 7

(one)

It was sunny and brisk in the high country of northern New Mexico. The front door of my house opened, and Ed walked in unannounced.

"Renée left me," was all he said at first.

"Sit down. I'll get you a drink."

He didn't sit down. He walked around the living room, his eyes darting to every corner. I handed him a glass of whiskey. He gulped it down and handed me the empty glass. I poured some more whiskey, and he drank that more slowly. I grabbed his arm, pulled him into the pantry, and showed him where there were eight or nine bottles of various forms of booze. Ed was into drinking just then.

"I'm restless as hell. Can we go for a ride?" Ed looked as though he had been peering over the edge.

"Let's go," I said.

Ed grabbed a couple of bottles. I grabbed a six-pack. We climbed into my old Chevy pickup and drove out into the beautiful plains southeast of Santa Fe, Ed slugging down bourbon right out of the bottle and chasing it with beer.

"Want to tell me about it?"

"It's been coming for a while. I knew it was coming. But it hurts like a sonofabitch anyway. Christ. I've lost her."

I looked over at him. His face was haggard, haunted. The creases between his eyebrows had deepened considerably since I had last seen him. He almost lost it, but then he rallied.

"Can I stay with you and Kath for a while?"

"*Mi casa es tu casa, compañero.* Always."

"I'm pretty fucked up."

"You been fucked up ever since I met you." I reached over and punched him on the shoulder, grinning at him.

He grinned back, fragile, his eyes brimmed with tears. "Thanks, *compañero.*"

Twenty-five miles later, I pulled over to the side of the road and stopped the truck.

"C'mon. I want to show you something."

Ed climbed out, taking a nearly full bottle of firewater with him. We went through the barbed wire fence and hiked up the eastern aspect of a long, narrow land formation with a serrated spine.

"What's up here?" asked Abbey, curiosity cutting through the pain for a moment.

"You'll see," was all I said. We hiked a way and stopped before a south-facing rock panel.

Ed saw the wonderful petroglyph carved in the face of the panel. There was a path trailing west, and he followed the path, stopping frequently to look at the rock art. After about a half mile I stopped and said, "Follow me up here."

I climbed up to near the top of the rock formation and waited for Ed. He took a long pull off the bottle, carefully set it down, and scrambled up after me. There, carved into the face of a broad slab of stone, were two huge figures, round, shieldlike, anthropomorphic in some weird fashion. Abbey just looked at them for a minute or two.

Then we both turned and sat on top of a flat-topped rock big enough to hold us both and stared out into the vastness that lay before us.

"I come here a lot," I said. "Especially when life looks shitty. It's pretty safe here, all things considered. Good place to get a sense of perspective."

"Give me a sense of perspective. I need it."

"Well, someone carved these petroglyphs here a long time ago. They're still here. But the rock carvers are a thousand years dead. Along with their emotions and thoughts and points of view. You hurt, Ed. But it ain't going to last forever. The rest of your life, maybe. But not forever."

"You're right, *viejo.* It's just hard to handle another failure."

"Shit. Just because something doesn't last forever doesn't mean it's a failure. It's just run its course. It's like an abandoned meander. It carved its place and moved on. Let's go home and eat. You're beginning to look like Abraham Lincoln on a diet."

Abbey grinned, threw an arm around my shoulders, and gave me a hug.

Still and all, it took Abbey many months to recover. He stayed at my house for two or three days, then went to the home of a doctor in the north country, from there to Debris's home, back to my home, and so on. Weeks later, he called me from Robert Redford's home in Utah and said that he was finally on the mend and looked forward to getting together in the fall.

Early autumn in northern New Mexico is splendid. It is a time to go camping, to ruminate on the purpose of existence; a time to take courage from the flow of Nature; a time to prepare for winter. My old friends Stewart and Lee Udall were in Santa Fe and collectively we were putting together a fund-raiser to help defray expenses incurred as Udall fought indefatigably on behalf of Navajo uranium miners and their widows. Abbey had volunteered to come to Santa Fe and read from *The Monkey Wrench Gang*. Pete Seeger was in town and had offered to sing, as had Eliza Gilkyson. John Kimmey was to be the master of ceremonies, and my friend and neighbor Reno Myerson and I were producing this event. It was to take place at the Paolo Soleri outdoor amphitheater at the Indian School.

A figure loomed tall in the western doorway. It was Abbey, clad in black pants, a T-shirt with the motto of the state of New Hampshire emblazoned across the span of his chest, a red bandanna tied around his neck, and a worn pair of GI jungle boots on his feet. He grinned, took two long strides across the room, and gave me a huge *abrazo*.

"I've got a surprise for you," he said. "I want you to meet Clarke." A young woman stepped into the room and smiled, shy yet at ease. How beautiful and clear she looked, all the way to her soul.

The magic of the moment was supplanted by a new magic. The Udalls came in the front door, and Pete Seeger came in from the backyard, where he had been absorbing the peace of the nearby mountains. Kimmey and Reno arrived. We made a hasty master plan and went to the outdoor theater. The event was sold out. Abbey read of resistance and revolution from his book, holding his audience in silent rapture. A beer in each hip pocket nurtured him through his reading. Udall spoke of the plight of uranium miners, whose bodies were inevitably riddled by radiation, and of radioactive particles blasted skyward, borne by the wind and sprinkled indiscriminately throughout the biotic community, perchance to cloud the clear waters of the collective gene pool. Pete Seeger performed music from the heart and brought to the occasion the consciousness and integrity that have been his hallmarks for over half a century.

The next morning before breakfast Seeger said to me, "Edward Abbey is a great man." Later in the morning Abbey pulled me aside, waving an inscribed copy of *Abbey's Road,* a gift he had given me that he had just pulled off my bookshelf. "Can I give this to Pete and I'll give you another one?"

"You bet."

He reinscribed it and gave it to Seeger. Ed didn't give me a replacement copy for many years. The evening of his sixty-second birthday, to be exact.

Abbey had indeed fallen in love. In a few more months, by the new year, he was whole once again and hoped to marry Clarke. She and Susie got along. "Susie and Clarke, the only women in my life anymore. And they are all that I need, the sweet dears. 'More precious than diamonds. More lovely than gold.'"

Abbey turned fifty-four in January 1981, a mature writer with more great works yet to be written. The University of Arizona hired him to teach nonfiction writing for the winter semester. He was not enthusiastic about this. He rued having relinquished his fire lookout on Aztec Peak. "Beware any job that requires new shoes."

Abbey began to plan a new book of essays tentatively titled either *Malice Aforethought* or *Down the River.* He intended to "give the book a riverine flow, a fluvial current, with repeated motifs and quotes (Joyce, Powell, Huck Finn, Thoreau, Conrad, Matthiessen, Whitman, etc., etc.,) conveying the fluid flow of my thought, ideas, excretions, etc."

Good News was not faring well with reviewers. Abbey felt that they misunderstood it.

> *Good News really is an optimistic book, in that it prophesies the imminent collapse of the military-industrial State. The title is not ironical but plain truth, which of course makes it incomprehensible to simple-minded reviewers who look for irony where none is intended. The collapse is followed by triumph of love, life and rebellion. The reviewers are self-deceived or baffled by my title.*
>
> *The Chief [the villain of the novel] a caricature? Of course he's a caricature. All such men—Nixon, Stalin, Truman, Hitler—are caricatures of human beings.*

Abbey was glad to have financial security and insurance benefits at the

University of Arizona. As much as he disdained academe, a corner of his mind delighted in being involved with a university. Perhaps he secretly rued not having pursued his Ph.D., perhaps not. Life for an artist over fifty does not lead to a peaceful, well-heeled retirement. Most artists die with their boots (or sandals) on. Most artists would have it no other way.

Abbey and Clarke went camping at every opportunity. Abbey's father, Paul, visited them during the summer months, and the old man was able to hike into the bowels of Grand Canyon and back out again, no mean feat for a man over seventy. Paul's hearing was on the wane, and he was becoming grouchy. He and his son argued incessantly—there was great love between them but also antipathy. They were too much alike to be good friends.

By early summer Abbey had sent the manuscript for *Down the River* to Jack Macrae at Dutton. Abbey supplied the original drawings for this book of essays, which he dedicated to Don Congdon, his agent. This may well have been his own favorite work of nonfiction. Many times he told me that it upset him that *Desert Solitaire* stole so much of his literary thunder from his other books; while he regarded it as a good book, he had certainly written better. *Down the River* was high on the list of his own collected works.

Abbey bought acreage at Vermillion Cliffs in northern Arizona. The land sat flat atop a *bajada* overlooking the vast span of terrain that cradles the Grand Canyon. Far in the distance, far to the south were the San Francisco Peaks. Directly to the north was the thousand-foot-high wall of the Vermillion Cliffs. Here and there were random "slow elk," wild cattle that Abbey regarded as possible food on the hoof.

Abbey and Clarke began to dream of building a home here.

Clarke loves the Vermillion Cliff's place. Good! . . . I am in a home-building mode these days. Can even accept the prospect of another baby without panic or terror. Hell, Clarke really is a good woman. The best I've ever known and loved.

It is strange, in this light, that Abbey began to have true intimations of his own mortality that summer eight years before his death. He wrote out his funeral instructions for Clarke:

Body to be transported in bed of pickup truck and buried as soon as

possible after death, in a hole dug on our private property somewhere
(along Green River, up in the La Sals, or at Cliff Dwellers). No under-
takers wanted; no embalming (for godsake!); no coffin. Just a plain pine
box hammered together by a friend; or an old sleeping bag, or tarp, will
do. If site selected is too rocky for burial, then pile on sand and a pile of
stones sufficient to keep coyotes from dismembering and scattering my
bones. Wrap my body in my anarch's flag. But bury if possible; I want my
body to help fertilize the growth of a cactus, or cliff rose, or sagebrush, or
tree, etc. Ceremony? Gunfire! and—a little music please: Jack Loeffler
and his trumpet; maybe a few readings from Thoreau, Whitman, Twain
(something funny), Jeffers, and/or Abbey, etc.; that should be sufficient.
No speeches desired, tho' the deceased will not interfere if someone feels the
urge. But keep it all simple and brief. Then—a wake! More music, lots of
gay and lively music—bagpipes! drums and flutes! the Riverine String
Band playing jigs, reels, country swing and polkas; I want dancing! and a
flood of beer and booze! a bonfire! and lots of food—meat! corn on the
cob! beans and chiles! cake and pie and ice cream and soda pop for the
kids! gifts for all my friends and all who come—books, record albums,
curios and keepsakes. No formal mourning please—lots of singing,
dancing, talking, hollering, laughing, and love-making instead. And I
want my widow to take a new man as quick as she can find one good
enough—for her.

On the very next page of his journal, Ed wrote: "It is not death or dying
which is tragic; but rather to have existed without fully participating in life—
that is the deepest personal tragedy."

In December 1981 Abbey embarked on a solitary adventure that had great meaning for him. He hiked across the Cabeza Prieta Wildlife Refuge and Air Force
Bombing and Gunnery Range by himself, alone with his thoughts. One hundred and ten miles through the heart of the Sonoran Desert, average rainfall
less than ten inches per year. True desert. Sparsely vegetated with creosote bush
and bursage. Randomly crisscrossed by dry riparian arroyos vegetated with
mesquite, ironwood, and paloverde trees, their sandy courses patterned with
the prints of the local wildlife. Empty living desert where few men tread, and
very few have trod across.

There is a road of sorts known locally as *el camino del diablo*—the devil's road! It is a pair of tracks leading through sand, over rocks, and across arroyos and is frequently impassable to vehicular traffic. A car-killing road where no one should go. A toll road where the devil takes his toll.

Abbey carried a fifty-pound pack, including water. His intent was to hike by night as much as possible to avoid the dehydrating daytime sun—even in December the desert is hot and dry. Abbey selected ten days that spanned the time of the full moon so that he could pick his trail. He didn't want to twist his ankle in the dark of a moonless night fifty miles from the nearest fellow human. He carried with him a much studied USGS map with marks where there were tanks and water holes. He wore a pair of canvas-topped GI jungle boots of the style that he favored for many years.

As he started the hike, he was afraid. But Abbey was a man of tremendous resolve. He was determined to hike across 110 miles of desert wilderness.

In his shirt pocket he carried a couple of pocket spiral notebooks in which he jotted his thoughts, his fears, and his hopes that indeed there would be water at the next *tanque* where there was supposed to be water, otherwise. . . . Beneath the intellectual level always lurked the dread thought that he would run out of water and die miserably. There has to be danger in every adventure, otherwise why bother? There has to be the random chance that one won't make it, won't survive, to give adventure the flavor of honesty. Abbey savored this as he examined the shadows that looked like crouching demons beside abandoned mines, or skimmed away larvae, bees, and ants from the surface of barely potable water before he could sip his share.

His feet ached and the soles of his boots wore thin, perhaps even flapped a bit before the end of his journey. But he reached the other side. And Clarke met him on the appointed day at the appointed hour. And they both rejoiced.

Abbey went back to the University of Arizona, where he taught through the winter of 1982. He felt somewhat dishonest, encouraging a class of young would-be writers when he thought they should be learning honest trades like carpentry or horseshoeing. He was convinced that the economic system would finally break down and that the only skills worth having were survival skills.

Late that winter Abbey telephoned to inform me that there is some justice in the world. He had recently read an article about a young man who had gone out into the desert with his shotgun, which he fired twice at close range at a giant saguaro cactus. The dying cactus retaliated by falling on top of the man and crushing him to death.

Ed was happy once again. His personal world was in some sense of balance. While he missed his two sons, he saw Susie daily. He loved her dearly.

My Susie: she is growing up so beautiful, so clever, so talented, so sweet and loving and lively—my Gawd but I love that kid of mine. She's the joy and delight of my decrepit middleage. A wonderful girl. If she only knew how much I love her—more than anything in the world—she'd never have doubts about me again. Bless her.

Though Abbey was ever reticent about his love, there is no doubt how much he loved all of his children. He mentioned many times that the great tragedy of his own existence was the distance between himself and his offspring. He loved both Josh and Aaron, though he barely knew the latter. He hoped that his genetic contribution, at least, would be worth something to them.

In May 1982 Ed and Clarke were married. Abbey realized his great good fortune years later when time and history had their way and Clarke was always there for him to the very end of his life—and beyond.

The Abbeys went camping for a while and then headed to Colorado in mid-July to spend the summer in a cabin owned by Jim Carrico of the National Park Service. Abbey was determined to immerse himself in his "fat masterpiece," *Confessions of a Barbarian,* soon to be called *The Fool's Progress.* The cabin was situated on the edge of the San Luis Valley within one hundred miles of the headwaters of the Rio Grande. Immediately to the east was the glorious fourteen-thousand-foot Blanca Peak, one of the great mountains in the southern Rockies. Nearby was Great Sand Dunes National Monument. The air was clear, pristine, and life held new promise.

Abbey was in good spirits and wrote the first few chapters of his "fat masterpiece." With his marriage to Clarke, he had entered the most prolific years of his literary career. It was as though for the first time he had committed himself to marriage, and with that commitment came the freedom of intellect and spirit to pursue his art. He retained his views concerning the biologic imperative of the male, but he had developed a strong resolve to maintain fidelity to his Clarke. He loved her and respected her. She had let him know early on that the only way she would be his wife was if he would be faithful.

In early August the Abbeys headed south to gather up Susie, who had spent the first part of the summer of 1982 at a camp at Verde Valley School in Arizona. They slowly wended their way north so that Abbey could resume work on his novel. On their way to Carrico's cabin, they stopped in Santa Fe, ostensibly for a visit with the Loefflers.

For some time Abbey had been feeling abdominal discomfort and indigestion and generally felt less than great. He had hoped to visit a doctor in Santa Fe before returning to Colorado. Coincidentally I was running the Rio Chama with our friend and doctor and didn't get home until the afternoon of the day following his arrival.

Ed helped me unload the river rats' equipment from my pickup. He told me that he kept getting pains in his gut. I told him I'd call our doctor friend right now or first thing in the morning. He opted to wait one more night.

The next morning after breakfast the doctor made a house call and talked to Abbey about his abdominal pains. He suggested that Abbey wait another day or two to see if the pains would go away. Abbey and I spent the day hiking up into Santa Fe Canyon. Occasionally he would stop and grimace, holding his gut.

Late that afternoon we sat on the porch to watch the sun set behind Mount Taylor about a hundred miles to the west. Abbey complained that he was feeling pretty bad. That evening he didn't eat much dinner and we all retired early. About 10 P.M., it was evident that he needed medical attention. We helped him out to my truck, and Clarke and I took him to the emergency room at St. Vincent's Hospital. Susie remained at the house with Kath.

Abbey was loaded onto a gurney, and Clarke and I registered him at the emergency-room desk. Hospital staff wheeled him into an examination room, and Clarke followed to be with him. I stayed at the desk to answer questions. A few minutes later a nurse came up to me with a hypodermic needle in one hand and an alcohol-soaked cotton swab in the other.

"Would you please roll up your sleeve, sir?" she asked.

"Why?" I replied.

"This is a sedative. It will make you feel better."

"I feel fine already. I don't need a sedative."

"But I was told that you had abdominal pain, Mr. Abbey."

"Abbey's in that room over there. I guess us guys with beards all look alike."

The nurse flushed and walked away without saying another word. I continued to stand at the admissions desk. Two hefty orderlies approached, firmly holding both arms of a young man who was obviously deeply disturbed. They brought him to the desk, where they stood him beside me. Then the orderlies walked off, leaving the man standing there looking at me, his eyes growing wilder by the second. Then he spun around and ran like hell for the door and away he went. The orderlies returned, looking for their charge.

"He went thataway," said I, pointing at the door.

"Oh, Jesus!" The two orderlies made for the door as fast as they could. I don't know if they ever did find that poor young wacko.

I went into the examination room, and Abbey told me they were going to keep him in the hospital overnight.

"Whatever you do, don't let anyone near you until you make sure they know who you are," I said.

"Why?"

"Take my word for it. It's good hospital procedure."

I took Clarke back to my house, and she, Kath, Susie, my young daughter, Peregrina, and I made the best of a worrisome evening.

A few days passed, and Abbey was subjected to various tests. The doctor had called in an abdominal specialist. More time passed, and the x-rays revealed foreboding shadows in the region of the liver and pancreas. Finally the specialist called Clarke. Shortly thereafter Clarke called me at home and asked me to come over to the hospital.

"Jack," exclaimed Clarke. "They think he has cancer of the liver and possibly of the pancreas and that he's going to die."

"Oh, shit." Clarke and I stood there in disbelief. Ed couldn't be that sick. Could he? I told Clarke to go back to my house and try to relax for a while, that I'd be along as soon as I could.

I went into Ed's room. He sat there on the edge of his bed. We looked at each other long and deep.

"Well, *compañero,* I'm here for your disposal," I said.

"At least I don't have to floss anymore," said Ed. He grinned at me.

"What the fuck's wrong with you?"

"The doctors told me there's a ninety-eight percent chance I have cancer and that I'll be dead in two to six months."

"How do they know this?"

"Well, they performed a biopsy on my liver and punched me here and there. Did you ever have a biopsy?"

"No."

"They take a needle about a foot long and stick it into you. Then they pull it out and you realize that parts of your guts are inside the needle in microcosm. Sort of like tree-ring dating."

"What did they find?"

"Nothing so far."

"Then how do they know you have cancer?"

"Beats me. Maybe a shadow on the x-ray. This afternoon I have to go in for a CAT scan."

"Look, Ed. What do you want me to do? I'll do absolutely anything you need me to do."

"Just don't let me die in this fucking hospital, Jack."

"I guess you're calling in the vow we made, aren't you?"

"I guess I am. Are you up for it?"

"You asshole! I gave you my word!"

"Well, you told me you'd bring tools up to Vermillion Cliffs and help me build a *ramada* [arbor]. Clarke and I waited for you for two days."

"When was this?"

"About a month ago."

"I told you I'd come up and bring some tools, but you never told me when you wanted me to meet you there, for chrissake!"

"I didn't?"

"No! Why didn't you call me?"

"I just thought you'd be there."

"What the fuck. Do you think I'm telepathic?"

We glared at each other and then started to laugh. It was either that or start to cry.

"Look, Ed," I said. "Let's get you out of here and back to the house. Figure it out from there."

"I want that CAT scan first."

"Okay, but let's get you the hell out of here as soon as we can."

"Thanks, *compañero*."

Abbey had the CAT scan, but it revealed nothing definite. Yet the doctors insisted that Abbey, in all likelihood, was doomed to death from cancer before the turn of the year.

Early the next morning Clarke and I brought Abbey home from the hospital. He went out into the backyard to stare at the mountains. I had joked with him as much as I could, trying to cheer him up. When he was out of earshot, Clarke planted herself in front of me and looked me right in the eye.

"Do you really care about him, Jack?"

I was utterly taken aback.

"Clarke, he's the best friend I have in this world. I would do anything for him. I love him."

Clarke started to cry. I held her for a few minutes until she stopped. From that moment on, Clarke has been like my sister.

Abbey came into the living room.

"Jack. We have to leave you in peace. We'll get a room somewhere until they finish the tests." Abbey's face was set in the dark mode.

"No way."

"C'mon, Jack." Abbey walked out into the front yard. I followed him. He went to his truck. I climbed in the passenger side. He fired up the truck and we drove away downtown to the old Hotel Fidel. Abbey parked, got out, and went into the hotel. I followed him. He asked the clerk at the desk if he could look at a room. The clerk gave him a key. Ed and I climbed two flights and found the room. It was modestly dreary.

"Goddammit, Ed! If you and Clarke and Susie don't stay at my house, I'm going get *really pissed off at you!*"

"Jack. I don't want to bother you with all of this. You and Kathy have your own things to do. You don't need this." Ed's eyes were tormented.

"Ed, you and I are *family*, for chrissake!" I went over and gave him an *abrazo*. "C'mon home, now."

We went home.

Abbey called his friend Wally Mulligan, a doctor then living in Tucson, who insisted that he get out of Santa Fe and back to Tucson immediately.

Ed wasn't fit to drive. We decided that Clarke and Susie would leave that afternoon, driving the Datsun back to Tucson, and that I would take Ed to the Albuquerque airport the following day so that Clarke could meet him when he arrived in Tucson. Kath and Clarke had already driven up to Colorado to get the Abbeys' possessions out of Carrico's cabin.

It was truly a poignant moment when Clarke and Susie left Ed and me standing there on the front porch as they embarked for Tucson. As she walked down the path, Ed started to weep—not for himself but for Clarke and Susie and for everyone he truly loved. Abbey and I were born into a generation where grown men don't easily weep in front of each other. But we had before, and we would again.

After Clarke had left, Abbey asked me for a drink.

"Are you sure a drink would be good for you?"

"Christ, Loeffler. Are you going to deny a dying man a drink?"

"Well, if you put it that way . . ."

It was a strange afternoon. Abbey was immersed in a terrible sadness. He told me that death held no terror for him. But the idea of a long, drawn-out, grisly death that put everyone through the stench of disease and indignity was distasteful to him. Kath and I began to worry that he might "wander westward" that night to save Clarke the grim torment of watching him fade from cancer.

The phone rang. It was Clarke. The truck had broken down in Albuquerque. She was at the end of her immediate reserve. I told her to sit tight. She had gotten a motel. We would be down first thing in the morning. I would tow the Datsun to Tucson, and the three Abbeys would catch the first plane out. This gave Ed something to look forward to.

On the way to Albuquerque, Ed talked about ways he could use his death wisely. He invoked the notion of the geriatric kamikaze unit. Let's see: there was the Glen Canyon Dam, the Navajo Generating Station; how about the bridge on Highway 95 or the conveyor belt at the Black Mesa Mine? Fine idea. Do something really useful for a change instead of scribble about it all the time. Whaddya say, *frijol viejo,* will you give a hand?

Yes!

As the fantasies began to mount, the spark in Abbey's eyes supplanted the stark cast of hopelessness.

We pulled into the Crossroads Motel in Albuquerque, and Clarke ran out to meet us. She and Ed were indescribably glad to see each other.

We hooked the Datsun pickup to the back of our Chevy with a tow bar. Clarke, Ed, Susie, Peregrina, Kath, and I squeezed into our truck, and away we went.

Abbey was admitted to the hospital two days after arriving in Tucson. He was subjected to another CAT scan, and a host of doctors went over him. They predicted liver cancer. Or cancer of the biliary ducts. There was talk of a laparotomy, a meaningful moment when the abdomen is opened and the innards strewn about and examined, thence stuffed back in the abdominal cavity, little pieces snipped off here and there to better the fit. This, we were collectively assured, would cause Ed minimal discomfort and establish precisely the nature of the problem.

Abbey wanted nothing to do with it.

We were grasping at straws, willing the shamanism of modern medicine to work magic on Ed. Ultimately we collectively cajoled him into going through ordeal by knife.

A few days later Clarke and I sat in the grass outside the hospital where Abbey was now undergoing major surgery. For six hours we talked about everything we could think of. Finally we were called in.

No, Mr. Abbey has no trace of cancer. There is evidence of pancreatitis. We removed his appendix and his gallbladder. There is evidence that the portal vein has thrombosed. Plugged by a stone. Accommodated by a new cluster of veins. But definitely no cancer.

When the doctor left, Clarke and I danced jubilantly around that part of the hospital, decorum abandoned. Ed wasn't going to die!

We took shifts by his bed. Abbey hurt like hell. Every few minutes spasms of heavy cramps rippled across the muscles of his violated abdomen. He would cry out and squeeze the hand that held his almost to the breaking point. "I want to kill the fuckers who did this to me!" he raged. But he survived.

For about two weeks, I looked death in the face and was not frightened. I felt a great sadness, yes, at being forced so suddenly, abruptly, prematurely, to leave my beloved Clarke and Susie, and the desert hills and sunsets, and music and books and my friends and my work, but—strangely—

*I felt no fear. Nor panic, anger, despair. Only a great sadness, and a
calm acceptance of what I'd always known to be inevitable. Continuity!
I was not going to die in a hospital, or by slow ugly humiliating degrees,
in bed, under sedation, at home either, by Gawd.*

*I looked Death in the face. Death has no eyes. I felt no anger, fear,
or dismay or any of the alleged 5 stages of the terminal patient (fuck
Kubler-Ross). I would hold out as long as possible, settle my affairs, do
what literary work I could, and then as pain and debilitation became
too much, I would take a walk, as Thoreau advised, out into the western
desert, "in the spirit of undying adventure, never to return."*

Abbey was left with a fourteen-inch-long curved scar across his abdomen. I
told him he should have a head tattooed on one end, a rattle on the other, and
Don't Tread on Me! inscribed across the face of his belly. Abbey laughed, but
not too hard. There was too much pain to laugh very hard.

That autumn, Ed noted on October 4, 1982, Glenn Gould died at the age
of fifty. Gould was one of Abbey's musical heroes.

As soon as his health returned, Abbey went back to work on the "masterpiece." He had so many notes for this autobiographical novel that he had to
weave an extraordinarily intricate web of plots within plots.

He didn't neglect his stance concerning the natural environment. He noted
that Arizona ever fell prey to developers. He concluded, "Arizona has the best
politicians that money can buy." He was disgusted with professional politicians and favored term limits. It was his opinion that a career politician couldn't
function without making irrevocable compromises. Thereafter, the parameters
had been established, and the politician was involved in the prevailing game.
In Arizona the game was the Central Arizona Project. Abbey didn't believe in
having to "play the hand you're dealt." Abbey believed in changing the game
even if it meant turning over the gaming table with six-shooters ablazing. This
was one of Abbey's most admirable qualities. He *would not compromise* for
personal profit.

Though the fires of youth may have been spent in many of Abbey's contem-
poraries, men of late middle age who elected to sigh, sit back, and accept the
otherwise unacceptable, Abbey refused to relinquish his sense of justice, his
environmental activism, his deep-seated commitment to anarchism. By now

Abbey was truly "the wilderness anarchist," relentless in his resolve to speak only the truth as he understood it.

During the early 1980s a small group of fellow environmentalists, haggard and worn by the political game, founded Earth First! These were radical environmentalists who were willing to break the law if the law was environmentally unethical. "No compromise in defense of the Earth!" Dave Foreman, one of the founders, had spent a decade as a hard-core environmentalist within the arena of "legitimate environmentalism." Foreman had read *The Monkey Wrench Gang* and was otherwise no stranger to Edward Abbey. As time went on, Abbey and Foreman became friends, and to a great extent Abbey became a spiritual adviser to Earth First! For the rest of his life, Abbey regarded Earth First!ers as America's true heroes. They were defending wilderness for its own sake, a path that, though extremely perilous, Abbey saw as one of the few paths of truth being followed in this nation.

In December 1982 Abbey fell ill again. He was bleeding internally because the cluster of veins that had formed to accommodate the flow of blood from the liver to the esophagus with the damming of the portal vein had weak walls subject to rupture. This malady, esophageal varices, is associated with alcoholism. Abbey was a moderate drinker, definitely not an alcoholic. The doctors had not clearly revealed the nature of this illness when they discovered it during Abbey's surgery. Abbey could well have bled to death on any of the strenuous hikes he had taken since then, for he had no idea of his condition and felt healthy.

He and I had planned a trek on the Baja peninsula, which we canceled because he was seriously weakened by the hemorrhage. We settled instead on a camping trip into the nearby Superstition Mountains, whence I could readily transport him to a nearby hospital should he begin to bleed again. As we sat by the campfire, he told me that he was now truly facing his mortality, that there was no real cure for his illness, and that it would undoubtedly carry him away at some time in the future. He grinned at me in the firelight. There was really nothing to say. The elation at having survived "mock cancer" was now overshadowed by a new specter. There was simply no way of knowing how long he would endure.

Abbey had already accepted his fate. He had digested it. Now he was telling me where he stood in relation to eternity, as best he knew. He asked me not to mention it to anyone. Only Clarke and his doctor knew the gravity of this sickness. Abbey understood that he was held in highest esteem by an ever growing cadre of young environmentalists. He knew that he was regarded throughout western America as a talented writer. There was no sense in tarnishing the patina of his reputation with the grim foreknowledge of his limited time left on the planet.

To which I replied, "Fuck!" and threw my beer bottle at a rock. (I later cleaned up every shard and hauled it out.)

The next day Abbey opted to remain in camp but urged me to go on a hike he recommended that should get me back by midafternoon. I strapped on my web belt with two canteens and my trusted piece to protect myself from armed badge bearers and others of their ilk. I had a wonderful hike, but my heart felt like a big ball of lead. At one point I happened into a pack of javelinas, who let me pass through their midst without exploding off in all directions.

I followed Abbey's instructions as best I could, but it was late afternoon and twilight was on me when I found my own trail back to camp. I examined the tracks in the sand and saw Abbey's following my own. They looked fresh, and I realized that he had probably gotten worried and taken off after me even though he didn't feel well. I pulled out my .357 and fired off a round, listening to the sound blast through the canyon. I started following Abbey's tracks, and sure enough, within five minutes I ran into Ed headed back down the trail.

"Figured you were lost, Loeffler. Figured I was going to have to rescue you as usual."

We grinned at each other as we had a million times before. But this time, when I looked at this tall, bearded finest of men, I realized how much I had grown to love him, how willing I was to spit in the eyes of those gods who would take him away, and that I would defend him against anyone or anything that ever threatened him. I am basically a coward, and my greatest fear was that I would lose my friend.

Clarke was pregnant! She radiated life, and Ed spent many poignant moments contemplating the beauty of existence. He was also sobered by the knowledge of his mortality. He had lived a full life and realized that a human lifetime is only briefly wrested from eternity, to which it will return. Life must be lived keenly, fearlessly, without regard for the dreary moderation practiced by those who have invested heavily in a possible hereafter. Having gazed calmly into the eyeless countenance of Death, Abbey was now resolved to hold Death at bay until his energy was utterly spent. He was determined to be a good husband and a good father.

Focusing again on his "fat masterpiece," he wrote copiously, flailing relentlessly at culture gone awry, whether it be American or Mexican or Japanese or Indian. His passion for expression in the English language was like a bonfire in his brain. Perspiration soaked his hair, dripping down his face, sometimes landing on the page he was writing.

In late January 1983 Abbey wrote a powerful letter to *The National Review:*

> Dear Editor:
> Thank you for publishing A. Solzhenitsyn's splendid indictment of the Soviet empire. His denunciation rings true, despite some contrary reports (on the economy there) by the CIA. The most disturbing aspect of S.'s attack on the USSR, however, is the fact that almost everything he says applies with equal force, at least in principle, to most of the rest of the world as well: the concentration of power in a hierarchy of the few; the destruction of our God-created environment; the insane lust to dominate manipulate control almost every part of both nature and human nature; the deliberate suppression, by military force, of every effort at popular liberation; the demoralization of the general population; that mad pursuit of military power at all costs.
> The gross evil of our time defies all labels.
> Yrs.,
> Edward Abbey

Abbey was outraged by the America of Ronald Reagan. During Reagan's tenure the rich got richer, the poor got poorer, and the land got raped. According to the 1983 Federal Reserve Board Report, Abbey noted that 2 percent of the families in the United States held 54 percent of the national wealth and that 10 percent of the families held 86 percent. America was an oligarchy disguised as democracy. The two-party system had to fit the needs of the powerful few at the expense of the general population. In addition, the United States had the highest rate of incarceration in the world and was the only major power without a national public health policy. Abbey's anarchism was honed by his outrage. He gave speeches before university audiences, he wrote letters to the editors of many periodicals. He noted in his journal:

> *There comes a time in the life of every woman, every man, when we must put down our books, leave the library or the kitchen or the shop or the field, and go forth on the road of life to meet the enemy face to face. One brave deed is worth a thousand books. In a nation of sheep, one brave man is a majority.*

Abbey and members of Earth First! were drawing fire from certain liberal or environmental periodicals, where they were regarded as "ecoterrorists." The FBI called them "soft-core terrorists." Ed was demoralized by these epithets. He was no terrorist, nor were the Earth First!ers. Their first rule was to cause no harm to any fellow human. They committed acts of civil disobedience. They spiked trees but forewarned the loggers and Forest Service employees that the trees had been spiked and were now dangerous to cut. They saw themselves as anti-terrorists. Their purpose was to halt the terrorizing of wilderness and natural habitat by extractors and corporate carpetbaggers. They contended that the government and private industry were the true terrorists.

"Martyrdom," wrote Abbey.

> *I don't want it. Don't really need it. Here I am, leading a soft easy sedentary lower middle-class life—why should I forfeit these easy joys and bland pleasures for a possible bullet in the face, a kick in the groin, solitaire in a prison cell? Makes no sense . . . what possible point to it? Much wiser to become a temporizer, an explainer and apologist like my fellow writers. To avoid the self-reproach of moral cowardice, one need only convince oneself that a new, more "reasonable," more "pragmatic" approach to the great conflict of our time—is correct. This is not too difficult when thought-modification is encouraged by fear. Then once this mental conversion is made, one is free to attack radicals and independents with zeal, in apparent good faith, with an enthusiasm made all the more fervent by the knowledge that your enemies' convictions, if true, brand you—thyself—with the mark of intellectual dishonesty and moral dishonor. Meanwhile too, of course, you enjoy all the safety, privileges*

*influence and not negligible material rewards of service and subservience
to the powerful, the rich, the dominant class.*

*Intellectual and active resistance, on the other hand, can only lead to
trouble, loss of job, poverty, insecurity, danger, prison, perhaps death.
Inevitably to death. For note: if I refuse to pay the income tax, for
example, my property is seized. If I attempt to defend my property against
seizure, I will be arrested. If I resist arrest, I will be clubbed, beaten,
jailed. If I attempt to defend myself against physical attack by fighting
back, I will promptly be killed—gassed, clubbed, shot, executed.*

*The death penalty is the State's ultimate weapon. The death penalty is
the original, fundamental act of terrorism. The purpose of the death
penalty is to inspire awe, and fear, and terror, in all subjects of the State.
Thus the cross, the stake, the gallows, the electric chair, the gas chamber.*

Abbey had agreed to run a river in Alaska in the summer of 1983 with a group
of environmental enthusiasts and personal admirers. No sooner had he agreed
than he wanted to withdraw his promise. The trip would come as a major
interruption in the writing of *The Fool's Progress*. Because this book was becoming a great autobiographical novel that dealt very little with the environment,
Abbey was loath to don the guise of the master outdoorsman even for a free
trip down an Alaskan river. His time was precious. But he had given his word,
and the outfitter was counting on him, so he mustered his goodwill and finally
headed north to Alaska, where he caught the flu but ran the river anyway. It
wasn't his favorite adventure, but he had done his best.

He returned to Tucson in midsummer of 1983 and went back to work after
a month-long hiatus. He had written an article for *Playboy* about Mexican
culture that was rejected. Abbey had Mexican friends, but he disliked Mexican
culture. He didn't regard himself as a racist or a bigot. He had spent time in
Mexico and had seen a culture that followed the *patrón* system, that turned on
its own, that trashed the environment, that was suffering a population increase
of 3 percent a year—the highest in the world! He considered the Mexican
police, who were armed in a land where the poor were denied the right to bear
arms, the worst kind of bullies. He called it the way he saw it. When challenged, he would refer to the history books. It was all there.

This was an unpopular stance among the liberals and the Hispanos, and

Abbey was widely criticized for his views. Yet he strongly advocated providing sanctuary for political refugees from Latin America. I have seen Abbey weep at the way the whores of a border town were treated by their fellow citizens. I have watched his look of astonishment as he observed a pesticide container draining into the puddle in the backyard of a jacal, a pig drinking from the puddle, and a naked child splashing the pig.

He regarded human overpopulation as the fundamental problem of our time; he came to condemn Christianity as one of its great evils. Abbey believed the biblical apothegm "be fruitful and multiply," once relevant for the continuity of a few thousand desert tribesmen, had been contemporized by a Christian pope whose subservience to ancient doctrine gravely threatened *life on Earth* while proclaiming it! Bad idea, this business of dominion over *everything* on the face of the Earth. After all, humanity is but a single species living in interdependence with myriad other species within the biotic community.

Abbey's faith lay in the process of evolution, incomplete as our understanding of it might be. He rued the superstitions that blind people to the evidence of the five senses. He didn't understand how humans fail to be overwhelmed by the presence of life on this planet. Abbey contended that it is the responsibility of every living being to live in balance with Nature, that human sympathy should be extended to all living things and beyond to include the air, the land, the water. To place faith in an after-death state is to be contemptuous of life.

Abbey also had little patience with the modern-day wave of scientific spiritualism:

Analogical argument: The reductionist fallacy of current, faddish, metaphysical science (for example "The Dancing Wooly Masters"): to assert that reality is nothing but the free dance patterns of organic energy is like saying that a human being is essentially a whirling buzz of electrons, or that a book is merely ink specks on paper. An obvious mistake. But the occultists and theologians will resort to any absurdity, however extreme, rather than face up to the real world of common sense and common living experience. An attempt (as in Dillard) to smuggle the presuppositions of traditional religion back into intellectual respectability under the guise of science. Since these people are doubly superstitious, they want not only to dig up the dead horses of Christian and Hindu theology,

but live also in idolatrous awe of science, especially physics. Biology, they
are not so keen about. These people (like Jung and Capra, et al.) do not
have scientific minds but are mightily impressed by scientific achievement.
We cannot repeal ten million years of primate biology.

Abbey was working on his novel and preparing a collection of essays to be
titled *Beyond the Wall*. In mid-September 1983 he and Clarke headed north to
see old friends in northern New Mexico and to visit the headwaters of the Rio
Grande in connection with his assignment to write the final chapter for an
anthology called *Great Rivers of the World*, to be published by National Geographic. They passed through Santa Fe, and Abbey and I ran the Rio Chama,
a major tributary of the Rio Grande. In Taos they visited Malcolm Brown,
Abbey's friend since his early university days. They hadn't seen each other in
years, but the bond between them was long and deep.

The Abbeys wended their course west by northwest to the historic mining
town of Silverton, in southwestern Colorado. The summer rains were late and
lashing at the mountains in a relentless deluge. Their road headed into the high
country, where they hoped to find the wellsprings of the Rio Grande.

Clarke recalled that adventure:

I was nine months pregnant. It was at the very end of September. Ed
was busy writing his chapter on the Rio Grande for that book about
rivers. He had wanted to go to both the source and the delta of the Rio
Grande. He had already flown to Brownsville, Texas. And now we had
come to see the source of the river. I should have known better than to
have gone on a camping trip with Ed when I was pregnant with my first
child. I guess it was maybe two weeks before I was due. We were in his
Datsun pickup with the camper. We were going over rough roads and
were beyond Silverton. We went up this slippery road to get to the very
first trickle of the Rio Grande. It had rained for quite a while and it was
pretty cold up there.

The rain was pouring and the road got really muddy so we stopped,
but we still had the windshield wipers on. We had been driving around
the side of a big hill with a steep embankment on one side and a sheer
drop-off on the other. We saw this huge mud slide come right down the

hill in front of the truck. So Ed quickly put it in reverse and looked around to see which way to back up the truck. I looked out my window as another mud slide came down right in back of us. I can't believe that neither one of them hit us, but they didn't. They were huge. We couldn't budge. We spent the night in the truck. We got up the next morning and it wasn't raining. Ed started digging in this slimy, slimy mud. Every time he dug out a shovelful, another ten shovelfuls would fall down in its place. Ed dug for the entire day. I was too pregnant to do anything. Ed was really scared that I was going to go into labor and have the baby there. He was really panicked. He dug and he dug and he dug and he finally had dug out two tracks through which he could back up the truck. He had me get out of the cab and walk across the mud slide. He backed it up over the mud slide and I watched as the front end of the truck almost slid over the cliff. But he made it.

Dangerous business, going camping with Abbey.
Then, a scant two weeks later:

Rebecca Claire Abbey was born at 11:20 P.M. Monday, October 10th, 1983. Looks human (beautiful!). A long ordeal for Clarke—almost twenty-three hours. We are both delighted by our Becky.

Whole nations, entire races
May crash in ruin
Before I'd sacrifice your smallest finger
To save them.
(The fanatic love of the parent
for the child . . .)

My daughter, Rebecca . . . grows more lovable, adorable beautiful every day! What an angel, what an imp, what a marvel and wonder and spicy bundle of vitality and joy!

I finally did something right.

I want to be a good husband, a good father, a good man, more than anything else that life makes possible. Fame and money seem trivial now. . . .

As Clarke said to me, "Becky brought so much into his life. Such incredible love. He would have been lost without that part of his life."

Abbey finished *Beyond the Wall* and continued working on *The Fool's Progress.* He went back to the University of Arizona to teach for the winter semester of 1984, although grudgingly. Teaching left him little energy for his novel. He decided to remain in Tucson for the summer of 1984 while Clarke and Becky headed north, first to Santa Fe, then to Salt Lake City, to avoid the blistering Sonoran summer sun. He polished 155 pages, which he sent to Don Congdon. Congdon passed a copy of these to Jack Macrae, who for many years was Abbey's editor. He waited anxiously for a reply. In the meantime *National Geographic* asked him to write an article about the Big Bend country of west Texas. He was interested in having an adventure and getting paid for it, for funds were running low. He wasn't so interested in actually having to write four thousand words. He was fast tiring of "the mechanical and uninspired drudgery of a scrivener."

(t w o)

Ed exited the plane into the September sunshine of Albuquerque International Airport. A tall man, six-foot three in his stocking feet, bearded, beaked with a great nose, penetrating green eyes, a full head of brown hair sticking out from under a sunshade that bore the legend Earth First! with a monkey wrench—his coat of arms—and bedecked in a pair of old blue jeans and a T-shirt with Live Free or Die! written across the front. He wore a pair of surplus GI jungle boots. He carried an old briefcase. He was grinning and waving. The rest of the passengers gave him a wide berth. When they saw me grinning and waving back at him, they gave me a wide berth, too.

He tromped down the portable stairway and walked across the tarmac to the gate where I stood.

"Hello, you old fart," he said, and gave me an *abrazo.*

"Howdy, *frijol viejo!*" said I, returning his bear hug.

We hadn't seen each other since June, and we both had stories and lies to tell. We hiked to the luggage carousel a couple hundred yards into the bowels of the terminal and stood watching luggage being regurgitated from below. We asked about each other's respective families, anxious to get the hell out of there.

Finally an old army duffel bag popped out onto the conveyor, followed by a backpack. We retrieved Ed's luggage, and away we went toward my old dented and bent pickup truck with the white camper. We tossed everything in the back, fired up the truck, and headed out down that long, dusty road. There was cold beer in a cooler at Ed's feet. He pulled out two, popped the tops, and handed me one, which was foaming over the side.

"*¡Salud, compañero!*"

"*¡Salud, hermano!*"

I chugalugged; Ed quaffed more elegantly. I squeezed my empty can into an aluminum ball. Ed handed me another fresh one.

"I remember when it took some strength to squeeze a beer can flat," said Ed. I pulled out onto I-25 south.

"We gotta stop in Belen and load up with some more beer," said I. It was a one-six-pack-for-two trip from Albuquerque to Belen. "We have a long way to go."

"How far do you think it is?" asked Ed.

"Probably about six hundred miles."

We were headed for Big Bend National Park in southwestern Texas, heart of the Chihuahuan Desert. It was just over ten years since we had run the Rio Grande in Big Bend country, and we were determined to return to paradise.

"Lemme know when you want me to drive," said Ed.

"Okay," I said, shuddering to myself. Abbey was the kiss of death to every vehicle he got near. He wasn't inept; he simply pushed the vehicle he happened to be driving to its limit and beyond.

Ed was about to write the article on Big Bend for *National Geographic*. He had called a few days earlier and asked if I wanted to go along. Hell, yes!! I offered to drive, load up on water and camping gear, meet him at the plane, and head out, just the two of us for ten days or so. It was all there in the back of my truck. Tent. Coleman stove. Twenty gallons of water. Cooking gear. Eating gear. Everything we needed but beer and food. Ed would buy all of that, plus the gasoline and oil, with his *National Geographic* expense money.

We had it made!

After loading up with beer in Belen, we continued to head south on I-25, barreling along as fast as my old Chevy would comfortably go. Much of the time, Ed read. It was noisy in the cab of the truck, and Ed's hearing diminished every year, so that by now it was difficult for him to converse in a noisy vehicle. Sometimes he would read aloud to me, but in the main we were comfortable enough in each other's company to travel wordlessly for hours.

It was dark by the time we reached El Paso, Texas. Beyond the expanse of moist sand euphemistically known as the Rio Grande (most of the water had been sucked into irrigation ditches farther north), we could see the sparse lights of Juárez, Mexico. At that time, Juárez had a population of over a million.

"Doesn't look like a million people could live there," said Ed.

"It's supposed to be bigger than El Paso," said I.

"Juárez. A terrible place. Hard to believe that much human misery could be packed into that small an area. Have you gone over there much?" asked Ed.

"Not really. Maybe five times since 1962. There's a good Chinese restaurant there. I was there one night when they set the ceiling on fire with baked Alaska."

"Baked Alaska in a Chinese restaurant in Mexico. Jesus." Ed laughed. "I'm getting hungry. Are you?"

"Yeah. We need gas, too."

We drove farther until we found a truck stop near Fabens. We went into a dimly lighted, depressing restaurant that featured a buffet in the middle of the room, where booths lined three of the walls. Ed and I sat in a booth and looked around at the truckers taking their evening meals.

"Be a hell of a way to earn a living, wouldn't it?" said Ed. "Driving all the time, looking at a landscape you never get to walk around in, eating in places like this all the time. Trying to stay awake at night. Hell of an existence. Almost as bad as writing for a living. Get about the same amount of exercise, maybe a little more steering a semi. Whatever happened to the time when a man earned his food honestly by hunting for it, for chrissake?"

"Relegated to antiquity," said I.

"Jesus, did you look at that buffet?" asked Ed. "Pure grease. It's been so long since most of that food was in a natural state, it probably has no nutritional value anymore."

"The apples looked pretty good."

"They're probably covered with herbicide," said Ed.

"What are you going to have?" I asked.

"Guess I'll get a hamburger. Hard to fuck up a hamburger."

We both ate hamburgers and drank coffee. We had a long way to go, and we wanted to get there.

By the time we got to Van Horn, Texas, it was close to midnight. From there, we would leave the interstate and take Highway 90 to Marfa. We spotted an all-night Safeway supermarket in Van Horn and decided this was our last chance to buy food for camping.

The supermarket was illuminated by ghastly fluorescent light that lent a deathly cast to everything.

"Jesus, you look awful," said Ed.

"You look like a refugee from one of Poe's nightmares, you po' bastard."

"Nevermore," said Ed.

The night manager gave us the once-over as we extracted a shopping cart from where it was crammed into an entire train of shopping carts. I held the train while Ed pulled. Finally it gave, and Ed went dancing backward, holding on to the shopping cart to keep from falling.

"I hate these goddamned things," he said. "They're badly designed."

We cruised up and down the aisles of the Safeway, each of us selecting arbitrarily what we thought we wanted to eat. There was a frozen meat section. We took two packages of frozen pork chops and some burger. Three days' worth of real meat—thereafter we would have to rely on processed foods, packaged foods, canned food, junk food. We went on to the canned meat.

"Do you know what the hot dog vendor said to the Zen monk?"

"No."

"Let me make you one with everything."

I started to laugh. Soon I was out of control, totally doubled up in front of the Vienna sausages. I was laughing so hard, I couldn't breathe. I thought I was going to faint. I looked at Ed. He was laughing, too. We leaned against the shelves, not daring to look at each other. The night manager of the Safeway stood at the end of the aisle, looking at us curiously, threateningly. I began to envision a night in the drunk tank in Van Horn. Not a good thought. Little by little, we reassumed control.

I addressed the night manager. "Just heard the funniest joke of my life. Sorry about that." He looked uncertain and walked away.

"Jesus, Ed. That was close," I said, drying my eyes with my bandanna.

We wandered through the store, piling an enormous quantity (

the shopping cart. We had regained our composure, lulled by the inescapable Muzak provided to soothe the supermarket shopper.

"Did you bring your flute?" asked Ed.

"I always bring my flute," said I.

"Not that flute, goddammit! Your wooden flute."

"I always bring both flutes," said I.

"Good. A real man should never be without his flutes."

"Two-flutes La Trek. That's who you are, Abbey! Two-flutes La Trek."

"Nope. I'm Two-*Shoes* La Trek. I forgot and left my flute at home."

"Touché, La Trek."

We pushed the all but overflowing shopping cart to the check stand. A tired-looking cashier started checking us through. The night manager stood off to one side, still suspicious of these two midnight marauders. *National Geographic* shelled out over a hundred bucks for whatever it was we were going to eat. As we pushed our shopping cart out the automatic doors of the Safeway, I turned and looked at the night manager and grinned.

I fired up my truck and we left Van Horn behind us. The next town was Marfa, about seventy-five miles ahead. It was well after midnight by now, and we were both getting tired.

"Want me to drive, Jack?"

"No, thanks. I'm doin' fine."

"You never let me drive your fucking truck. Why the hell not?" demanded Abbey.

"Because it is a gentle beast, not to be ridden like a bronco," said I.

"Horseshit!" retorted Ed.

We drove on for a while in silence. By now we were both looking for a place to pull off the highway where we could camp for what remained of the night.

"There's no public land in this godforsaken state," said Ed. "All the land around here is privately owned."

"Jesus. It's too far to try to make it to Big Bend tonight. See if anyplace looks good."

We both peered into the night, trying to find someplace where no one would give us any grief. The drive seemed endless. finally, sometime around 3 A.M., we pulled into Marfa.

"Do you want to see if we can get a motel room?" asked a weary Ed.

"No. Let's get south of town and just pull over. We have to find Route 67 around here and turn south."

Ed spotted the junction, and we turned south into darkest night. Soon there were no lights anywhere.

"There's a dirt road. Let's pull off there," said Ed.

We crossed a cattle guard and drove maybe half a mile into open rangeland.

"This good enough?" I asked.

"Hell, yes, it's good enough," said Ed.

I pulled off the dirt road about a hundred feet or so. We stopped the truck, got out, and peed. Then we opened the back of my camper and Ed hauled out his duffel bag. He opened it and pulled out his folding wooden-and-canvas cot.

"Jesus, you really travel light, don't you?" I said.

"I can't stand ants crawling in my ears. I hate fucking ants."

Ed started to assemble the cot. The only time Ed ever borrowed money from me was to buy this cot. He had gotten it years before when he and I were in a surplus store in Tucson. He had found it hidden behind a pile of army jetsam in a corner. He had come over to me and asked if I could stake him to this cot because he didn't have any money with him. I did. He paid me back later that same day. From that time on, anytime we went camping, he always took his cot with him. He always mumbled about "fucking ants" whenever he assembled it.

We collapsed at exactly 4 A.M., Ed on his cot, I in the back of my truck. I don't like "fucking ants" crawling in my ears, either. Or scorpions, centipedes, and rattlers crawling in my sleeping bag, for that matter.

Shortly after dawn I woke up. I heard horses and men talking. I looked out of the back of my camper and saw three vaqueros, Mexican cowboys, astride their horses, looking at Ed on his cot. He was stirring in his sleeping bag. His head emerged, and he cocked a baleful eye at the cowboys. They grinned and rode off.

"Christ," said Ed. "I'm tired."

"So'm I," said I. "But chances are zero we'll get any more sleep."

"Let's get up," said Ed.

We piled out of our respective fart sacks, as our old friend Karl Kernberger used to call them, and faced the day. A beautiful day it was, the sun just rising. Too bad we'd only gotten two hours' sleep.

I rummaged in the back of the camper and dug out the Coleman stove, the coffeepot, and two cups. Ed searched through the food boxes until he found one of the rectangular tins of coffee, chocolate, and sugar that we both loved. We said nothing. We were too wasted to talk. In a few seemingly interminable minutes we each had a cup of Swiss mocha, hot and steaming. We sat on the tailgate and drank two cups each before we had the energy to start packing up. Sugar and caffeine. Chemicals, as our friend Doug Peacock would say. More chemicals.

"It's beautiful here, in a flat, boring sort of way," said Ed.

"I've seen antelope around here. Lots of antelope."

"Too bad there're so many cows here. There should be thousands, millions of antelope. I've read somewhere that there used to be bison around here," said Ed.

"Yeah. It was in that article I wrote that I loaned you," said I.

"Then it probably wasn't true."

"It was true. I read several accounts of bison migrating around Big Bend. The Indians used to come in and hunt them. Comanches and Apaches, I think. The Indians didn't get along too well with each other. And they raised hell with the ranchers."

"Too bad they didn't drive them out and keep them out," said Ed. "I have nothing against the men who become ranchers. Many of them, most of them, are hardworking men, unlike you and me. It's their cows I hate. And what the cows have done to the land. And the fact that the cattlemen own the land, or think they own the land. There should only be public land. Wildlife should be considered part of the public who owns the land. The wildlife should keep humans off the land. And you and I should be part of the wildlife. We should live off the bison and antelope until some wildcats come along and eat us. If we're fit to eat, that is."

Ed fell silent, and we sat there looking out over the grassland, imagining great herds of bison and antelope. And Mexican wolves. And Mexican grizzly. And pumas. And us and our families and friends.

"You know, Jack, if I were rich, really rich, I'd buy a great big ranch and fill it up with bison. I'd post big signs that said, All Trespassers Will Be Violated. I'd invite you and a few other friends to live there and we could all revert to hunter-gatherers."

"I hope you get really rich. I'd give just about anything to live like that. Be a nomad with a sack full of jerky, wandering the west with my wives. Knowing the springs. Learning the flora. Making music and dancing naked around the bonfire at night, watching the naked women dancing with me. Performing pagan rites with the young beauties. Pretending to be wise, hoping I was clever enough to outsmart the younger bucks for a few more years, at least. We wuz born in the wrong millennium, Abbey."

"Too true, La Trek. Too true," said Ed. "Let's go to Presidio and get breakfast. On *National Geographic.*"

Presidio, a small town on the Texas side of the Rio Grande, marks the confluence of the Rio Grande, which has its headwaters in the San Juan Mountains of Colorado, and the Rio Conchas, whose headwaters come from the Sierra Madre Occidental of Chihuahua, Mexico. Here the Conchas replenishes the waning waters of the Rio Grande. I had brought my copy of Paul Horgan's *Great River,* a superb human history of the Rio Grande.

"According to Horgan, it was around here somewhere that Cabeza de Vaca met the Jumanos Indians," said Ed as we drove into town.

"Now, there was a true adventure," said I.

"Took him six years to hike from Galveston back to his own people in Mexico after the shipwreck," said Ed. "Accompanied by the Moor, Estévan. He became some sort of a medicine man, they say, or conned the Indians into believing he was. Maybe he was. Who knows? Must have been a hell of a long walk. He was naked most of the way."

"No shoes, La Trek," said I.

"Let's eat," said Ed, spying a small home-style Mexican restaurant of promise.

After a fine breakfast of red chile meat burritos, we cruised the streets of Presidio. On the Mexican side of the river is the town of Ojinaga. We parked on the American side of the bridge and strolled across into Mexico.

Ojinaga seems larger than Presidio. There was a parade dominating the whole town, or so it seemed. Ed and I watched from a distance as a couple of marching bands and clusters of children, probably grouped by their classes in school, trouped past the spectators, their parents.

A mustachioed man of middle age approached us, smiling, obviously wanting to sell us something. I have never lasted more than four minutes in any border town without being hustled. Neither had Ed. Both of us hated to be hustled.

"*Señores. ¿Taxi?*" The man gestured behind him to reveal a ten-year-old Plymouth, highly polished, which was for hire.

Ed and I looked at each other.

"Do you want to ride around Ojinaga and see what's here?" asked Ed.

"Sure. But we'd better establish the price first," I said.

"You talk to him," said Ed.

"*¿Señor, cuánto cuesta para ver Ojinaga?*" I asked in my own bumbling, stumbling Spanish, wishing Kath were there to speak for us.

"Ten dollars, señor."

"*No, no. Demasiado. Yo voy pagar cinco dollars. No más.*"

"*Ocho dollars. No menos.*"

"Eight bucks to drive us around," I said to Ed. "I offered him five, but he won't take it."

"Hell. *National Geographic* can afford eight bucks to finance our education abroad," said Ed.

"*Bueno, señor,*" I said to the taximan, and Ed and I climbed in the backseat. The driver took a back street around the parade, and soon we were witnessing Ojinaga, a pleasant-looking town that wasn't dominated by its proximity to the United States—it existed for its own sake. I was watching for a *tienda*, or store, that might sell *pañuelos*, or bandannas, which I've favored as neckwear for decades. They make a hell of a lot more sense than their descendants, the neckties.

We realized that we were heading out of town.

"This doesn't seem right to me," said Ed.

"*¿Señor, a donde vamos?*" I asked of the driver.

He smiled slyly into the rearview mirror. "*¿Quieren ustedes la puta, señores?*" We were driving up a hill beyond the edge of town.

"*No, señor. Queremos ver Ojinaga, solamente. Es todo,*" I said.

"What did he say? What did you say?" asked Ed.

"He wants to know if we want to get laid. I told him no," I said.

"Shit. Tell him to turn around and take us back." Ed was genuinely uncomfortable.

By now we had entered a tiny barrio, or neighborhood, that consisted of two or three long adobe structures, neglected and dusty in their demeanor, like a motel that has been abandoned and subsequently resurrected for other, less savory purposes.

"I don't want to be here," said Ed.

The taxi slowed, and in the harsh light of late morning six or seven woman of varying ages appeared in the doorways of several of the cubicles. Their carelessly painted lips, disheveled hair, pale skin, strained smiles, revealing discolored and decaying teeth, their clothes askew, the general ambiance all suggested a sexual combat zone.

The taxi had stopped. The women beckoned to us. The driver sat like a sly, lewd Buddha of carnal enlightenment in the front seat. The bright morning sun seared the dusty roadway, the whores beckoned, their arms and bodies undulating in invitation like tendrils of anemones, imprinting an image in my mind that can never be erased. I glanced at Ed, whose eyes expressed disgust, compassion, torment, disbelief. The instant between arrival and departure seemed infinite.

"Let's get out of here. Tell him to drive us out of here. Now! I can't stand this." Never before nor since in our adventures and misadventures through life and death have I ever seen Ed so totally distraught.

"Ándale, señor! No me gusta aquí. Tenemos que regresar a la puente. No tenemos interés en las putas aquí." I focused all my attention on the driver and put force in what I had said to him—that we didn't like it here, we wanted to return to the bridge, and we had no interest in the whores. He watched me in the rearview mirror, looking surprised at our reaction to his little fuck nest in the desert. Then he shrugged. "Okay," was all he said.

We drove back through town in silence. When we got to the bridge, I dug eight bucks out of my wallet and passed them to the driver. No tip for this pimp!

"C'mon, Ed. Let's go." I grabbed my buddy's arm and pulled him into action. He was still stunned by what he had seen. He stumbled out of the cab and followed me to the bridge. We walked back to America and were motioned through U.S. Customs.

"Jesus, Jack. That was terrible. Don't tell Clarke." Ed wiped tears from his eyes.

We climbed into my truck and drove off toward Lajitas.

"Christ, that was awful," said Ed. "How can people be like that in this time? The people of Ojinaga have actually relegated those poor women to having to live there in that terrible place. To having to sell their poor bodies in order to live. To eat. To survive. They all looked diseased. Sick in the soul. What becomes of them? Ah, Christ. It makes me sick. We should never have gone over there."

"Maybe we should have gone over there," I said. "Maybe we need to see things like that to really understand just how fucked up life can become."

"Those women must live in a state of total despair, having to rely on fucking to survive. It's a dead end. When they lose what little beauty and youth they possess, they're thrown out. Then what? What becomes of them? Do they starve? Does anyone take them in? Do they get sick and die? It's hard to believe that anyone would select a life like that of their own accord." Ed was passionate, gesticulating, punching me on the arm. "Our whole species is diseased. We are a disease, a cancer that eats away all that is beautiful and natural. Within our species we have a hierarchy where all the scum rises to the top and the dregs sink to the bottom. We float around somewhere in the middle with little or no direction other than responding to our own experience. What kind of meaning can there be in that, for chrissake? Not much. Especially when you think about those poor women back there. What kind of meaning does life offer them? None. None whatsoever." Ed opened a beer and handed it to me. He opened another for himself. "Jesus, Jack. Is that what we came here for? To see that? Hell. Maybe so. Maybe that's why we're here. Maybe in the long run it all comes to the same thing. Old age, sickness, and death. Death for sure. What's that you always say? About existence?"

"We are born. We live. We die," said I. "Loeffler's seven words of wisdom."

"Maybe that's really all there is to existence. I always thought you were a simple bastard. Simpleminded. Maybe you're smarter than I thought." Ed was starting to come out of it.

"Well, I'm smart enough to hate like hell what we saw back there. But I'm sure too dumb to know what to do about it," I said.

"I guess there's really nothing we can do about it. Except never go back. Try to forget it. Hell, I'll never forget it. But let's try to forget it for now."

"You're a good man, Abbey," I said, deeply moved by Ed's empathy for the whores of Ojinaga. "There are a lot of women who would never have any idea just how deeply you feel about these things. Here's to you, *frijol viejo.*"

I reached over and poured my beer over his head. He jerked around, looked at me, and we both laughed as we drove along the northern side of the Rio Grande.

Ed and I headed straight for the high country after we reached Big Bend National Park. Emory Peak is the highest point, at 7,825 feet above sea level. Regarded by some as the southernmost extension of the Rocky Mountains, for us it was a refuge from the heat of the floor of the Chihuahuan Desert. We fell to hiking for a few miles to work out the cramps bounced into our muscles during the long drive from Albuquerque.

Ed carried a small spiral notebook in his shirt pocket, where he jotted his observations along the trail. Although he complained bitterly about being regarded as a naturalist, he was undeniably on intimate terms with the local biota. He had made his first visit to Big Bend some three and a half decades earlier. As we walked along, Ed's sharp eyes sought every clue. Frequently we knelt to look at tracks in the sand to see if we could determine what had passed before us. We watched the sky for birds. Ed examined rocks and escarpments. He listened to catch birdsongs. He marveled at the beauty of this environment that grew out of the floor of the desert five thousand feet below.

We hiked to the end of this particular trail and gazed out through a formation known locally as The Window. From there, we could see hundreds of square miles of desert extending out to the northwest. As we began our return hike with the afternoon sun more or less at our backs, we could look across the area known as the Great Basin and beyond to the peaks of the Chisos Mountains. It was still. There was no man-made sound except for the crunching of our boots. We later noted that we had spent several days and never once heard the sound of an airplane. That was the last time I experienced that phenomenon.

When we returned to the truck, we had hiked four or five miles. There was a nearby campground, but neither of us had any intention of spending this precious time cloistered with other campers. We had previously decided to camp at the base of a *tinaja,* a natural basin that held water, that my great friend Bill Brown had taken me to years earlier. Ed had never been there, and his curiosity was mightily piqued.

By late afternoon the venerable pickup was crawling over a wonderfully rutted series of potholes that passed for a road. There were no fresh tire tracks—they had all been turned to corduroy by the wind. Ed and I were weary from too many miles, too little sleep. We passed over a rise and came to the end of the road.

We had had the foresight to gather some dead firewood back in the mountains, which we had crammed into the back of the camper. We were alone in the desert, at home for the night. I turned off the engine. My ears rang in the silence. I turned to Ed.

"Does the ringing in my ears disturb you?" I asked.

We laughed and exited the beast and stood in the lowering sun. It was hot. We both wore shorts and little else. We were walking around barefoot, feeling the sand against the soles of our feet. There was a gentle breeze. We stood there in silence for several minutes, taking wind baths in the golden light. At peace in paradise, allowed to be lazy at last.

A few hundred yards past the end of the road was a circular depression, beyond which lay the mouth of a beautiful canyon. We decided to make our camp in this depression. We made a few trips back and forth between camp and the truck, carrying firewood, ice chest, cooking gear, camping gear, the collected accoutrements of the happy camper. This was a drill we had performed countless times in the past. We were sinking gratefully into the nepenthe exuded by this desert garden tended by the winds of time.

"How 'bout some pork chops and spuds?" offered Ed.

"Great," said I. I dug two hefty spuds out of our food stash, rinsed them off, and wrapped them in foil. It was too sandy to try to make mud. I buried them beneath the earth Ed had enclosed in a circle of stones. He built an Indian fire, small but sufficient to create a hefty bed of coals. Then we decided to explore our demesne.

We walked up canyon and soon came upon another *tinaja*. We came to yet another and another until we found a real pool big enough to swim around in. We shared it with a garter snake. Ed wanted to hike on up the canyon. I was content to splash around in the pool. I had developed a pain in my foot for no known reason, and I wanted to stay off it for the time being. Later my foot would grow numb. It's numb to this day, almost twenty years later. Every time I reflect on my numb foot, I think about Garter Snake Tank and my old buddy who climbed out of the water and commenced to do some interesting rock climbing in order to pursue his endless curiosity.

Half an hour later Ed was back, having climbed as far as he could easily go. It was dusk. He jumped into the tank, we had a water fight, then we climbed out and headed back to camp dressed only in our dripping shorts.

After a good meal, after scrubbing our utensils in sand, after making ourselves a couple of cups of cocoa laced with a taste of Wild Turkey, we ruminated on what we had seen in Ojinaga that morning.

"I'll never forget those poor women," said Ed.

"What was going on in your mind when we were actually there?" I asked.

Ed stared into the fire. A slight grimace of inner pain passed over his face.

"I guess mostly I was outraged and frustrated. Outraged that anyone, man or woman, should be reduced to such a terrible condition and frustrated that there wasn't a goddamned thing I could do about it. Then I got to thinking about Clarke and Becky and Susie and how much I love them. I couldn't stand the thought of anything happening to them. I want to be a good father and a good husband. That's a hell of a lot more important than being famous or rich. Y'know, Jack, I'll be dead one of these days. Not this year or even next year. But I won't be around too much longer. You and I both know that. I can feel it. Right here in my belly. Little by little, I'm dying. Between now and then, I want to do right by my family. When we saw those women this morning outside of Ojinaga, I thought about how they had been abandoned. By their lovers and husbands. By their families. By fortune. I don't want to abandon my family. I want them to be able to live comfortably, never be threatened. I don't want anything bad to happen to them. I guess that's been nagging at me all day."

We both stared into the fire for a while. Then Ed looked over at me.

"I know you've seen misery before. What did you think when we were there?"

"I guess what really got to me was the familiarity of it. That here was yet another chapter in the tragedy of human existence. This kind of misery takes many forms. For example, in Mexico City there's a whole subculture that ekes out an existence at the Mexico City dump. I've seen beggars hitting on beggars. I've visited state prisons in Georgia. I've hung out with the mentally deranged of St. Louis after they had been turned out of mental institutions, bereft of both shelter and medication. I've been at home on derange. Christ, you were a welfare caseworker in Hoboken. We've both seen a great deal of misery, and we'll probably see a great deal more. But I had to get the hell out of there, too. It's a problem with no real solution. As long as there are many times too many of us on this planet, human misery is bound to prevail. I guess that's the rub. Maybe pain and suffering are at the heart of the human condition. Hell, maybe the whores of Ojinaga enjoy their work."

"Maybe so," said Ed. "Maybe that's what's so disturbing. I hope I don't dream about it."

We rolled out our sleeping bags. Ed had left his cot in the truck. He stuffed cotton in his ears. I pulled out my pistol and placed it in easy reach.

Ed watched. "You didn't happen to bring one of those for me, did you? I didn't want to bring my piece on the plane."

"I did, as a matter of fact." I took out a .22-magnum pistol and handed it to Ed. I had swapped him a .357 magnum for it years earlier.

"My old piece. Thanks for remembering to bring it. It's comforting to know we can hold off the bandits." Ed grinned, put the pistol in easy reach of his left hand, and bade me good night.

Off in the distance night birds sang with coyotes.

"How long since you took the river road?" asked Ed as we gazed south from Nugent Mountain.

"Been a good twelve years or so. I had that new Land Cruiser you borrowed back in '74. Wanted to see if it really worked."

"Did it?" asked Ed.

"Did till you borrowed it. Never could figure out what the hell you did to it," I said.

"Hell, I just drove it."

"Where did you drive it, anyway?" I asked, curious.

"Just into the Maze," said Ed. "Wanted to see if it really worked."

"Did it?" I asked.

"Did till I drove it back out of the Maze. Never could figure out what the hell happened to it."

"You happened to it, for chrissake!"

"You're not pissed off about that, are you?" asked Ed, concern showing in his face.

I laughed. "No. I'm just putting you on. Actually, it worked just fine. I discovered that I was taking it where I shouldn't take anything. I was driving off the road right out across the desert. Woke up one morning lying in a patch of prickly pear ten miles from the dirt road. With a hangover. Realized I couldn't be trusted with a four-wheel drive. So I finally traded it in for this truck with two-wheel drive. Anyway, that's the last time I took the river road. How about you?"

"It's been years. Told you about that trip. Took my lady love and her new car down the river road. Made it to Castolon. Then the car died. She left. There I was with a dead car. Had been a nice car. Comfortable. Probably shouldn't have taken it down the river road, though. That was the end of the car. And the end of the line for my lady love and me. There I was with less than two bucks in my jeans. She had all the money. I had to hitchhike home."

"Ah, the vagaries of existence," I said.

"Yep. I was a vulgar vagrant, all right."

The river road. Fifty miles of wonderful dirt road. I looked at Ed. Ed looked at me. We climbed in my pickup and headed out. We had to find out. Had to. Find out what? Find out if we could make it down a road that had two warning signs. The first one said, Four-Wheel-Drive Vehicles Only. The second sign said, Road Closed to All Vehicular Traffic. We had to find out why the road was closed, of course.

It was a great road. We had to do a fair amount of road work—move boulders, shovel dirt, drink beer. Finally, after about twenty-five miles or so, we came to an arroyo where the road was such that we knew we could probably make it up the other side, but if we had to turn around and try to go back the way we came, we'd be SOL—shit out of luck. Take up rabbit hunting for a living or find our way to the river and hijack river runners. Become outlaws. Real outlaws. We'd talked about this eventuality for years. There was nothing for it but to do it, as the old cliché goes. I gunned the motor, released the clutch, shot down into the arroyo, bounced high, and landed with all four wheels on the opposite incline, and kept gunning the motor as the rear wheels slowly got enough of a bite so that we could crawl up the other side, the smell of burning rubber melding with the cloud of dust.

"Made it, goddammit!"

We stopped the truck, climbed out, and looked through our dusty wake.

"Glad we're headed south instead of north," said Ed.

"S'pose we'll make it?" I asked.

"Who knows? Hard to say," Ed replied. "You've been here since I have."

"We might make it," I said optimistically.

"Or then we might not," said Ed, just as optimistically.

We climbed back in and started onward. We passed Chicotál Mountain and stopped at Glenn Springs for a hike, both of us fascinated with the place but for different reasons. Ed rummaged through the debris that marked the encampment from which had sallied forth the first motorized brigade in the history of warfare, or so I told Ed. I had read it in the cited *The Tin Lizzie Troop*. I searched the ground for peyote, the cactus sacred to many Indians for its hallucinogenic qualities. It was said to have been found in this vicinity. I didn't find any. I have always thought that if everyone partook of that sacred cactus, everyone would know beyond doubt that the planet is a sacred, living entity and that thereafter she would not be desecrated by strip miners, dam builders, land developers, and other criminals of similar ilk. That's probably why peyote (and marijuana, for that matter) is deemed an illegal substance. Those who govern don't want the masses to get any ideas that might jeopardize the conversion of the biotic community into money. Bad for the economy.

Ed and I cruised the road a few miles farther until we rounded a bend and came to the edge of the Rio Grande. Much of the bank was obscured by a stand of tamarisk. We could see the river beyond the tamarisk, its water rich with silt and biotic detritus, its allure almost overwhelming to two hot and dusty desert rats lodged in the sunlight of a Chihuahuan midafternoon. The road climbed a grade and bore to the right. We were above the river, scheming on finding an access so we could go swimming. We dropped into an arroyo and shot up the other side and screeched to a halt in front of a wooden roadblock. We got out of the truck and walked around the roadblock to examine the possibilities. The river had seriously undercut the bank directly beneath the road.

"Whaddya think?"

"Might make it. Might not."

"Well, we can't go back."

"True enough."

"Let's do it," I said, starting to move the barricade.

"Let's go swimming first," said Ed.

"Why? We're here now. The motor's running. Let's do it."

"I wanna go swimming first. Do this later."

"What the fuck's wrong with you, Abbey? Let's do it now. We can go swimming in five minutes. Either that or the bank'll cave in and we'll be swimming in one minute."

"*No!* I want to go swimming first." Ed and I were both getting pissed off.

"Fuck you! I'm gonna do it now and go swimming later."

"Goddammit! Let's go swimming first and then do it."

I didn't bother to answer. I climbed in the truck, shifted into high gear, let out the clutch, and shot forward, hoping like hell that the bank would hold. I lurched around the bend, hugging the right side of the road for dear life.

You bastard!" Abbey yelled at me as I left him in a cloud of dust.

Then it was over. I'd made it.

Ed trotted up to the side of the truck. "You didn't even wait for me, goddammit!"

"Bullshit! I didn't want to wait around while you go fucking swimming!"

I got out of the truck and walked around in circles. We were both mad. Mad as hell. I looked over at Ed. He stood with his feet spread apart, his fists balled on his hips, glaring at me. I stopped walking in circles and glared back at him. Then I started to laugh. And laugh and laugh. The more I laughed, the more Ed glared. Finally I went to the cooler and pulled out a couple of cold beers, popped the tops, and handed one to Ed. I moved over into the shade of the hill and drank my beer.

Two hours passed without a word. I had finally pulled a book out of my *bolsa* and started to read, by now sitting in the shade of the pickup truck. Ed finally came over and sat down beside me and handed me a fresh beer.

"I apologize, Jack. Don't know why I got so angry," he said, looking me straight in the eye.

"I'm sorry, too, Ed. Sometimes I get a wild hair up my ass."

"Still *compañeros?*" he asked.

"Jesus Christ! You're like my brother. Can't we ever get mad at each other, for chrissake?"

"Hell, yes, we can get mad at each other. We just did."

"*Salud!* You old bastard!"

"*Salud!* You old fart."

We clinked our beer cans and guzzled, reassured that no matter how mad we ever got, we'd always be there for each other.

"I wanna go swimming."

"So do I."

We grabbed a couple of fresh beers, stripped except for our hats, and waded out into the river until we were neck deep. The water swirled by, washing away any vestiges of pissed-offedness, and soon we were grinning at each other.

"You know, the last time we had a fight was right here in Big Bend," I said.

"Oh, yeah. I remember that time. Just before we put in to run the Lower Canyons ten years ago."

It had been at dusk. A group of us had assembled upstream from Boquillas Canyon, intending to put in the following morning. Ed and I had gotten into a half-kidding, half-serious argument about something neither of us could re- member. Ed had jumped me, and we wrestled around until we rolled right over the edge of the embankment into the river. There had been several people standing around, witness to this minimelee between two grown men. It hadn't been a real fight at all. We were horsing around like high school boys at football practice. We floated down the river, still wrestling, trying to dunk each other, yelling at each other, calling each other names until we finally worked it out. Then we climbed out of the river, our clothes, boots, wallets soaked through. We were happy, content. Neither of us had won. Neither was supposed to.

"That was the trip you brought the amazing blond lady on. Boy, was Kath pissed at you!"

"Yeah, I guess she was," said Ed. "Why the hell was your wife pissed off at me? She's your wife, for chrissake, not mine."

"Circumstances, old bean. Circumstances."

"What circumstances?"

"Well, you were married at the time, and our wives were friends."

"Oh. Well, what the hell. Interesting what'll make a woman mad."

"At least it ended well."

"It was pure grace that we got out of that one."

"Amazing grace."

"Remember the Frogs? Gawd, she had beautiful tits."

"Yeah. I had as much fun watching you watch her as I did watching her."

"Remember when we went off telling everyone we were going bird watch- ing and we spotted those naked girls swimming in the river?"

"Yeah. You spotted that beautiful rosy-butted skinny-dipper."

"Yeah. Remember when Kernberger tore the bottom out of his raft because the Frogs had brought thirteen cases of beer and wine and they were all loaded in his raft?"

"Everybody got pretty loaded on that trip. Except for the kid, Tony Anella. He wanted to float the whole Rio Grande."

"I wonder if he ever did."

"I heard that he did."

"Jesus. Nearly two thousand miles."

"That was the trip when you bent my wooden oar. Never could figure out how the hell you did that. Talent, I guess."

"Did I ever buy you a new oar?"

"Nope. No need to. It still works. Been trying to bend it back for ten years now. Can't seem to. Charter members of the Fraternal Order of the Bent Oar. FOBO for short."

"Let's get de fobo outta here and find us de campsite."

"Ten-fobo."

That night we camped in the Sierra del Chino, high enough in elevation to provide relative coolness. We were less than a mile from Mexico, and we imagined life in this area seventy years earlier, when Mexico was engaged in a revolution that would release millions of peasants from the peonage that had dominated the land through much of the nineteenth century. We recalled the jungle novels of B. Traven, which described the horrors inflicted on the Indian peoples.

"A fine writer, B. Traven," said Ed. "One of my favorites."

"Mine too. I became aware of *The Treasure of the Sierra Madre* in the late forties when the film came out, and since then I've read all of his books but one. Too bad most of his books are out of print."

"You'll remember that you gave me a leather-bound copy of that book. Judy had given me one when she was still alive, but I lost it somewhere or someone borrowed it and didn't give it back, the swine."

"You're one of the very few I'll lend books to anymore."

"Same here. I still have your copy of *Mutual Aid,* by Kropotkin. I'm not finished with it."

"Hang on to it as long as you want. I've got several of his books."

"What else do you have?"

"Let's see. There's *The Conquest of Bread, Ethics, Memoirs of a Revolutionist,* and a little anthology called *Kropotkin's Revolutionary Pamphlets.*"

"What other anarchists do you have in your library?" asked Ed.

"Let me think. There's Bakunin, Guérin, a book about Proudhon, Paul Goodman, Emma Goldman, Edward Abbey, Gary Snyder, Hannah Arendt, and Sir Herbert Read."

"Ah. Herbert Read, the beknighted anarchist."

"Gary Snyder's a good anarchist. A communitarian anarchist. He told me he regards Earth First! as the first significant anarchist incarnation since Kropotkin. He has a real handle on anarchist theory, although he claims he's no authority on anarchist history. I sort of consider you and Gary respectively as modern-day counterparts of Bakunin and Kropotkin."

"I've always wanted to meet Gary. We've corresponded a few times. I think I must have offended him when I told him in a letter that I didn't understand how he could be so hung up on all that Zen and Hindu bullshit. I respect his work."

Gary Snyder had responded to Abbey's letter with a long letter that provides an informed cultural background for the evolution of Buddhism. Near the end of the letter Snyder wrote:

> Thinking back on what I've just written, in response to your notions about Asia, I swear it's like you had exactly the same view of Buddhism and China as my Texas Methodist aunt. Stereotypes die hard.

Snyder continued in the final paragraph:

> I loved *The Monkey Wrench Gang,* me and my boy laughed all the way through it. So in the letter I wrote [Dave] Foreman . . . I was not knocking *The Monkey Wrench Gang* as literature, or theater, or device, but as you know, questioning how we want to handle, seriously, the point of possible violence in the movement. I stand by what I said there—we need warriors not rhetoricians. And anybody who is truly intent on radical action doesn't go shooting off their mouth about it, like some of those guys do. But I love their energy

and consider myself essentially in the same boat. I hope you consider me in your boat as I consider you in my boat, and hope we can walk some ridge or canyon together somewhere, sometime. . . .

As Ed and I sat there, looking out over the canyon carved by the Rio Grande, Ed asked me what I knew about Buddhism. I said, "I don't know all that much about Buddhism. But I know that compassion is a major component of their point of view and that a lot of them can extend that compassion to include all living creatures. They also favor detachment from material possessions."

"Well, that's a start. When I was a young man, I read through Lao-Tzu's book a few times. Some regard him as the first anarchist. I like what he had to say about keeping government to a minimum. His buddy Confucius was a real bureaucrat. Made up lots of rules."

"Really added to the confusion, did he?" I said.

"Jesus, Loeffler. I don't know why I hang out with you."

"Sorry 'bout that."

"Seriously, Confucius lived too long ago and in a culture too alien for us to know how he really thought. But someone like Marx, who was alive in the last century, knew full well that the main function of government apparatus is coercion through monopoly of power. Power attracts the worst and corrupts the best. The power junkies compete for seizure of control. Government and corporate powers are the right and left hands of an oligarchy that controls not only the human population of this country but the land as well. And the water and the air. We're like a bunch of fucking Helots, peons, serfs, slaves, bonded to a system that lulls us into a stupor by feeding us processed food and hypnotizing us with television and videos. We're slaves to excess. We're hyped by Madison Avenue into believing that this mass overindulgence is morally acceptable. As a result, we're too torpid to resist. You can only resist when your belly's empty. How long has it been since your belly was empty, for chrissake? Or my belly was empty. We're too goddamned comfortable to resist effectively. We've been opiated by TV and the media. Takes too much effort to step out into the wilderness—our true home—and look around to see what's happening to it. To see how the fucking swine are gobbling it up and spitting it out as money. Is there a beer handy?"

I handed Ed a beer from the cooler and took one for myself.

"I know it looks pretty dismal," I said. "Especially when you see how the human population is caught up in this sway of excess. It's a diseased attitude, a psychological pandemic. It can't last. It's bound to crumble sooner or later."

"The sooner the better," said Ed. "If I was a praying man, I'd pray for it to fall apart this minute."

"Remember when we knelt on the bridge and prayed for an earthquake to take out the Glen Canyon Dam? It didn't work."

"Maybe we didn't pray hard enough. Maybe prayer doesn't work. Who knows what works? Revolution works, but it's hard to get people to revolt when they're too comfortable. There are just too goddamned many of us, and we have no sense of balance. We're stripping it all away to satisfy a cultural gluttony. What was it Dave Brower said? 'We're stealing from our children.' It's true. Even you and me. We're too lazy to actually get up off our asses and go to war. All we do is sit around and talk about it. At least most of the time, anyway. We should be busy throwing a monkey wrench into the endless gears of bureaucracy. Christ. We're anarchists. We're supposed to be out there dismantling bureaucracy and ensuring that it can't be recycled. Bureaucracy is death to the human spirit and brings death to this poor helpless planet, this organism that has its own life and its own reasons and to which we are incidental, maybe accidental, maybe fatally accidental."

Ed was sweating even though the air was cool with the coming of evening.

"Ya know, Jack, it's as though we've lost track of our origins. We've hidden our origins or maybe buried them, killed them and buried them so we don't have to look at them and honor them for what they are. Instead we've created the illusion of purpose, which is false. At least it's false from any biological point of view unless our purpose really is to kill off this planet. To be a cancer that eats away all that is alive and healthy."

"Do you really believe that? That we're a cancer eating away the planet?"

"Who wants to believe that? But when I sit up on Muley Point and look out over the desert that we've known and loved our entire adult lives and see how Navajo sheep have overgrazed it, or when I look at that dismal agglomeration called Page, Arizona—shithead capital of the Colorado Plateau—or that fucking Glen Canyon Dam, or Phoenix, or any number of similar disasters, I certainly see a corollary. I certainly ain't saying that all humans are like cancer cells. Some are and some ain't. The ones that are are the ones that love power

for the sake of power. Power for its own sake. Generals. Dictators. Many politicians. Who knows. Maybe most politicians. And the developers. And the
technocrats. There's something insidious there. The techno-military-industrial
complex. It's like a giant octopus or squid. And the more it grasps, the greater
it grows. The greater it grows, the more it grasps. Most politicians serve it, are
its lackeys, are mastered by it. Its mind is like a computer, apparently incapable
of fathoming anything organic. And we're its slaves, its serfs. Most of us live in
this serfdom, dominated by a system controlled by the power mongers. Now,
we're all slaves to financial necessity—money. We earn just enough money to
buy food and basic necessities. TVs, pickup trucks, motorboats, houses—and
we pay it off on the installment plan. Rarely have any money to spare. Some of
us don't have enough to live on. But a few of us have vast resources of money.
Have specialized in the acquisition and control of money. Gain money by stripping our planet—this wonderful, tiny, fragile living organism—of its resources.
Why? Because money buys power and more power. Power is the root of all evil,
for chrissake!"

"Jesus. You make it sound hopeless. Do you think it's hopeless?"

Ed looked long into the fire. "No. I don't think it's hopeless. I think on
some level or other, life will survive. Probably man will survive. But I don't
think that humanity can survive within these conditions too much longer.
Sooner or later the techno-military-industrial system and its overreaching oligarchy must fail and break down. The sooner it does, the better the chances
we'll survive. But the first order is to decentralize. That would neutralize the
current power base. Centralization of power, political power, military power,
corporate power is what sustains oligarchy. Decentralization into modest communities where individuals assume responsibility and the community is directed by consensus seems to me to be the most sensible way. Get rid of the
police state altogether. Stop hiring thugs and giving them badges. Instead arm
everybody. Give everybody a gun and teach him or her how to use it. And
assume responsibility for policing our communities ourselves. It seems to work
in Switzerland. Decentralize into communities of freeholders, free men and
women whose communities are founded on mutual aid, like Kropotkin said.
Therein lies the true spirit of anarchism. Anarchism in its highest sense is synony-
mous with democracy in its highest sense. We don't live in a true democracy—
we live within a system of standards that has shifted far away from Jefferson's

ideas. It didn't take long for that early government to be manned by politicians first, citizens second. That was a critical time in American history. America has been on the wrong track ever since."

"I can imagine the megalopolitan areas breaking down and becoming totally chaotic," I said. "Actually, I can't imagine them not breaking down. But I think it'll take a long time for a collective sense of responsibility to evolve so that autonomous communities founded on the principles of mutual cooperation can prevail. First, the human population of this country far exceeds the optimum population. To me, the optimum human population allows for a state of balance between our species and all other species within a given biotic community. There probably shouldn't be more than fifteen or twenty million humans on this whole continent. We've probably got twenty-five times that many of us as we sit here drinking beer. Pray for a pandemic, goddammit! We'll take our chances. Shit, man, we've gotta really thin ourselves out or the planet's fucked!"

"Well, Jack, could be the planet is fucked. But just imagine a given watershed. Like the Upper Rio Grande. Your watershed. Imagine small communities based on family and traditional ties. And as you say, an optimum human population is maintained. There is no centralized power in Washington, D.C., or even Santa Fe. Geopolitical boundaries no longer exist. The only meaningful boundaries are watershed boundaries. And the concept of wealth is based on the health of the watershed. Not money or excessive possessions. From each according to his means. To each according to his needs. Anarchist communism. Not bureaucratic communism. Any governing is by committee. Rotating committee. Like jury duty—it's a community service, not a profession, not a career. Old Prince Kropotkin had a pretty good definition of anarchist society. You've got it written on your wall at home. Where did it appear originally?"

"In his essay called 'Modern Science and Anarchism.' Do you know where I first saw that?"

"Nope."

"In 1972 you gave me a copy of *Anarchism*, by George Woodcock. It's a copy you got in Hoboken in 1964. Woodcock included Kropotkin's definition near the beginning of his own book. Kropotkin wrote the article about anarchism for the 1911 edition of *Britannica*. Woodcock wrote the article for the current edition."

"I wrote my master's thesis on the morality of political violence," said Ed.

"What were your conclusions?" I asked.

"When all other means fail, I believe the true patriot has the right, is obligated to defend his country against the government. When a government terrorizes its people and, by extension, terrorizes living creatures to serve its own ends, I believe violence is justified. The violence of self-defense. I would defend Clarke and Becky and Susie, and even you, you old fart, from a criminal who was threatening bodily harm. You defend your loved ones. And you can extend that protection to include creatures who live free in the wild. To include all life. All life is kindred, and all life belongs to this living organism that is the Earth. You defend the Earth from exploiters who want to turn its life and its so-called resources into money."

"How do you distinguish between terrorism and sabotage?" I asked.

"That's simple enough. To me, terrorism is the act of threatening or committing violence against living creatures. Could be planting a bomb in a plane. Could be strafing villages in Vietnam. Could be chaining piñon or juniper trees to make way for cattle grazing or strip mining. Could be setting cyanide traps to murder predators that pose a threat to ranchers. These are all forms of terrorism: terrorism against life, terrorism against the planet. Sabotage is the dismantling of the tools of terrorism. I believe that the government commits great acts of terrorism. And they justify these acts of terrorism through legislation, calling what they do legal.

"Yet eco-defense or monkey wrenching could lead to a whole new level of police action. Police are hired by an oligarchy for protection—someone to do their dirty work for them. It's called fascism. Fascism is when a government becomes fully centralized and autocratic and develops enough power to oppress the opposition. Finally it totally controls industry, finance, and commerce. You know the process is complete when they start burning books and breaking up public demonstrations that denounce their own principles. Censorship. Regimentation. Death to outlaws like you and me. You can bet that the FBI has kept track of us and our friends for years. Still and all, we have to resist the bastards. 'Resist much, obey little,' as old Uncle Walt wrote."

"Great man, old Uncle Walt."

"I've always looked forward to the time when the system itself collapses, whether from its own accord or from a nudge here and there from the likes of us. We have to go back to a more natural, more normal life. Get rid of this seemingly boundless capacity for technologizing ourselves into a corner so that technology finally serves only itself and enslaves humanity. We really are slaves, you know. Even you and me. We're slaves to a system that we can't get away from no matter how hard we try. And this system becomes ever more insidious, more self-serving, more greedy by the minute. There's no real solution. Humanity has to reduce its own population by several magnitudes until we're more in balance with the rest of the species so that maybe some of them have a chance to eat us for a change. I really believe that we took the wrong fork in the road when we invented agriculture, when we tamed some beasts. When we stopped being hunter-gatherers. That's when we invented the system that would eventually enslave us, every last one of us. And I'm not talking about just our bodies being enslaved. Our minds are enslaved as well. Television, for example, has been the greatest force of centralization so far invented. That kind of centralization leads to the most insidious form of slavery of all, the enslaving of the human mind, redirecting this wonderful product of millions of years of evolution toward the most banal, shallow, meaningless level of intellectual and spiritual ineptitude. One of most wonderful sights I've ever beheld is that wonderful scene in your friend Godfrey Reggio's film, *Koyaanisqatsi,* where a huge pile of television sets was blown up in slow motion. That inspired me to go home and shoot a hole right through the screen of the TV set. That's a great film. Maybe one of the greatest."

We ruminated on the embers for a while, both of us frustrated at having been born into a time when the cloud of human bureaucracy cast its shadow ubiquitously, relentlessly across the land.

"We have to fight back, Jack. We can't ever give up the good fight of free men. We have to fight for wilderness if for no other reason than so we and others can have a place to disappear into when they come looking for us. We have to fight to preserve islands of diversity. We have to fight to maintain what little self-esteem we have left. Christ, we can't let the bastards have it all. We have to stop 'em somehow."

"I know we have to fight," I said. "But we have to watch our step. It's really easy to get busted. Especially you, goddammit. Why the hell did you have to go and get famous? It really crimps the style of the silent revolutionary."

"I ain't that famous," he said. "Only regionally. I admit there was a time when I wanted to be a famous writer. Experience the thrill of it. But now I really get tired of scribbling all the time. What do I really want out of life? Anymore, I want to be true to my family and a few good friends who are true to me. And be free to live where I can roam an empty country without always stumbling over the spoor of some developer or step in some cow shit and slip into a strip mine."

"Well," said I, "it could be our monkey-wrenching days are over, *frijol viejo*. Remember that time back in '73 when you showed up in Santa Fe with a gunnysack full of splitting wedges? Kath and I were building our house, and you wanted to drag me over to Black Mesa and help you stick the wedges to the Black Mesa railroad and see if we could derail the coal train."

"Yeah, I remember," said Ed. "Instead you roped me into helping you build your house for two weeks. We never did get to try that experiment. We always have these excuses, for chrissake."

"Well, at least I got a place to live outta the deal."

"You owe me two weeks when I build my house," said Ed.

"I was bo'n to serve, massuh. Yassa, I was bo'n to serve."

"You know, Jack, we really can't give up the fight. Not till we're dead, anyway."

"I know that, Ed. And we ain't gonna give up the fight. Just have to figure out what fight to fight. These days it's uncool to go take out a D-10 Caterpillar and then drive away in a truck with a bumper sticker that says, Hayduke Lives!"

"You never have any bumper stickers on your truck," said Ed.

"That's right. I haven't had a bumper sticker for many years. The last one said, Save Black Mesa. Then it got to where every time I got near Black Mesa, all these funny-looking cops kept stopping me, looking at the tread on my tires. I still have a pair of boots of yours that you didn't want anymore."

"Didn't you throw them away?"

"No. I wear them every time I blow up a bridge. Then I walk around in the dust in 'em. Then I change my shoes and bury your boots in the back of my truck where no one could find them."

"Did you really do that?" Ed looked almost horrified. He was serious.

"Abbey, you're so fucking gullible, it almost kills me. No. I didn't do that. I wouldn't do that for anything. It just makes me feel good to have a pair of your boots in with my boots. Don't you understand?"

Ed looked at me and grinned. "Yeah. I understand. It's the same reason I always wear that brown corduroy jacket you gave me. It feels good. Clarke hates it. Says you have terrible taste. But I love it. It feels right."

"Wanna last beer before we hit the sack?"

"I ain't gonna turn it down."

We were still beer rich. I dug out a couple of cold ones, and soon we were sipping, sharing a reverie, mellow at last, half believing that we were two hardened anarchists, reliving our too few deeds of derring-do, scheming on some future accomplishment, forever planning to celebrate a black sabot.

For some of us first light comes far too early; for others, it doesn't come nearly early enough. I had spent an uneasy night, uncomfortable with the pain in my leg that resulted in numbing my foot. I looked over at Abbey, who sat hunkering on the edge of his cot. Neither of us had slept well.

"How's your leg and foot?"

"Lousy."

"Want to hike around Emory Peak?"

"Don't think I'd better try. Why don't you go on, and I'll stay in camp and read?"

"Okay by me. Can I borrow your walking stick?"

"Sure. Want to take this little flashlight just in case?"

"Naw. I'll be back by dark, easy. How about driving me up to the trailhead, then meeting me there before sundown?"

"Fine."

We drank our early morning coffee, and Ed filled two quart canteens that hooked into an old army surplus belt. He stuck an old pair of leather gloves into a belt pouch along with a modicum of dried food. He put his dime notebook and ballpoint pen in his shirt pocket and donned his old cowboy hat with the hatband made of beer can popped tops. He laced up his jungle boots after having examined his perpetually discolored big toenails. He brushed his teeth, then stuck his toothbrush, bristle up, under one of the windshield wipers on my truck. He looked at me and grinned.

"Let's go, monkeyfucker."

"Up yours, Abbey."

We fired up the old Chevy and headed for the trailhead to Emory Peak, several miles away.

"Great country, Loeffler, especially when you consider that Mexico is right over there. Could probably hide here indefinitely if there was a need."

"Yeah. We could probably make a halfway decent living holding up the smugglers and river runners. Put the fucking border patrol out of work, where they belong."

"Then the illegal aliens would take over. They're streaming out of that forsaken country of theirs and want to take over ours. Garrett Hardin's right. You probably don't agree."

"I agree in principle. But I don't restrict it to illegal aliens. We've all overpopulated. I think we have to defend the home ecosystem, especially from ourselves. More people moving in kills it. But when you actually see some poor bastard dying of thirst who's hiked a few hundred miles across the desert to try and escape an intolerable system, you sure as hell want to help him out."

"I agree," said Ed. "But you want to help him out by feeding him a few square meals, arming him well, and heading him back south filled with the intent of overthrowing the system he's trying to escape. Otherwise not only is he truly defeated, he puts even more of a drag on the system north of the border. California has millions of illegal aliens now. Soon there will be more people who speak Spanish than speak English. What do you think about that? Do you prefer Mexican culture to American culture?"

"If the truth were known, I'm a great believer in cultural diversity. I happen to like Mexico. Some of my best friends are Hispanos and Native Americans who have been willing to share their music and lore with me. Nobody's perfect, Ed. You're not perfect. Hell, I'm not even perfect."

"C'mon, Loeffler. You're skirting the issue. Do you want Peregrina to have to take a bilingual program in school to accommodate the presence of millions of Hispanos who have poured into this country because they've made their own country unlivable? That's horseshit."

"Consider this. When your ancestors and my ancestors came to this continent, we were displacing cultures that had been evolving along quite nicely here for millennia. We fought the Mexicans for this turf that we're driving on right now. And both the Mexicans and ourselves displaced the Jumanos Indians, who lived here before we got here. What you're doing and what Garrett Hardin is doing as well is defending the territory that the culture you were born into *currently* controls. This so-called culture is a northern European transplant. It's biased against the southern European transplant that *currently* controls the territory known as Latin America. Both transplants are biased against the so-called indigenous cultures, which undoubtedly supplanted earlier cultures, and so forth. I believe that the time is ripe to overthrow the whole goddamn European-American transplant system and begin anew."

"That's very profound, Loeffler. In the meantime, do you want Peregrina to have to learn Spanish just so she can communicate with several million illegal aliens?"

"I have nothing against Peregrina learning Spanish so she can communicate with Spanish-speaking people in their own tongue. What I can't stand is human overpopulation and what this overpopulation does to the land. Especially when the humans who have overpopulated believe they have a God-given right to be fruitful in order to dominate the land. Christ, Abbey. You've yet to convince me that you're still not some Presbyterian fundamentalist who still condones all that biblical anthropomorphism."

"Stick to the point, for chrissake. Mexico is a wasteland thanks to the Mexicans. Now they're leaving in droves for the United States so that they can turn it into a wasteland as well. When Renée and I flew down to the Barranca del Cobre, we saw what had happened to the land. Slashed and burned. Overgrazed. Clear-cut. Polluted from end to end."

"Sounds like much of the American Southwest."

"That may be true in part," said Ed. "But in Mexico it's true for the whole country. The Mexicans have ruined that land. Made it unbearable. Now they can't stand it themselves and they're coming north, ten to a family. In a generation or two what's left of the United States will be just like Mexico is today."

"What's your solution?" I asked.

"Like I said. Catch 'em, feed 'em, arm 'em, and head 'em back south to clean out their politicians, get rid of the Catholic Church, and clean up the mess they've made of their land."

"Maybe we should do that here."

"Hell, yes, we should. Then we'll be free to start over and live on the land properly. But first we have to clean out the politicians and the priests and the military-industrial complex and the developers and the extractors. We have to initiate the use of contraceptives and cut our human population by a factor of ten. If we don't, America as well as Mexico will be unlivable."

We pulled into a parking area where the trailhead for Emory Peak was identified. Ed climbed out of the car, grabbed my walking stick, and looked at the mountain. I climbed out and went over and stood beside him.

"Well, Ed. I hope you have a great day out on the trail."

"I won't have a great day if I don't want to." He grinned at me, turned, and hiked into the brush.

The sun crossed the blue dome above the Big Bend country, where Comanches and Apaches had fought each other and fought Mexicans and fought Americans. The Chihuahuan Desert endured as an ecosystem unto its own, sensing, perhaps, human presence, but not dominated by it like other less fortunate ecosystems. I thought of my friend circumambulating Emory Peak, stopping to stare off into the great distance spanned by his wonderful mind. I remembered another time, another camping trip we had taken into the Superstition Mountains, when Ed was healing from the very first attack of the malady that would one day carry him away. It was his turn to rest in camp and mine to wander a trail around a peak that Ed had urged I wander. It had been a wonderful day for me.

During the course of the day I had scouted another campsite for us and had returned well before sunset to meet him. I chewed on some jerky and limped up the trail a mile or so. The sun set, and there was no sign of Ed. Dusk settled in. I hiked back down to the truck and got out my flashlight. I waited. It got dark, and two hours passed. I was finally, truly worried. I went over to the visitor's center and scouted down a ranger and told him that I had a friend out on the mountain who was supposed to have come in hours earlier. The ranger looked thoughtful for a moment and asked me if my friend was trail worthy. I said he was as trail worthy as anyone I knew. He asked me my friend's name. I reluctantly told him. "Oh, shit," said he. "I'll get a rescue team together." I told him I'd meet him out at the trail. I went back out, straining my ears, listening for Ed. Crash. "Shit." Stumble, crash. "Goddammit!"

"Is that you, Abbey?" I hollered.

"Who the hell do you think it is, for chrissake? Do you have a flashlight handy? I can't see the trail."

"Hang on." I gimped up what little trail I could see, the beam of the flashlight dancing in front. Then I could see him. He was leaning on my walking stick, looking somewhat trail worn.

"Shit. I was worried about you."

"Why?"

"Oh, I thought you'd run into a bevy of tawny-breasted crotch squatters and had sprained your member."

"Screw you, La Trek."

We both hobbled down the trail and went into the visitor's center. I found the ranger, who was looking efficient. I told him Ed had just come in.

"Oh," said the ranger. He looked disappointed.

Ed had gone over to the book rack and was perusing titles. I went over to him. "How ya doin,' *frijol viejo?*"

"Tired and hungry."

"Let's camp."

The following morning was somewhat overcast. We brewed our coffee and looked out over the desert.

"I miss Clarke," said Ed.

"Let's split," I said.

"You sure?"

"Yeah. My foot feels weird. Time to go home."

We looked at each other and grinned. "Just a pair of pussy-whipped fellows," said Ed.

"You wanna drive?" I asked.

"Are you serious?"

"Sure. Why not?"

"You never let me drive your truck."

"My foot never felt this weird before."

"Ha. We go."

We loaded everything into the back of the truck and headed out. I fell asleep. When I woke up, we were near Fabens, not far from El Paso.

"This here's a pretty good truck," said Ed. "It goes at eighty miles an hour on the flat."

"Oh, Christ. And you wonder why I don't let you drive my truck. It's fragile, like an elderly gentleman. It's got over two hundred thousand miles on it."

"Not anymore. The speedometer cable broke a couple of hours ago."

I thought about this for a while and changed the subject.

"Do you want to catch a plane from El Paso?"

"I'd rather take the train," said Ed.

Within the hour we had found the train station and learned that a train would be headed west toward Tucson in a couple of hours. Ed bought a ticket, and we unloaded his gear onto the platform. We opened a couple of beers.

"*Salud, hermano.*"

"*Salud, hermano.*"

"Great trip."

"A swell trip."

"Thanks, *compañero.*"

"Thanks, *frijol viejo.*"

"*Adios.*"

"*Adios, muchacho.*"

I turned and walked off toward my truck, happy to be headed home, sad as hell to part with my friend.

(three)

A week after Abbey returned from Big Bend, the word came that Jack MacRae had rejected his *The Fool's Progress.* In his own words, "My heart is temporarily broken. I really thought MacRae loved my work, foolish enough to believe he'd publish anything I wrote, no matter how lengthy, bizarre, morbid, or reckless. Guess not."

Abbey didn't abandon his novel, but he was shaken. The truth is, his readers (including his editor) were accustomed to Abbey the desert rat, the environmentalist. When they encountered Abbey in the light of his Appalachian upbringing, they were disconcerted. Abbey went to his filing cabinet and pulled forth a tattered manuscript of yore, presently titled *City of Dreadful Night.* He retyped it, editing and adding, shaping and nurturing, and he sent it off to Congdon in November.

He had finished another book, his "Abbey Reader," which was released as *Slumgullion Stew* and featured excerpts from all of his novels to date and most of his books of essays. It's a superb book that was later released by Sierra Club Books as *The Best of Edward Abbey*.

He wandered north to Utah, where he was joined at Spanish Bottom by his friend Ken Sanders, who was soon to publish a hardcover edition of *The Monkey Wrench Gang*, illustrated with cartoons by R. Crumb. Abbey "discovered (maybe) a very elegant arch near Doll's House-Confluence Trail." This adventure bolstered his waning spirits and none too soon, for shortly after he returned to his home and Clarke and Becky, he suffered a major internal hemorrhage.

The Loeffler family spent the winter of 1984–85 in Tucson and were witness once again to Abbey's plight. It was grim to watch his vitality and vigor be spent by the dread varices. But there was nothing for it but to provide moral support while he rallied. This particular bout seemed to temporarily alter his metabolism, and his normal reticence gave way to a six-month period where he became uncharacteristically talkative. After he was well enough, he and I walked almost every day that we were both in town. It was a delight to listen to him tell his tale. It was almost as if his chemicals had momentarily been rearranged, and he was on a natural high.

One morning Abbey called and invited me to join Clarke and himself as they went in quest of a good, used pickup truck. We cruised the city of Tucson, want ads in hand, until we found a beautiful 1974 Ford pickup, newly painted, rarin' for adventure. Clarke drew me aside and asked me to help her convince Ed that this was it, the new Abbey-mobile. Later that day Abbey drove their new truck home. Indeed, it carried him through many adventures and kicked up thousands of miles of desert dust. When he bought it, it bore not a dent. It is to the truck's extraordinary credit that though it is deeply scarred and only faintly resembles the shiny blue truck he bought that day, even now it would bear a driver across the devil's road, if that driver were Edward Abbey.

As his body healed, his mind raced. For many years he had wandered through the "cow-burnt" public lands of the American West. He had ridden herd on cattle when he lived in New Mexico. Some of his friends were cowboys. The great hero of two of his finest novels was a cowboy—Jack Burns, who rode through two more novels and was finally revealed to be the father of his other great hero, George Washington Hayduke.

Ed loved the freedom of spirit of the mythic cowboy of the American West. But as he looked out over the land, he saw habitat laid waste by overgrazing, by fences. He saw human killers hired by the U.S. government enter the landscape to kill off the natural predators—the wolves, the mountain lions, the coyotes—so that cattle and sheep ranchers could cut their losses. He discovered that about 35,000 cattle ranchers controlled nearly four hundred million acres of public land in the eleven western states, an area roughly twice the size of France. Years earlier, as caretaker of the Aravaipa Wildlife Preserve, he was witness to the level of government subsidy that was provided to public land ranchers and determined that western cattle ranchers were one of the most highly subsidized special-interest groups in America. They paid ridiculously low grazing fees. Their grazing rights took precedence over the rights of the wildlife whose habitat was being destroyed by cattle and sheep. He discovered that only a tiny fraction of America's beef came from public land ranching and that if all of the cattle were pulled off public lands, the consumers would barely notice their absence at the meat market. True, it would put 35,000 people out of work. About like 35,000 autoworkers being laid off, or the U.S. armed forces being reduced by 35,000, or 35,000 Navajo Indians being relocated, or 35,000 coal miners being laid off, or 35,000 Hispanos having to leave Santa Fe because too many rich gringos had come to town. True, it would be tough on these cattle ranchers, many of whom were third-, fourth-, or even fifth-generation public land ranchers. In Abbey's opinion, public land "cattlemen were the worst welfare parasites in all of U.S. society."

As this growing body of information based on hard research and personal observation stirred in the cauldron of his mind, Abbey realized that he was going to have to address the evidence. He was scheduled to deliver a lecture at the University of Montana in Missoula on April Fool's Day, 1985. Although he was scheduled to speak about American literature, when he stepped up to the podium, he announced the subject of his lecture: "cowboys, ranchers, the beef industry. I used to be a welfare worker. Some of the things I say tonight may be construed as critical." He pulled out his knife and stuck it in the podium. "I want you to know I will be available for questions and answers afterwards. If you've got the questions, I've got the answers."

Abbey opened his lecture with a long story about his youthful days at the University of New Mexico, his cowboy friend "Mackey," and their adventures as poker players in a cow town of southern New Mexico. He spoke of his early days as a summer hired hand and how he had gone on to be a fire lookout, backcountry ranger, and wilderness nomad. He had come to know the backcountry at close range, so to speak.

Abbey went on to say that in his nearly four decades as a westerner, he had met dozens of cowboys and ranchers, and in the main, as individuals, they were fine men, and, as is the case in most instances, much better than the class to which they belonged. He attacked institutions, claiming that when a person becomes nothing more than a working member of a larger body, he becomes less than human. He denounced centralized government and stated that the sovereign community was his ideal.

He then launched into an attack on the cattle industry, stating that western cattlemen had been having a free ride on public lands for a long time and that the time had come to phase it out. He gave his reasons. America didn't need the tiny proportion of beef that grazed the public lands of the eleven western states. Vermont grew more beef than the entire state of Montana. Reclaimed strip mines of Appalachia grazed more cattle than all of the desert Southwest. Federal tax dollars went toward tree chaining, mesquite poisoning, sagebrush clearing, predator control, BLM salaries, and the salaries of university professors who taught range management. And cattle were responsible for the ruination of an enormous amount of public land in the West, land that by rights should be preserved for wildlife. Public lands were infested with herds of cattle.

He attacked especially the corporation ranchers, who were unwilling to relinquish their hold over public land. They were a powerful lobby who controlled politicians. Cattlemen contended that cows didn't compete with deer. But in years when grass isn't abundant, browsing cattle do compete with deer. Their presence will drive out elk, antelope, and bighorn sheep. He recommended the book *Sacred Cows at the Public Trough,* by Denzell and Nancy Ferguson, for any who wished to gain more introductory knowledge of this subject.

He likened overgrazing to strip mining, clear cutting, and damming of rivers in the intensity of its devastation. He cited figures that indicated that public lands were, in the main, deteriorating due to the presence of cattle—figures cited by the BLM, which he called the Bureau of Livestock and Mining.

Solution? Cut down on the number of cattle on public lands. Go hunting for them. Not great sport, but effective. Then restock the lands with buffalo, antelope, bighorn sheep, and elk. Moose. Javelinas. Wolves. Mountain lions. Grizzly bear. And eat less beef.

He likened the myth of the American cowboy to a fairy tale. In truth, he pointed out, the cowboy is really only a hired hand who sometimes gets on a horse to do his work. Many ranchers do not. They are simply businessmen farming public lands for private profit. They have become disproportionately powerful. Abbey lauded several ranchers whom he had known and mentioned them by name. He said that he had no quarrel with them as fellow human beings. Indeed, they were hardworking, honorable men. But they had had a free ride at the public expense, and it was time to seek another line of work. In closing, he exhorted all of the cowboys and cowgirls sitting there in the audience to get their sacred cows and dead horses out of his elk pastures.

The applause was stupendous.

It was a great act of courage for Abbey to deliver that lecture before such an audience. The lecture set up waves of reactions. He refined it and published it in his final book of essays, *One Life at a Time, Please.* It was instrumental in bringing the subject of public land ranching and its effect on the natural environment before the eye of the American public. It also drove a wedge between ranchers and environmentalists, people who should be natural allies. But he had delivered a swift, hard right hook to the nose of an industry that some wildlife biologists (not in the pay of Cattlemen's Associations) regard as causing the gravest environmental jeopardy to the American West.

In June 1985 Abbey finally received a contract from Henry Holt for his novel *The Fool's Progress.* He called me in Santa Fe and asked if I intended to hold a *cabrito,* or goat, roast that summer. I knew why he was interested. He wanted to include a *cabrito* roast in the final version of the novel. I invited him and his family to come to Santa Fe and we would have a party.

The Abbeys arrived. I had bought a goat on the hoof from my old friend Roberto Mondragón, a good folk musician and former lieutenant governor of

New Mexico. Ed and I dispatched the goat in the proper fashion, that is, by suspending it from its hind legs and slitting its throat. We gutted it, saving the good edible organs. We skinned it and let it hang outside overnight, covering it over with cheesecloth to keep the flies off. We prepared a marinade of beer, chile, honey, garlic, and oregano and soaked the carcass all the following day.

About sundown Ed, artist Sam Scott, and I built a fire in the pit we had dug out in the backyard. We lined the pit with stones and built a bonfire from the wood of fruit trees. We buried more stones in the fire, which we fed for hours. About midnight we pulled the embers out into one pile and the top layer of rocks into another pile, lined the pit with green alfalfa, and loaded the marinade-drenched, cheesecloth-enswathed *cabrito* (complete with an enormous pork roast that we had stuffed into its abdominal cavity) into our "cabritorium." We covered it over with more alfalfa, shoveled in the embers, loaded in the rest of the hot rocks, and covered the pit over with soil until not a single hot spot could be found aboveground.

We drank a beer and went to bed.

The next day a few dozen good friends came by, bringing pots of chile and beans, tortillas, salads, pies, cakes, and case after case and keg after keg of beer. There was wine and tequila. At 3 P.M. Ed, Sam, and I quaffed some beer, took shovels, and unearthed the *cabrito*. We gently brushed away the detritus that clung to the scorched cheesecloth, raised it from the pit onto a giant cutting board, and carried it to the table on the back porch, where we deposited it. We unbandaged it and looked at it, salivating. The feast began. The food was delicious. The pork haunch that had roasted within the goat was perhaps the finest eating I have ever experienced. We ate and drank. The musicians played and sang. John Nichols and Tom Pew, each ten beers down, revealed their extraordinary repertoire of sixties rock 'n' roll. Jeanie McClerie and Ken Keppeler played great folk music, including foot-stomping Cajun tunes.

Abbey became very shy and disappeared. But not until he had eaten of the *cabrito*. Clarke remained, and she and Kath made sure that order prevailed. Loeffler had become Zorbatic, as usual, and was last seen playing a wooden flute while dancing up the side of the nearby mountain.

By autumn 1985 Abbey had written about half the final text of *The Fool's Progress*.

His blood count was back within normal range, but his energy level was at half-mast. By now he was working with film director and cinematographer Carroll Ballard on a film script for *The Monkey Wrench Gang*. Paramount was paying him, modestly by Hollywood standards. Abbey wanted the film made as did Ballard, one of the more sensitive and ethical artists associated with Hollywood.

Abbey had conceived of a book of his own favorite baubles of wisdom. His journals contained a lifetime of reflections, experiences, ideas for novels and essays, and some sense of chronology. He referred to them as he wrote his books. Sometimes they contained entire outlines, sometimes only suggestions. They provided both an outlet for his chronic melancholia and an account of his published works, complete with moneys received. Abbey began to sift through them for his best one-liners, his best "stings."

His new acquaintance Ned Judge was a producer for NBC. He had arranged to meet Abbey at Arches National Monument to shoot footage for a video vignette of Abbey in red rock country. Abbey had borrowed a red convertible and donned his rust-colored corduroy jacket and broad-brimmed cowboy hat bedecked with the hatband of woven beer can tabs. Ned Judge produced the finest piece of live footage ever taken of Abbey.

The winter solstice passed, and Abbey needed a break from endless scrivening. He thought of taking up an honest trade like boot making, carpentry, or even smuggling. He had recently read *Adventures of a Red Sea Smuggler*, by Henry de Monfreid, and regarded it as a fine account of a noble calling. It was time for an adventure.

(f o u r)

Two old pickup trucks, each bearing a white camper shell, rested in decrepit dignity side by side beneath the winter sun in the Sonoran Desert. One was a 1974 Ford, the other a 1976 Chevy. The Chevy sported an array of scrapes and dents and a once buckled hood. The Ford also sported an array of scrapes and dents, but it was the grill and front bumper that were buckled, not the hood. Vehicular combat scars. These two trucks had once collided with each other—the only two vehicles in hundreds of square miles. But more often they had been of mutual assistance—jump starting, gas siphoning, pushing, pulling, towing, parts hauling—and they still had many miles of eating each other's dust left in them.

This Christmas Day they were packed for an expedition, an adventure into old Mexico to where the desert meets the sea. Each truck carried at least twenty gallons of water, thirty-five gallons of gasoline, fifteen days' worth of food, tools, camping gear, beer, ice chests, and sundries for two families of three each, including toys for little girls.

"Ed."

"Jack."

"Are you gonna take your piece?"

"Are you gonna take yours?"

"I dunno."

"I dunno, either."

"Do you suppose we should?"

"Do you suppose we shouldn't?"

"Suppose we get stopped by *banditos?*"

"Suppose we get stopped by *federales?*"

"Can you tell the difference?"

"Is there a difference?"

"Shit, I dunno."

"I dunno, either."

"How much money you got with you?"

"About three hundred bucks. How about you?"

"About the same."

"I guess we probably shouldn't."

"What if we need 'em?"

"Shit, I dunno."

"I dunno, either."

We didn't take our .357 magna on that trip into Mexico. But we wished we had. A sack of grenades would have come in mighty handy, too.

Finally we were ready. Clarke and Becky climbed into the Abbey-mobile. Kath and Peregrina climbed into the Loeffler-mobile. Ed and Jack stood in the sun and opened two cold ones.

"Salud."

"Salud."

"Do you wanna lead or follow?"

"Doesn't make me any difference. How about you?"

"I don't care one way or the other."

"I don't believe you guys," shouted Clarke. "Just get in the truck and let's go!"

"Sometimes she beats me," said Ed.

We both laughed, got in our respective trucks, and headed out.

Soon we were cruising south through the Altar Valley, past Baboquivari. South of Baboquivari is the village of Sasabe, a town that straddles the U.S.-Mexican border. We crossed in tandem and stopped at the office of the *aduana,* where we had to get our visas in order to travel legally in Mexico. No one was there. I walked around the building and looked into the barren backyard. There stood two officials, not talking, unperturbed, merely standing—facing west.

Curious.

"Buenas tardes, señores."

"Buenas tardes."

"Están abierto?"

"Sí, sí, señor."

"Bueno. Gracias."

"Por nada."

Thanks for nothing. Indeed. I had asked if the office was open, and they had said yes but not as yet budged.

Within a few minutes Ed and I were standing in the office, conferring with the officer in charge. He looked familiar somehow, and Ed and I both realized about the same time that this was the same *aduana* who had given us visas several years earlier.

He was typing the Abbey visa on an old typewriter. Ed was nervous. His Spanish was minimal, his hearing was on the wane, he hated bureaucrats and authoritarians, and in his experience, Mexican bureaucrats were the worst of the lot. There he stood, trying to communicate in a foreign language with a bureaucrat. Kath and Clarke, our wives, both of whom spoke Spanish with some fluency, were outside with the kids. The *aduana* looked up at Ed from his typing.

"¿Profesión?"

Ed quickly looked at me. My Spanish is limited but a hell of a lot better than Ed's. "He wants to know your profession," I said to Ed.

"Writer," said Ed to the *aduana*.

"Ah, un escritor. ¿Qué escribe, señor?"

Ed looked at me. "What did he say?"

"I think he wants to know what you write," I said.

"Novels and essays," said Ed to the *aduana*.

"Ah, que bueno. Un escritor." The *aduana* typed in a single word on the official-looking paper passing through his antique typewriter.

"His typewriter looks just like yours," I said to Ed quietly.

Ed turned and scowled at me and mouthed the words, "Be quiet!"

"¿Tiene usted una maquina de escribir como lo mio?" said the *aduana*.

Ed looked at me. "What did he say?"

"He's asking you if you have a typewriter like his," I said.

"Yes," said Ed to the *aduana*.

I looked at the smiling *aduana*. *"¿Dispenseme, señor, pero habla usted inglés?"* I asked.

"Sí, señor, poquito," replied the *aduana*.

"What did you say? What did he say?" asked Ed.

"I asked him if he spoke English. He said he did."

"Well, why doesn't he speak English, then?" asked Ed.

"Because we're in Mexico and Spanish is his native tongue," said I.

"Tell him I'd rather speak in English," said Ed.

"Señor, mi amigo quiere que habla en inglés, con su permiso," I said.

"Okay," said the *aduana*. "I am finished with your visa. Please sign here." Ed turned and looked at me, his expression conveying volumes. Then he bent over the proffered paper and signed his name. He stood up to his full height and sighted down his nose at the *aduana*. Ed said nothing, but I could sense that he was fuming.

The *aduana* spoke to Ed. "To be a writer. That is a very fine profession, Señor Abbey. Have you written many books?"

"Yes, I have," replied Ed.

"Are you visiting Mexico to write about it?"

"No. We're here to try and have a good time," replied Ed.

"I remember that you all came through here one other time," said the *aduana*.

"You remember that?" said I, amazed.

"Oh, yes. But you had no children with you before. It must have been several years ago," said the *aduana*.

"You have a quite a memory," I said with some admiration.

"My memory is not that good. Not many people come through here to get visas. But I remember you both. You seem like you like to have a good time, no?"

I was warming to this most unusual *aduana*. "Yes, indeed. I think that much of the purpose of being alive is to have as good a time as you can."

"Would the two of you join us for a beer?" asked the *aduana*.

"That would be very nice," I replied. The *aduana* and his companion, the vehicle inspector, took four bottles of Bohemia from a carton in the corner. They ceremoniously removed the caps and passed beer to Ed and me. We all four were standing now, and we toasted each other and drank. In all my years on the planet, and my passages through international boundaries and myriad police stations, only once have I been offered refreshment by the local constabulary. It was here in Sasabe. I was deeply moved. So was Ed.

"*Señores,* to your lasting good health," I said, raising my bottle.

"And to yours," said the *aduana*.

I glanced at Ed. There was an unusual look of happiness and pride on his face—happiness in a moment of unexpected fraternity and pride in being well regarded by this Mexican official because he was an *escritor*.

We finished our beer, thanked the *aduana* and wished him the best for the holiday season, and went with the car inspector out to our trucks. We each gave the vehicle inspector a *mordida,* or bribe, of two dollars to not inspect our vehicles—proper form at many international boundaries. The car inspector skillfully pocketed the *mordidas* without looking at them and then proceeded to place stickers on the windows of our trucks proclaiming right of passage. He gave us more papers to carry in our cars. We all shook hands, loaded up, and headed south, this time without benefit of pavement. This was sixty miles of plain dirt road wending through a forest of great, columnar *cardón* cactus that resurrected memories of revolution.

We were bound for Caborca.

"Meet me in Caborca, Lorca, meet me at the fair . . . ," Ed sang lustily, having hooked his arm through mine as we walked down a sidewalk in this city in

Sonora, situated in an agricultural zone less than a hundred miles from the northern reaches of the Sea of Cortez. I wanted to buy a bag of *bolillos,* those small loaves of Mexican bread, or *pan,* which, when freshly baked, are delicious. We rounded a corner and encountered a *panadería.* In we went, all six of us, the girls wide-eyed with wonder at the *pan dulces,* sweet cakes and cookies covered with colored frosting and sugar sprinkles. Clarke and Kath each took a large round metal platter and a pair of tongs. Then, with our *niñas* carefully monitoring, they selected an assortment of goodies destined to bring great prosperity to our respective dentists. Ed and I stuck to our goal of procuring *bolillos.* Ten minutes later we were back on the street, trying to figure out whether we had received the proper change.

I spied a store that advertised *licores y cerveza.*

"Let's get some more beer," I suggested.

"*Cerveza* in Caborca, Lorca . . ."

The local citizens were beginning to stare.

Finally, laden with far more than we needed, having filled up with *gasolina* at the Pemex station, and having inquired as to the location of the trailhead of the back road to Puerto Libertad, we abandoned Caborca, that last out-post of civilization, and nosed ever southward into the hard-core Sonoran Desert, following a single pair of ruts that wound around *cardones,* paloverdes, mesquite, and ironwood through cow pies, cow flies, and the dust of millennia.

We had finally entered paradise, and as far as we could tell, we were the only ones there.

There is a perfect rhythm to driving a nominal dirt road, a perfect speed, a perfect method that involves coordinating two hands, two feet, two eyes, two ears, and all parts in between. One is constantly steering, shifting, accelerating, braking to accommodate road conditions. But one is also watching for wildlife or unusual vegetation or nearby or distant landmarks. One listens for changes in the sound of one's truck. Changes are usually bad—always bad, actually. One is aware of new smells against the olfactory background of dust, local vegetation, water (rarely), or cattle dung. One doesn't want to register the smell of hot rubber, or hot oil, or hot anything. One remembers, too late, that one didn't check one's spare tire to make sure that it held air.

Through the dust, dead ahead, I saw brake lights. I slowed down and stopped behind Ed's truck. We converged behind his tailgate.

"What's happening?" I asked.

"I smell gas. I bottomed out pretty hard a while back," said Ed.

We both lay down on our backs and edged under the truck. There was gasoline dripping out of what looked to be a small hole in one of the two gas tanks.

"Shit," said Ed.

"Do you have any gasket cement?" I asked.

"I don't think so," said Ed.

"Maybe I do. Try to plug the leak with your finger while I go look." Ed pressed a finger against the hole, and I crawled out from beneath his truck. I opened the back of my truck and dug out an army ammo box where I carry tools and various artifacts I might someday find useful. I emptied the box on the tailgate and found no gasket cement. But there were some metal screws. And a screwdriver. I dug into the ice chest and pulled out three beers. By this time all six of us were outside the trucks. Kath and Clarke were standing near Ed's feet, which extended out from beneath his truck. Becky and Peregrina were squatting in the shade of a paloverde tree, poking at something of interest. I opened three beers and went over to Ed's truck. I gave one to Clarke and one to Ed, who still lay in the dust under his truck, holding his finger over the hole in his gas tank.

"No gasket cement. Hold on. I just remembered something." I went back to my truck and started unloading everything under the bed inside. The last item was a huge army duffel bag. I crawled in, grabbed its handle, and pulled it out. I opened it and looked inside to see my rolled-up Avon raft. There on top was a can of Barge glue used for patching leaks. Eureka! I took the Barge glue, the cork from inside one of the Bohemia beer bottle caps, and a metal screw and crawled back under Ed's truck.

"Is your finger tired?"

"Fuck you, Loeffler."

I dug out my Swiss Army knife, opened the corkscrew, and punched a hole in the bottle cap cork. I then closed the corkscrew and opened the screwdriver blade and screwed the metal screw through the hole in the cork. With some effort I finally uncapped the Barge glue can and, using my finger, slopped some glue on the cork.

"Shove over, Abbey." Ed moved out of the way. I managed to get the point of the screw in the hole in the gas tank. I started screwing it in with my pock-etknife, and it worked. Soon the screw was all the way in, firmly holding the glued cork to the hole. The gas had stopped leaking.

"Pretty good, Jack. Where'd you learn that?"

"Down in the Barranca del Cobre. By necessity. Jimmy Hopper and I were down there one time, and we kept punching holes in our gas tank. Down there we used gasket cement. But the Barge glue should hold."

We lay there in the dust, looking at the patch on the gas tank, and finished our beers. Victory was ours.

It took a while to get everything repacked under the bed in the back of my truck. It was hot. Everyone was getting tired. The kids were getting a bit grumpy. Kath and Ed exchanged a few caustic remarks. As ever. Clarke was cheerful. I was happy but concerned about everybody's well-being. Someday I hope to learn that everyone is responsible for his or her own well-being and that I really have nothing to worry about on that score.

"Where the fuck are we?" I asked.

"Around here somewhere," replied Ed, recalling an ancient joke.

"I think we should camp," said Kath.

"I think so, too. The kids are getting tired, and it's been a long day," said Clarke.

"Let's find a spot well off the road," said Ed.

"I'll follow you," I said.

"You don't have any choice," said Ed. His truck blocked the road.

Ten minutes later we had found a place a few hundred yards away from the road near a cluster of trees on a little rise where we could look off in all directions. We parked our trucks well away from each other, making sure that they were level. Shortly we had transformed a spartan idyll in the giant Zen garden of the Sonoran Desert into a chaos of water jugs, ice chests, folding chairs, Coleman stoves, flashlights, Ed's cot, bird books, binoculars, shovels, hatchets, trash bags, food bags, clothes bags, and toys. The Joads on the road at home for the night.

The first night out on any camping trip involving more than two people is nothing less than pandemoniacal. People resolutely pursue minor endeavors for no apparent purpose. Ed was usually the first to function on behalf of the common good. He would don his gloves and go off after firewood. Clarke would unfold a camping table and organize cooking gear. Kath would open some bag or can containing something instantly edible. I would open another beer and gather stones with which to build a hearth. The kids were thirsty and tired of riding in trucks and launched themselves gameward. Little by little, order would come to prevail and a heretofore foreign landscape would become a familiar territory, a place to be rightfully defended should the need arise.

Ed and I had hatchets, knives, and machetes, but our .357 magna were in Tucson. We both felt naked and defenseless in this country, which had been going through such major economic upheaval that it now took about twenty-five hundred pesos to secure the purchasing power of one buck. This very day the peso had once again been devalued, and Ed and I didn't know but what we might appear fair game to *banditos*. I, for one, had been shot at and missed in old Mexico. "I wish we had at least one pistol," said Ed.

"We do," said I.

"We do?"

"Yep. It ain't much, but it's comforting."

"Lemme see it," said Ed, demanding proof.

"C'mon over here," said I triumphantly.

We walked a few paces away from camp. From my hip pocket I withdrew a five-shot .22 derringer pistol. It held four hollow points, and the hammer rode on an empty chamber.

"I'll be goddamned," said Ed. "A throwaway piece. It would do the job in a pinch. Better than nothing."

"Probably not much better than nothing. But the surprise factor might count for something. That and the noise."

"Can you hit anything with it?" asked Ed.

"Not yet, but I've only shot it five times."

"How far from the target?"

"Maybe fifteen feet."

"Jesus. Well, it's sure better than nothing. I'm glad you have it. Especially because the kids are with us."

That night, after we had eaten and cleaned up, well after the sun had set, Ed and I lit out for a walk. It was a dark night, moonless but star ridden, and we hiked back along the road we had driven in on.

"How do you like being a father, Jack?"

"I love it. I'm not very good at it. But I love it."

"I think you do fine," said Ed. "I wish I'd done a better job of it."

"Why, you're great with Becky. You take her on walks, you read to her, you tell her stories. She loves you, Ed."

"I love her, too. I love all my kids, although I barely know my two sons. I haven't done a very good job as a father. Poor Susie's practically had to raise herself."

"Jesus, Ed. Susie still wore diapers when her mom died. That was a long time ago. She's turned into a fine young lady."

"No thanks to me."

"Bullshit, Ed. You've done the best you know how."

Ed said, "You know, Jack, I don't think Susie knows how much I love her. One time she and I were camped out in the Owens Valley. I woke up early and decided to go for an early morning walk. When I got back to the truck, Susie was gone. I found her walking along the dirt road toward the highway. She was carrying my briefcase with my papers and all our money. She was on her way to try to get help. Poor little kid. When I caught up with her, I wanted to weep. She was still pretty young. Some memories are harder than others."

"A friend of mine and I have tentatively concluded that enlightenment and amnesia are one and the same," said I.

Ed laughed. "Could be."

Ed and I trekked on in silence for a mile or two, ruminating on parenthood. Ed had recently proposed that we resurrect our now ancient notion of purchasing land in common with one or two other families and assuming responsibility for the education of our collective children. Ed was convinced that children should not be held responsible for the guilt incurred by our species for having caused such massive destruction to the natural environment and our fellow humans. He believed that if children were educated within a set of principles based on mutual aid and individual freedom within the context of a handcrafted lifestyle, the children might indeed be exonerated from "the sins of the fathers." As ever, he envisioned an anarchist commune styled loosely after the system of ethics propounded by Pyotr Kropotkin. It was inspiring to see this man, now approaching sixty, still caught in the sway of his ideals, still consumed by fires kindled in his own childhood that ever burned on behalf of justice and freedom.

I stopped in my tracks. "What was that?" I said.

"What was what?" said Ed. He hadn't heard it.

"Sounded like a scream," said I.

"Jesus," said Ed. "We're two or three miles from camp. Are you sure you heard it?"

"I think I'm sure."

Ed looked at me disgustedly. "We'd better head back. Do you have that popgun with you?"

"Yep."

We turned and started walking briskly. The moon had come up, and the desert shown in silver luminescence. We both felt that sickening knot that comes when one senses danger to one's family.

"Exactly what did you hear?" asked Ed.

"It sounded like a distant scream. But I think we're too far from camp to have heard anyone there. What do you think?"

"It's pretty far. I don't know how far a scream could carry."

"I heard a mountain lion once up near an Indian camp in Jicarilla country. I thought it was the Apache woman who was herding sheep. It was at night. I grabbed my .30-30. and headed out toward her camp. Must have been about five hundred yards away from my cabin. I got about halfway there and I heard the scream again. It was close, and it sure as hell wasn't the Apache woman. I turned and hightailed it for my cabin. The next morning I found mountain lion tracks. Maybe just now I heard a mountain lion scream."

"That's comforting," said Ed.

We made good time straining against our frustration, but even so, it was nearly an hour before we rounded a bend and were able to catch the glow of firelight held in the leaves of the trees by our camp. We slowed and crept as quietly as we could toward the fire, agonized by what we might find. And lo, we heard the mellifluous song of ladies laughing. There by the fire sat our wives, talking and drinking cocoa.

"Hi," said I, striding casually into camp. "How ya doin'?"

They were startled by our reentry.

"Fine," said Kath. "Except that was pretty scary. We didn't hear you."

Ed stood on the edge of the firelight. His eyes combed the camp.

"Are the kids asleep?" he asked.

"They've been asleep almost since you left. Did you have a good walk?" said Clarke.

"Yes," said Ed.

We eased in, staunch guardians against the shadows of imagination.

"Anything exciting happen while we were gone?" said I, still casual.

"We saw a beautiful meteor," said Clarke.

Just then we all heard the sound of a truck bumping along the ruts of the road a few hundred yards away. As it drew abreast of our camp, we heard loud, cheerful mariachi music blaring from its radio and barely perceived its shape in the backlight of its dim headlights. It had one taillight. It bounced along just ahead of its wake of dust. It dropped over the edge of the next rise and was gone.

"Glad you're back," said Kath.

"Thanks. Glad you missed us," said I.

"Oh, we didn't miss you," said Clarke, grinning. "We were finally having a good time."

"Gee! What a pal," said I. We all laughed. I looked at Ed. He looked at me and shrugged. Who knows what I heard. A night bird? A wildcat? A woman in distress? Perhaps it was La Llorona, the ghost of that beautiful weeping woman who treads nightly through the collective psyche of *la Raza. ¿Quién sabe?*

Doug Peacock had told me of a campsite he had found near the Sonoran coast on the mainland side of the Sea of Cortez where the boojum trees grow in abundance. He had also told Abbey. We had a map scrawled in the pen of Peacock, sparse in information but enough to get us there, so we were told.

It was early afternoon, and Abbey and I leaned over the buckled hood of my old pickup truck, an aeronautical map spread out before us, Peacock's weird rendering on top of that.

"Don't look like we're where we oughta be," said I.

"Just where the hell oughta we be?" said Ed.

"Come again?" said I, looking at Ed. For some reason, we both started to laugh and laugh and laugh. The empty desert spread around us endlessly, reeking of mesquite and dust, hot under the midday sun.

We had been driving for hours, following the twin ruts that had forked a few times, aimlessly, it would seem, for in over a hundred miles we had passed but a single structure, an adobe house set back in the *cardones,* a windmill and a corral nearby. There were a few horses in the corral and one wearing a saddle and bridle tied to a hitching rail in front of the house. A middle-aged vaquero stood near the horse, a gun belt buckled around his waist. I had waved as we drove by. He hadn't waved back.

That *ranchito* was a good thirty-five miles behind us. Ahead of us, miles ahead, was a low range of hills.

"I bet Puerta Libertad is just beyond that range," said Ed.

We had both switched to auxiliary gas tanks. One doesn't get great gas mileage in the lower gears. We hadn't been in high gear since Caborca. Not once. And Caborca lay in our distant past. From here, Caborca had the characteristics of a spasm of imagination, no longer clear to the mind, a mere mirage lingering in memory.

"Where the fuck are we?" said I.

"They just gotta be around here somewhere," said Ed. We started to laugh again, stomping around in the dust, doubling up.

"C'mon, guys. Don't get weird. Let's go." Clarke and Kath are two of the greatest mothers alive on the planet. Their kids were hot and tired of driving through this eternal desert. Their husbands were demonstrating that irresponsibility for which they were both distinguished. It was time to push on.

My truck was in the lead. The Abbey-mobile hung back a good half mile or more to avoid the cloud of dust aft of my truck. The range to the fore looked like the series of ranges behind us. We bumped along the corduroy, those ridges of dirt in the road wrought by the wind that rattle parts loose and wear out shock absorbers. We avoided sharp rocks, which inevitably lay in the direct course of ever balding tires. We straddled ruts deepening into arroyos, although where the water came from to facilitate this phenomenon remains a mystery. This desert was dry. And big. In proportion we six humans were minuscule. From the point of view of that place, we didn't account for much. Hell, we didn't count for nothin'. An interesting perspective when one tries to consider the nature of eternity. Which is what it seemed to take to finally arrive at the next range.

We topped out after steering through the circuitous parts, and there ahead of us, sure enough, was the distant community of Puerto Libertad.

The last few miles flew by. The road was straight and graded and we raced toward town, nuts and bolts bouncing off our trucks like figments of the imagination of R. Crumb. The town was dominated by a power plant whose fuel is hauled on barges through the Sea of Cortez. May the local deities spare that beautiful sea, which extends between the western aspect of the Mexican mainland and the nine-hundred-mile-long peninsula known as Baja California.

We reached the edge of town and pulled over to the side of the road to survey what lay ahead. The power plant with its smokestack was the center around which the community was haphazardly assembled. An enormous web of power lines supported by ugly towers spread across the desert. Clustered directly beneath the tangle of wires near the point of origin was the main body of the town. A few houses were well constructed and obviously inhabited by the well-to-do, the bosses and their families. The rest of the structures were slapped together from broken plywood and corrugated tin left over from the construction of the power plant. *Jacales* constructed of mud and wattle whose elegance lay in their blending with the natural environment of which they were crafted had been abandoned in favor of these ugly shanties.

Ed and I emerged from our trucks to take stock and confer. The look on his face reminded me of that time when he and I had, through absolutely no design of our own, passed through the whorehouse section of Ojinaga.

"Man, this scene is truly funky," said I.

"This is disgraceful," said Ed. "Let's do what we have to do and get the hell out of here."

"I don't see any gas station," I said. "There's a *tienda*. Let's ask."

We pulled our trucks into the middle of town and stopped before a relatively prosperous-looking store. All six of us went into the *tienda* and found some oranges, cookies, and cans of juice, which we took to the lady at the counter. Ed paid her with a ten-dollar bill, and after some mental calculation, she gave him thousands of pesos in change. He pocketed his change in amazement. Evidently the peso had been devalued yet again.

"*¿Hay gasolina en Puerto Libertad?*" I asked.

"*No. No hay gasolina.*"

"*¿Hay una estación cerca de Puerto Libertad?*"

"*Sí, señor. Hay un Pemex treinta y cinco kilometros al sur en el camino a*

Hermosillo," replied the woman.

"Muchas gracias, señora," I said.

"De nada," she said.

We went out into the sun, somewhat disoriented.

"What did she say?" asked Ed.

"She said there's no gasoline here. But there's a gas station about twenty miles south on the highway," replied Kath.

"I've got enough to make it. Do you, Jack?" asked Ed.

"I think so. I can always siphon a gallon or two out of your tank if I run out."

"Well, according to Peacock, we want to camp near here if we want to see the boojums. Whaddya say?"

"Let's do it. His map says Cabo de Lobos, which must be over there," I said, pointing to the southwest.

"Okay. Let's get out of this hole," said Ed.

We had crossed pavement of a sort that must be the highway to Hermosillo. According to Peacock's map, we should follow the pavement for a short distance before cutting off on yet another dirt road, which we were to follow for five miles. Ed was in the lead, and shortly we found our way through a cluster of rocky hills. We rounded a bend, and lo, there grew the boojum trees, looking like great inverted parsnips bearing tiny green leaves. The boojums are a bizarre form of flora that call to mind the weird imagination of Lewis Carroll, hence their name. So much for taxonomy.

We drove through the boojum miniforest down to the edge of the Sea of Cortez. The road ended at a small cove with a beach. Here was camp and a respite from the intensity of the desert road. We burst forth to the beach to see what mysteries would be revealed. Becky and Peregrina were beckoned to the water's edge; the rest of us stood on a rocky hillock and gazed westward over the sea.

In the middle of the beach was a large scattering of broken glass.

"The fucking Mexicans are worse than the fucking Americans," said Ed. "Look at that. What kind of people would trash a beach with their broken bottles?"

Kath looked at Ed. "I've seen you throw your share of beer bottles out the car window."

"That's different," said Ed.

"What's so different about it?" asked Kath.

"Roads are made to throw bottles on. Besides that, every beer bottle thrown out of the car window brings us that much closer to a bottle law," replied Ed.

"Bullshit!" said Kath. "I remember that time in Green River. . . ."

Kath and I had been on a camping trip in southern Utah. On our way home, we had decided to visit Ed and Renée in Moab. Renée wasn't there, but Ed was, and he was ready to party. At the time he was unemployed, having recently been fired from his caretaker's job at Aravaipa by the Defenders of Wildlife for having taken his work so seriously.

"Have you got any real beer in your camper, Loeffler?" There was a glitter in his eye.

"Not much. Only a couple of cases," said I.

"That's a start," said Ed. "Do you drink beer yet, Catalina?"

"I don't drink alcohol," said Kath.

"Good," said Ed, grinning. "I was gonna go up and meet the Quists on our land near Green River and have a cookout. Whaddya say?"

"Let's go," said I.

For some reason, we all piled into Renée's old tomato soup red VW Bug. There were just the three of us. Susie was with her grandma far to the south. We had loaded our coolers full of beer into the backseat of the VW. Kath crowded in beside the coolers, and Ed and I sat in front, Ed driving.

We drove through the late afternoon light northward until we finally reached Green River. Ed and I drank beer all the way. Every time Ed finished a beer, he tossed the empty bottle out the window of the car, spewing glass in his wake. I had grown used to this behavior over the years, but Kath couldn't stand it. She said nothing, for the time being.

That evening was full of good cheer. We shared a great meal with the Quists, a family of second-generation Colorado River runners. We were camping on land jointly owned by Ed and Ed's friend Ken Sleight.

It was a wonderful time. We ate, we sang (Kath had brought her guitar), we told lies and jokes, and we quaffed quantities of beer.

And then it was time to head back to Moab. We got to our feet, and Ed headed off in the wrong direction. A bit too much beer, perhaps?

"The car's over here, Abbey," I hollered into the night.

"I know that," replied Ed, veering out of the shadows, generally toward the VW. "You're too drunk to drive, Loeffler. Here're the keys." He tossed me the keys and somehow found his way into the passenger seat. Kath looked at me.

"Can you drive all the way to Moab?" she asked, only slightly disgusted so far.

"Yep!" said I, holding the driver's seat forward so she could crawl in back.

I got in the car, that Nazi-mobile. Hitler's pride. Who am I to be self-righteous? I've owned five of 'em. I fumbled.

"Where the hell do the keys go?" I said to no one in particular.

"Christ. Can't you do anything right? Fucking beatnik." Ed stuck his finger into the depression that signaled the ignition. I got the car started.

"At least I can drive your wife's car," said I.

"Izzer any beer left, Catalina?" asked Ed.

"Yes."

"How 'bout passing up a coupla beers," suggested Ed.

Kath complied. And so it went. I drove us back to Moab, fifteen or so beers to the wind and still going strong.

"O Tannenbaum, O Tannenbaum, O Tannenbaum, O Tannenbaum." Crash. Tinkle. Ed sang lustily of Tannenbaum, drinking beer and tossing his bottles into the night, then requesting yet another couple of beers from the lady in back.

"You're really an asshole sometimes," said Kath to Ed.

"O Tannenbaum, O Tannenbaum, O where's the fucking Christmas tree?" sang Ed in disregard of Kath.

"Quit throwing your bottles out," said Kath.

"Nope. I can throw beer bottles out whenever I want to," said Ed.

"Behind every great man is an asshole," said Kath.

That got to Ed and me and we both started to laugh uncontrollably, Renée's car weaving through the night on a course of its own.

"What kind of a people buries broken glass in the beach?" said Ed.

"The same kind of people who throw beer bottles out along the highway," said Kath.

"Why don't you two get married?" said I.

"Come on. Let's clean up the beach so we can have a good time," suggested Clarke.

"Okay," said I.

But it didn't really take all that long to clean up the tiny beach. There was no escaping the reality that the pristine had been violated by mankind in every corner of the planet, even here on this remote beach, an area that couldn't have been more than a hundred yards square. The beach was flanked on either side by rock escarpments, and behind it lay a low hill with a rocky crest. I was policing the southeastern quadrant when my nose caught the scent of something long dead. I had found the remains of a giant sea turtle, its carapace decorated with mostly rotten flesh and seaweed.

"Sorry, Jack. All this time I thought it was your breath," said Ed.

We both stooped and looked at this beautiful piece of natural design. Soon all six of us had gathered around the remains of the *tortuga*. Becky and Peregrina were both fascinated and offended by it.

"I want it," I said. *"Tortuga* shells make incredible drums. The Indians often use them that way. Turtle shell drums are in great demand among the initiated."

"The voice of the turtle," murmured Ed.

"I'm going to strap it to the top of my truck and take it home," said I.

"No, you're not," said Kath. "It stinks."

"But it's beautiful. Maybe we can clean it up some so it won't stink so bad," I whined.

"Either that turtle stays or I stay," said Kath.

"Go for the turtle," said Ed. "I'll give you a hand."

Kath gave Ed a shove.

"Come on, guys," said Clarke, the peacemaker.

We all laughed, and I dropped the subject. But to this day I rue having left that handsome artifact on a distant beach where it has probably whitened to dust in the desert sun, dissolving into its elements, blending with an environment in which it more truly belongs.

This beach had been our destination when we left Tucson. With Peacock's map we had found our way across many miles of Sonoran Desert. We had reached the boojum garden and lived in it overnight. Ed and I had hiked around it and through it, selfishly abandoning our wives to tend the kids in favor of exploration and adventure. We had found tracks of the coatimundi, a raccoonlike mammal that ranges from the southwestern United States into South America. We recalled that DePuy claimed to have spotted a Mexican wolf near the beach where we were camped. That had been many years before. Presently the dominant form of fauna seemed to be the osprey, the sea eagle whose four-fingered talons are so arranged as to be able to hold the fish it catches as it skims the top of the sea. We spotted osprey nests cradled in the *cardones.*

We rounded the end of a rock formation a mile or so from our camp. To the northwest we saw the ugly smokestack of the power plant at Puerto Libertad, several miles distant.

"Y'know, Jack. I think that woman at the store gave me change for twenty dollars instead of ten. Last night before I went to sleep, I counted my change again because it seemed like I had way too many pesos."

"What do you want to do?" I asked.

"I want to give her her money back," said Ed. "But I'm not sure that I have enough gas to go back and then turn around and try to find the gas station."

"Well, do you want to camp here for a few days, go get gas, and then go back to town and give her her money?"

"I'd like to get away from here, maybe head farther south. Try to get her money to her on the way back north. That's a dismal, fucking town, and I don't like it at all." Ed was in a morose mood and had been ever since we had arrived.

"I'm up for that," said I. "This place has a dark feeling about it."

"It'd be a great place if the goddamned Mexicans hadn't gotten here first. That's the problem, Loeffler. Neither you nor I has ever gotten anywhere first. Born a hundred years too late. At least." Ed scowled at the blight to the northwest. "Let's get the hell outta here."

We hiked back to camp, where Clarke and Kath were sitting on a rock, watching our daughters play at the water's edge. We eased over to the rock.

"Ed and I were thinking we might find a better campsite farther south. Would you be upset if we moved on to someplace more open?" I addressed both of them.

"Aw, we've been sitting in the car for days and the kids like it here," said Clarke. "But I'll go along with whatever everybody else wants. What about you, Kathy?"

"Well, I wouldn't mind camping somewhere more open if we didn't have to drive too far," said Kath. She hadn't slept well or felt comfortable here.

"That sounds fine," said Clarke. "Ed, do you remember that beach where we camped that time north of Kino Bay? Maybe we could go there. That had a great beach, and it can't be too far from here."

"We'll have to get gas before we go much farther," I said. "I'm running pretty low."

"There's supposed to be that gas station south of here on the highway," said Ed. "But in this forsaken country, they probably lost it."

"Think positive," I said.

"You think positive. I'll think negative. Sometimes I like to think negative."

"Gawd, you're a cheerful bastard," I said.

"Let's go tell the kids," said Clarke.

We broke camp, making sure that we left no trace of our presence. I looked longingly at the stinking turtle shell but said nothing. It's true that we indeed left that campsite much cleaner than we had found it. And as much as I love the Mexican people, I have to admit that they had surely trashed the country-side. On that score I had to agree with my surly *compañero*.

We drove in tandem back out to the paved road, which we assumed had to be the highway from Puerto Libertad to Hermosillo. We headed south, finally found the Pemex station, and filled up with gasoline. Invincible once again, our trusty steeds fed and ready to spew exhaust to the four quarters. Just who the hell were we to criticize anyone, anyone at all, about fucking up the environment? We did as good a job of it as any Mexican ever born.

We were bound first for Lower Desemboque, where Kath had lived with the Seri Indians fifteen years earlier. We found the dirt road that headed west from the pavement not many miles south of the Pemex station. We bounced over the endless corduroy, spotting all sorts of birds, many of which I couldn't identify. Clarke would know what we were spotting. She hails from a family committed to ornithology. But she was in the other truck. Kath tried to look up the birds we spotted in our Mexican bird book but had to give it up because she was getting carsick from bouncing along and trying to read at the same time.

Once again we were driving through a low mountain range, hoping that we were on the right road. At one point we stopped and made a picnic in the slender shade of a *cardón* cactus. A truck stopped beside our own parked trucks, its attendant cloud of dust passing over us and our food, leaving a buff, gritty patina in its wake. The driver leaned out his window.

"*¿Tienen problemas?*"

"*No, gracias, señor,*" I said. "*¿Es este el camino a Desemboque?*"

"*Sí, sí.*"

"*Muchas gracias, señor.*"

"*Por nada.*"

He drove on.

"*Muchas garcías,*" said Ed to the back of the receding truck. We laughed. The cloud had lifted, and we were back in our adventure again.

An hour later we entered the village of Lower Desemboque, the main village of the Seri Indians, who traditionally fished the Sea of Cortez for much of their sustenance. Consisting largely of *jacales,* the village was visually much more attractive than its northern neighbor, Puerto Libertad. It smelled strongly of fetid fish. The people were a handsome lot and excited by our arrival. As many as two dozen Seris swarmed around our cars, delighted somehow and curious. Their skin was dark, their hair jet black and frequently worn long. They grinned at us, and we could see that many of them suffered tooth problems. They carried wares crafted by hand with which they tried to entice us. The Seris have become well known for animal figurines carved from native ironwood, so called because of its density. They had come to rely largely on these carvings for income when the Sea of Cortez, once abundant with life, began to be fished out. Ironically, non-Seris who lived in the region perceived that their Indian neighbors had a good thing going with their ironwood carvings and decided to capitalize on it by making ironwood carvings of their own. Who was to say whether that bird, porpoise, or turtle was handmade by a Seri Indian? Carvings are carvings, and money is money. Competition for survival among the vast population of poor people in Mexico is fierce. Here in Desemboque, we were sure sources of *dinero.* And why not? We had the money; the Seris had the ironwood figurines.

Both Kath and Clarke got out of the trucks. Kath was happy to return to this village, where she had spent time as an anthropology student years before. In no time she had both recognized old acquaintances and been recognized by many of the Seris, and everyone was talking and being shy. Kath introduced Clarke and our kids. Ed and I stayed in our trucks, waiting for the melee to pass. At one point Kath pointed to me and talked to the Seris, who all looked at me and giggled. I rustled up a smile and waved, hoping I'd passed muster. Ed hunkered lower behind his steering wheel. I could monitor his countenance in my side view mirror. Finally, after much good cheer, it was time to leave. We fired up our trucks and slowly drove on beyond the accumulated Seris, who all waved and wished us well. Good people, the Seris.

The Abbey-mobile took the lead along a good dirt road that extended from Lower Desemboque to Kino Bay. Ed and Clarke had followed this road before, but from the other direction. They had explored many miles of beach that were rarely visited except by itinerant fishermen, who usually approached from the sea. We had traveled about thirty miles when Abbey turned west down a nondescript pair of tire tracks that led to a level area about twenty-five feet above the beach. Home for as long as we chose to live there, where the desert turned into a narrow, beautiful beach. West of camp and a little bit south, several miles at sea, stood Tiburón Island. Shark Island. The very heart of the domain of the Seri Indians, who were among the last of the hunter-gatherers still living on the North American continent.

Our camp looked out over a bay known in the nineteenth century as el Estrecho Infiernillo, or the Strait of Hell. From our immediate camp we could see no fewer than five inhabited osprey nests, and by day there was rarely a time when we couldn't spot osprey aloft. We dubbed our camp Osprey Bay. There we remained for the better part of two weeks, hiking, floating in the rubber raft, avoiding stingrays, eating, drinking cold beer and warm beer, and even considering thinking about working. At one point Ed drove off alone in his truck in quest of firewood and didn't get back to camp until well after dark. He had gotten stuck in the sand, true to form, far from the main road, where we had no idea where to look for him. But he brought back enough firewood to keep us in campfires for three nights. Ed was indeed a master firewood getter, the best I have known.

Clarke Cartwright Abbey started a tradition on our camping trips. She would buy a turkey frozen so solid as to shatter if dropped. She wrapped the turkey and placed it in its own cooler except for as many cans of beer as could be crammed in around it. This was the last beer to become warm, the turkey taking several days to completely thaw. At that point we would stuff the turkey with dressing Clarke had prepared in advance. Ed and I would dig a fire pit, line the pit with large rocks, and place some more in with the fire. At the appointed hour, usually just before midnight, we would use our shovels to carefully pick the rocks and red-hot coals out of the fire pit and put them aside. Then we placed the stuffed turkey, well wrapped in aluminum foil and wet burlap, atop the few rocks lining the bottom of the pit, covered the bird with hot rocks and coals, and filled in the pit with dirt. The following afternoon we would unearth the bird and feast to our hearts' content.

We had had such an afternoon. Clarke, as ever, had outdone herself. We were full and content. Too content. The fire was burning well; darkness had covered the land; the sound of the surf was lulling us into a collective reverie.

"Wanna go for a walk?" said Ed, cocking his eye my way.

"Sure," said I, trying to disguise a belch.

We roused ourselves, grabbed our walking sticks, bade our wives and kids adieu, and started walking east toward the mountains a few miles away. The moon was bright. The air was warm. There was no wind. The conditions were ideal for a nighttime stroll near the Strait of Hell.

We spoke very little for the first mile or so. We finally crossed the main north-south road and followed a trail continuing east. We were able to walk abreast and listen to the night sounds.

"Jack."

"Ed."

"Do you consider yourself a mystic?"

"Wow. I have to think about that for a minute. Do you?"

"Consider you a mystic? Yes."

"Consider yourself a mystic."

"I asked you first."

We stumbled along the trail for a bit.

"Probably no more than you do," I replied vaguely. "Is there any vestigial Presbyterianism left in you?"

"Oh, maybe a remnant or two left over from my childhood. My mother played the organ in the church back in Home. She still does. I remember when I was a boy, I would lie in bed at night and listen to her play before I went to sleep. I suppose any vestiges of fundamental Christianity come from associations like that. I'm no Christian. Any more than you are. But I was asking you if you were a mystic."

"It's ironic. When I was at college, I was one of the two professed atheists on the campus. It took me years to realize that my sense of atheism was mostly the result of semantics. I certainly didn't and don't believe in an anthropomorphic god in any biblical sense. It seems that somehow I've intuited the presence of some principle or urge that the English language, at least, isn't prepared to define. I suppose any religious feelings I have stem from the way I feel about the Earth and about consciousness. I've suspected for a long time that the planet is the living organism and that life is the way the planet perceives. We're just a step along the way. Humans, I mean. We're really not all that important when you think about it."

"Yeah. I know what you mean," said Ed. "But what about a sense of purpose? I wonder if we have any purpose in a higher sense. It seems like you spend years trying to absolve yourself from your childhood biases. If you're really interested, that is."

"What about you, Ed? Have you ever had a sense of the mystical?"

"Well, as you know, I've always tried to follow the truth no matter where it leads. And intellectually, I've tried to come to terms with reality by examining the evidence of my own five good bodily senses that I was born with, using my mind to the best of my ability. But there was a time back in Death Valley where I had what I guess was as close to a mystical experience as I've ever had. That was years ago. I was a young man. I've never had anything quite like it since. As close as I've come is after I've been out camping somewhere for at least two weeks. It takes at least that long for me to really get into it and leave all the baggage behind."

"Can you describe what happened back then?" I asked.

"Well, it's not something that's easy to remember intellectually. It was more the way I felt. As I recall, I felt like I wasn't separated from anything else. I was by myself at the time. It was as if I could almost perceive some fundamental activity taking place all around me. Everything was alive. Even the rocks. I was part of it. Not separate from it at all. I wept for joy or something akin to joy that I can't really describe. It was a long time ago. It's not something that can be remembered in the normal way. Or at least normal for me. The only time I can get close to it is out camping. I don't get to do that enough. Not nearly enough."

"Had you taken anything? Acid? Peyote?" I asked.

"No. I took LSD once, but it didn't take me. Not really. I've tried pot a few times. Hell, you've been there most of the times when I've tried to smoke pot.

I can't get it down. It almost always makes me cough. Malcolm gave me some once when we were on the river. I guess I got high. But that was nothing like I was telling you about when I was out in Death Valley. That was on the natch." Ed stopped walking, and so did I. We stood on either side of the trail about halfway between the base of the mountains and our camp. Ed resumed talking, gesticulating, his normal reserve abandoned for the moment. "In a way, that was one of the most important experiences of my life so far. I've tried to get back to it, but I don't know how. You've had experiences that are at least similar. How did you do it?"

We started walking again, toward the mountain.

"Well," said I, "I used to eat peyote a fair amount. I'd go up to Pyramid Lake, up at the north end. There was a cave up there where a bunch of us used to go beginning around 1960. We used to eat peyote together after the manner of the Native American Church. But it worked better for me when there weren't other people around except my first wife, Jean. We'd fast for a few days. Then in the morning we'd eat some peyote or drink peyote tea and throughout the day, we'd watch the Earth through peyote eyes. I can't describe it except to say that it was as though the Earth was totally alive and we were a part of it. As though our molecules were the same and that there was communication or some kind of interaction that always left me with the profound impression that any sense of purpose, human purpose at least, was to tend and nurture the Earth any way we can. Am I making any sense?"

"Yeah. That's a lot the way I remember what happened to me in Death Valley. But have you ever had anything like that happen to you when you weren't high on something?"

Ed and I had talked about this before many times. But in my memory, he had never been as intense as he was that night hiking near the Strait of Hell.

"Well," I pondered. "I used to get pretty deeply into it on the fire lookout. You never saw my old lookout. There was no tower. Just the top of a rock. After four or five months camped on top of that rock, watching birds and talking to wildcats and snakes or lying on the bare rock at night, feeling the warmth left over from the sun and staring straight up into that part of the universe, I felt pretty close to God. Although I've never believed in an anthropomorphic god. It was more like I belonged to the spirit of it all."

"Yeah. I know that feeling. But I never feel that way unless I'm camping.

And it takes a while. It's getting more important to me all the time. I don't know how much time I have left. Not much, I think. I haven't really felt right since that night I got sick at your house and you and Clarke took me to the hospital. You know that." Ed pointed to his upper abdomen. "I've wondered if they put me back together right when I had the laparotomy. But that's not the point. I guess it just gets harder to feel that spirit, as you call it, as I get older. I've gotten too involved in a world of inconsequential things to be able to be free enough to move out into the goddamn desert and just become a hermit."

"Your family's not inconsequential," I said.

"No. Of course not. I love them very much. And I feel responsible for them. I'm trying to do a better job with Becky. Poor little kid. Drawing me for a father. And I love Clarke, and I'm also very fond of her. But I feel like I'm missing some fundamental point. What the hell is the purpose of being alive, of being human? Is there any purpose? Or is it just some accident that you and I are walking here talking to each other at this moment in time? Whaddya think?"

"I think the whole thing is pretty random," I said. "I don't know if there is any conscious design to existence. I know that there have been times, a lot of times, when it felt like there was—that there was some spirit that pervades it all. When I'm in that mood or whatever you call it, there's a part of me that knows there is a spirit pervading it all. But I can only get into that mood when I've been camping out for a while. Just like you. When I'm involved in day-to-day existence and I'm not camping, I don't feel it. Meditation helps when I'm at home or on the road. But I have to admit that meditation isn't the same. It's good for me. Hell, it's great for me. But somehow I don't think that meditation is my path, at least, to the big answer."

"What's it good for, then?" asked Ed.

"Well, basically, anymore all I do is meditate on detachment. It's good for clearing my mind and making me feel good. I get into someplace where I seem, at least, to be totally empty. Like my mind has shut down."

"Brain-dead, eh?" said Ed with a wicked grin. "You can't afford to let your mind shut down too much. There isn't enough of it there to start it back up again."

"Asshole."

"Seriously, Jack. Could you teach me to meditate?"

"It ain't really all that hard. First, I get into a comfortable position, either sitting with my legs crossed and my back straight or lying flat on my back with my arms and legs extended and so that my skin isn't touching anywhere. I even try to put space between my fingers. I focus my attention above the bridge of my nose. Then I use a breathing exercise. On my exhalation I think of a word like *detachment* or *emptiness*. When I inhale, I think of *peace* or *serenity*. I do that a few times, letting my body relax, and pretty soon I get into a state of mind that's relaxed but focused. When I come out of it, I have a sense of well-being. That's about it."

"Did you ever study yoga with any teacher?" asked Ed.

"Not really. I've read a few books. One that affected me early on was Huxley's *Doors to Perception*. I'll get you a copy. In the long run, though, I think that one has to be one's own teacher when it comes to things like that. Maybe in everything. There was a time when I considered myself a student of Oriental philosophy. But that was all book learning. Did you ever study it?"

"Oh, I read a few of the basic works back when I was a student at UNM. Most of it seemed like bullshit. I enjoyed reading Lao-Tzu. They had me halfway convinced that he was the earliest anarchist. I think I even mentioned him in my master's thesis. I can't remember now. One of my professors actually studied Chinese philosophy. Wrote about it some."

"Archie Bahm?" I asked.

"Yeah. Wonder what happened to old Archie. Wonder if he's still alive."

We hiked on for a while, still headed east. The mountains were near. Ed broke the easy silence between us.

"I guess my own sense of it is that we really are part of a whole. I think of myself as an egalitarian. An absolute egalitarian. Everyone really is equal in some basic way. It's true that we're each different, one from the other. I'm smarter. You're dumber. I'm handsomer. You're uglier. But we're equal anyway under the eyes of God, whoever she is. I think that by virtue of being alive, we're all equal. And we should be able to extend that sense of equality to all living things. We should be able to sympathize or empathize with all living creatures—the birds, the beasts—because we all share the fundamental state of being alive. And we should be able to go beyond that and extend our sympathy to those mountains, to the sea, to the air, because it's all part of a whole. We're simply a part of a whole, a part of this planet, which is itself a part of the solar system, which is in turn part of the galaxy, part of the universe, and so on. We should be able to extend our sympathy to the whole of existence."

"Sure sounds like you have a pretty profound vision of the universe. That could have come from any number of treatises that originated in the Orient or India—some Hindu mystical vision," I said.

"That's what I sensed or came to understand, somehow, that time in Death Valley. Now I can intellectualize it, understand it rationally. Back then I felt it on some level that affected me very deeply. I'd like to get back to that by camping for an extended period."

"Same here," I said. "I need to be out in it more than I am. Sometimes I feel like I'm fading. Not intellectually but spiritually."

We were approaching the base of the mountains, and our trail was gradually ascending.

"You know, Ed. Sometimes I think about the second law of thermodynamics. You know, entropy. Where everything runs out, gives out, comes to the end of the road. Then I think about life. The urge to life. And I wonder if that urge isn't some attempt to balance entropy. Turn it around. I don't mean an individual life, yours or mine. But life in general. Biologically speaking, life seems to favor the complex. Evolution. Life is a form of energy that seems to be expanding or growing rather than running down. Of course, the evidence indicates that life needs inorganic material to work out in, and if entropy has its way, there won't be anything for life to cling to. Unless life or consciousness or whatever can extend beyond the need for matter as we understand it, to continue to exist. Intellectually, that doesn't hold water. But intuitively, it does. Or at least it has."

"Interesting. Could be, I suppose. What do you think about an afterdeath state?" asked Ed.

"Right this minute, I'd say that the odds favor that consciousness utterly ceases when the body dies. That's what my intellect tells me. But when I've eaten peyote, that hasn't seemed the case at all. It was perfectly obvious that some intrinsic part of myself would continue. What do you think?" I asked.

"Well, I've imagined that maybe at the moment of death, the mind experiences the glory of eternity in that very instant. In that flash between life and death. And then everything shuts off but doesn't know that it shuts off because the last conscious perception was the realization of eternity. Then the body decays and its elements meld with other forms of matter."

"As the bumper sticker says, 'Old musicians never die. They just decompose,'" I responded.

We both laughed.

"Yeah. Something like that," said Ed.

We stopped and looked back to the west. The sea was far away, miles away. The night was absolutely still. We stood there for a while, enjoying the stillness. The only lights visible were the moon, the stars, and the eerie illumination cast by the moon on the sparse desert landscape. The mountains were in shadow, not quite sinister in their darkened proximity.

"We probably better start back," I said.

"Whatsa matter? Scared?" said Ed.

"Naw. We're a long way from camp, and I'm a worrywart."

"So'm I," said Ed.

We started back toward camp.

"You know, Jack, one of the big reasons I love the desert, any desert, is because there's enough space to let my mind go free. I have little desire to leave the deserts of the Southwest, especially since I had that experience in Death Valley. I always imagine that I could be a hermit and ponder the imponderable for the rest of my life. Someday when Clarke kicks me out, I'm gonna be a hermit. Why don't you join me when Kath kicks you out?"

"Then you wouldn't be a hermit anymore," I said, laughing.

"We could do what we always talked about," said Ed. "Although instead of buying land, we could get a couple of Airstream trailers, put in woodburning stoves, and camp on public land. Once or twice a week we could visit each other and go for our hikes. When the fucking bureaucrats kicked us off, we could move on to another campsite. Neither one of us needs to live anywhere in particular to earn a living. Whaddya say?"

"I'll tell ya, Ed, the older I get, the better that idea sounds. Christ, we could live almost anywhere in the whole Southwest. Have you ever spent any time up in the Black Rock Desert?"

"Nope. We should go up there this summer. I can see it now. Just a couple of old geriatric nomads sneaking around, avoiding the law." Ed warmed to this subject. "We could take our guns and live off the land. Live off the rich. Christ, we could pull off a train robbery. We could hold up one of the narrow-gauge lines in Colorado. We wouldn't make much money, but we could have a hell of a good time. Then we could hole up somewhere out in the desert and meditate on detachment. Now, there's a life for a real man. Then I could stop this infernal scribbling all the time. I'm nothing but a scribe. A scrivener, for chrissake! I'm getting tired of all this scrivening, goddammit!"

"Ah, a scrivener riven from his writing is a sorry lot," said I.

"Great alliteration there, Loeffler."

"Yes, I'm quite brilliant."

"That's a great idea. Getting a couple of Airstreams. We've been trying to be neighbors for twenty years, for chrissake. This way we could be neighbors and the whole Southwest could be our neighborhood. Live anywhere we wanted. We could build a couple of barges and mount our Airstreams on 'em and float rivers, live on that putrid puddle, and figure out a way to blow the fucking dam!"

"What about the Indians who live in the bottom of the canyon?"

"Hell, it'd take at least a couple of hours for the water to get there. We could call 'em on the phone just after we blew the dam and they could hike out. No one would be hurt. And you and I could have a hell of a river trip. The greatest river trip of all time! Just think of it! We'd ride the crest on our Airstream barges. Maybe it would take out Hoover Dam as well. Christ, with any luck at all, we might make it all the way to the Sea of Cortez. We could park our trucks near the delta, fire up the outboards on the back of our barges, steer over to our trucks, unload our Airstreams, and haul ass for some country in the banana belt where we couldn't be extradited. Whaddya say, Loeffler? Do you think it would work?"

"Hell, why wouldn't it work? We might have to work out a couple of details here and there. Like figure out how to steer the barges down the river, for example. Be a pretty swift trip, Ed. Bet we could do it in ten hours. We might want to pick a night with a full moon so that the Park Service or BLM wouldn't notice what was happening. Of course, it would be pretty hard to stop us anyway, I suppose, once we really got going. We might want to mount lights so we could see where to steer. Especially through certain rapids, like Lava Falls. Might wanna wear life jackets just in case."

"Hell, yes. We could build little captains' cabins on top of the Airstreams and mebbe mount barbers' chairs in 'em like that one on your back porch.

Then drill holes in each wall so we could run the oars through. Put gaskets around 'em so they wouldn't leak. Put in stereo systems and listen to Beethoven's symphonies, one right after the other. Put skylights in the tops of the cabins so we could watch the sky when we weren't steering through the rapids."

"I'd rather listen to *The Art of the Fugue.*"

"Go fugue yourself," said Abbey, enthralled by this new vision.

We wandered on, stumbling along the trail, assessing the weird shapes revealed by the moonlight, the great *cardones* with their arms extended skyward like silent sentinels guarding the desert. Our minds were fully alive pondering ideas, Ed undoubtedly factoring notions into his book in progress, I finally content in my personal desperation because, for the moment at least, my friend and I walked through a plane outside the parameters of a system we both deplored. It was like a rare melody barely caught that can only be heard when the stillness is complete. I felt utterly at home there on the edge of the Strait of Hell.

"This would be a good place to live for a while," I said.

"Yeah. We could get our Airstreams here easily if we came around the other way," said Ed. Already he was lodged in the fantasy that we would never relinquish, neither of us as long as we lived. "We could strap a boat on top of one of our trucks and live off fish we caught out there in the sea. DePuy could come down with a sack of that good jerky he makes and some Earl Grey tea. That bastard's already got his Airstream. He's got the drop on us."

"I wonder how old Debris is doin'," I said.

"He's undoubtedly up in Utah somewhere, painting and contemplating existence as seen through the eyes of Debris. He is unique. Totally mad. A great friend. I would much rather look at DePuy's paintings of landscapes than any photographs. He's a true artist. Peacock saw him not too long ago."

"Another madman," said I. "Fascinated by bear shit. Seems like all my friends are weird."

"Except me, of course. I alone am sane in a world filled with madness."

"Do you really consider yourself sane?" I asked.

"Heh, heh, heh, heh." Ed turned, grinning maniacally, raising his arms and hands like a werewolf ready to lunge. He started to chase me down the trail and into camp, where the campfire had burned to embers. Everyone had gone to sleep.

We had run out of beer and ice, and we were nearly out of food and water. The time had come to head back. Ed and I had discussed the possibility of driving down to Kino Bay, over to Hermosillo, and then up through Nogales and saving ourselves nearly two hundred miles of driving over bad dirt road.

"Can't do it, Jack. I have to give that woman in Puerto Libertad her money back. I wouldn't feel right about gypping her out of twenty-five thousand pesos. I know it's only ten bucks, American. But I gotta do it."

We loaded our gear, fired up our trucks, and headed north, sorry to abandon our camp at the Straits of Hell. I didn't want to leave; I never do. I had just begun to really get into the spirit of place where I long to live and only get to visit occasionally. I know Ed felt the same way. We had talked about it.

The road was just as rut ridden as it had been on the way down. We passed by the village of Desemboque but didn't stop. We found our way to the highway and topped off our gas tanks at the sole Pemex station, and by midafternoon we pulled into Puerto Libertad.

We found the store, but the proprietress wasn't there. Instead there was a younger woman, attractive and clear of eye. Kath, whose Spanish is many times better than mine, addressed the situation squarely. She told the young woman that we had passed through ten or twelve days earlier and that some other lady had been tending *la tienda,* and that the tall hombre had subsequently come to discover that *la otra señora* had given him too much *cambio* and that he would like to give her her *dinero* back. The young woman's eyes grew wide as Ed counted out the stack of pesos.

"Muchas gracias, señor," she said, in a cross between awe and disbelief. She said that she would give this money to her aunt when she came back *mañana* and that she truly appreciated Ed's great honesty. Kath translated for Ed, who smiled nobly, gave the hint of a bow, and walked out of the store.

"Don't let it go to your head, Abbey," said I.

"Who, me?" said Ed. Clarke, Becky, Kath, and Peregrina came out minutes later, carrying a package with fruit and juice. The *panadería* was nearby, and they all went in to get some *bolillos y pan dulces.* Kath later told me that she had talked with the baker, who had told her that he started baking late at night and then loaded up his three-wheeled bicycle well before dawn and began his daily round of deliveries. He worked between twelve and eighteen hours every day, which he had done since he had first opened his bakery nearly ten years earlier.

He was a happy man. Once again we loaded up and began the long haul through the seemingly endless desert that extended northward to Caborca. We found our old campsite, made a modest meal, and sipped from a bottle of wine Clarke had saved for the occasion of our last night out.

The next morning a grim-faced Ed woke me before first light to say that Clarke had gotten extremely sick to her stomach in the night and that Becky was in screaming agony with serious pain in her neck. We loaded up as quickly as we could and started driving at daylight. By midmorning we reached Caborca and stopped only for gasoline. Clarke's stomach had improved slightly, but Becky's neck was possibly getting worse. Our goal was to get to Tucson as soon as we could and get Becky to a doctor.

The Abbey-mobile was in the lead. Ed was following a gray truck. Somehow we had missed the turnoff to Sasabe and were bound, unbeknownst to us, for the village of Saríc. We drove for miles, three trucks in tandem. Finally the road forked. The gray truck in the lead bore left and stopped. Three men jumped out and aimed guns at Ed's truck. Ed drove on by, and then the men aimed their guns at us.

"Don't stop!" shouted Kath. She had experienced life-threatening encounters with *aduanas* and *federales* during previous travels in Mexico.

I didn't. Instead I leaned my head out the window and grinned and waved. The three *banditos'* faces dropped in surprise. Why wasn't the *gringo chingado* stopping like he was supposed to, *ese?* We drove like hell and, as luck would have it, rounded a bend within a couple of miles and entered the village of Saríc.

We parked in the center of town in the relative safety of numbers of people. Kath stopped a pedestrian and asked if the road we were on would take us to the border. No, it wouldn't. We would have to turn about and backtrack a few kilometers and turn right on a road that would take us to Sasabe. Right where the *banditos* had tried to stop us! I looked around and spotted a municipal building, which was said to house the police station. I told Kath to sit tight and keep Peregrina with her. I walked by Ed's truck, wherein the three Abbeys sat, looking distraught.

"I'll be right back," I said.

I walked over to the police station and entered. The building seemed empty, but I walked down the hall and tried to rouse the local constabulary. Nobody home. Out to lunch. Son of a bitch.

I went back outside and looked around. Kath was talking to a Mexican man of middle age and honest countenance. I started back over to where we had parked. I heard a motor and turned to see the gray truck pulling into town. It parked in front of the police station. The three *banditos* climbed out of the cab of the truck and went inside, completely ignoring us and our trucks. What the hell?

I went directly over to where Kath was talking to the Mexican. She was pointing to the gray truck. The Mexican looked across at the truck and started talking to Kath. This conversation went by too fast for me to digest. Finally the Mexican turned and went into a nearby house.

"What did he say?" I asked Kath, my stomach in a knot, wishing for my .357 magnum and a sack of grenades.

"He said that these police are also bandits and that they're crazy. They try to hold up all gringos and steal their money. They won't do it in town. Too obvious." Kath seemed in control. "He said that he and his family are about to leave for Sasabe and that they can't all fit in their car. If his two daughters can ride with us, we can all go together to Sasabe and the police or bandits or whoever they are will leave us alone."

"Outta sight!" said I.

I went over and told the Abbeys of our plan. They looked relieved, but not very.

Within a few minutes the Mexican had returned with his two teenage daughters. Kath and Peregrina climbed in the camper through the window that extends between the cab and the camper and the two teenagers climbed in beside me. The Mexican had opened his car, and the rest of his family, including an old woman whom I supposed to be his mother, climbed in. He started his car as did we, and we all turned around and headed back out of town. I looked in my side view mirror and saw one of the *banditos/federales* come out of the police station and watch us drive away. He didn't follow.

The farther we drove from Saríc, the less anxious we became. After about an hour we felt downright relaxed. The girls in the seat beside me said we were only a few kilometers from Sasabe.

Just about the time I thought we might even make it back across the border, about fifteen uniformed men emerged from the *cardón* forest, all of them aiming guns at us. Some of them looked no more than fourteen years old.

The Mexican whose daughters rode beside me got out of his truck and began to talk to the soldiers. Some of the soldiers looked in and aimed their pieces at us in the friendliest-possible fashion. I got out of my truck and sought out the most officious-looking bastard in the lot.

"*¿Qué pasa?*"

"*¿Tienen carbinas o pistoles en su troque?*"

"*No, no tengo armas.*"

He walked around my camper, looking in at Kath and Peregrina. Then he walked over to Ed's truck. I went with him.

"What do they want?" asked Ed. By this time his face was as morose and grim as I had ever seen it. Clarke was pale. Becky had been crying because her neck hurt.

"They want to know if we have any guns," I said.

"I wish we did," said Ed.

"Shut up, Ed," said Clarke.

The soldier told Ed he wanted to look in the back of this truck. Ed got out and opened his camper. The soldier looked in, rearranged the camping gear, and was soon satisfied that we weren't smuggling guns. I have never understood why they thought we might be smuggling guns out of Mexico.

The soldier indicated that we could proceed. I looked at the army encampment. There were clotheslines strung between the *cardones,* underwear hanging turgidly, fatigues dangling forlornly. Military domesticity.

"Let's get the hell outta here," grumbled Ed.

We drove into Sasabe a few minutes later and bade our Mexican friends grateful farewell. We turned in our Mexican papers to a different *aduana* and crossed the border into Arizona. The American customs officer waved us through, and soon we were headed north on real pavement.

Ed floored his accelerator and sped away. Kath and I drove at a more leisurely speed, wildly relieved that we had made it through too many armed bandits/cops, whoever they were. Relieved as I was, I was also totally pissed off, ready to go to war.

Later that day, much later, we pulled up into the shadow of the Abbeys' home. They all sat on the front porch. It turned out that Becky had a pulled muscle in her neck and was now feeling much better. Clarke had recovered from her malaise. Ed and I walked out of hearing range of our families.

"Whaddya think, Ed?"

"I think we should get some friends and go down and clean up that rat's nest in Saríc. I would gladly kill any one of those bastards. They aimed their guns at our kids."

"I'll go if you will."

"I'll go if you will."

We never did.

(five)

Abbey, with the specter of mortality riding on his shoulder and his endless obligations to publishers, the university, lecture halls, and even family and friends, began to fantasize about spending part of his life in a hand-hewn hermitage where he could concentrate on peace and order. He was getting grumpy. Part of this was caused by the shift in his bodily chemistry as a result of his illness. Part of it was his personality. He was never satisfied with his own existence.

> *My heart longs for the open country, a cabin on the rim, woodsmoke,*
> *horses, saddle leather, inner and outer exploration. I am tired of writing.*
> *Childish work for a grown man. . . .*

Abbey headed east with his friend Dick Kirkpatrick in April 1986 on a trip to Pennsylvania. He recorded his impressions and visited with his family, gathering a fair amount of material for his novel. The trip lasted two weeks. Then he returned to Tucson, not to work on his novel but to continue to write a screenplay for *The Monkey Wrench Gang*.

In June the Abbeys moved to Moab for the summer, living in a cabin owned by the Sleights. Clarke went to work at Pack Creek Ranch as a waitress in the restaurant, a job she loved. Abbey focused on his writing.

The June 15 issue of *Time* magazine featured some quotes from *Desert Solitaire*. He wrote them the following letter.

> Dear Editors:
>
> Please include me out of your "American Best" celebration. The national parks which you imagine as havens of wilderness have been largely taken over by the profit-minded developers of industrial tourism. Those venture capitalists you praise are the types who would sacrifice all human and natural values to the god of commercial avarice (a mortal sin). The technonologists you cite as the envy of even the (robotic) Japanese are the servants in the main of big business, government and war—not of human well-being. The end result of this orgiastic self-aggrandizement has been the reduction of the majority of Americans to the status of indentured employees— helpless dependents on government and industry. They may be the best cared-for and lavishly entertained serfs in history but they are serfs all the same. That pop culture of TV, rock "music," home video, mechanical recreation and plastic architecture—from Sinatra to Springsteen, from Disney to . . . ?—is the culture of helots. Whatever became of Jefferson's vision of a society of self-reliant, independent freeholders? of Lincoln's dream of a true democracy— government *by* the people? Lost, crushed, buried beneath an avalanche of greed and garbage.
>
> Yrs.
>
> Edward Abbey, Moab

The high country of southeastern Utah agreed with Abbey. The storms, the chill of the night wind, the silence focused his stare outward. He was happy again. He was with his family.

I look upon my Becky sleeping and feel such a rush of unlimited love, boundless tenderness and will to protect and nurture and cherish . . . that it nigh transfigures me. We are at our best when we live for others. No doubt about it. It's that quality of caring so much for others that makes my Clarke such a fine distinguished woman. Like my mother. Like her mother. Most women really are better than most men. No doubt about that, either.

Abbey immersed himself in the novel. He and Clarke hiked the high country around Pack Creek Ranch. In mid-July, Clarke became pregnant for the second time. Abbey was fifty-nine-and-a-half years old. Myriad emotions rippled through his system—concern that his time left was short and that if he died, his family would be left without income; pride that he had sired another child; love for this family that was his joy.

Undaunted, he continued to write. On September 12, 1986, Abbey sent the 901-page manuscript titled *The Fool's Progress* to Jack Macrae at Henry Holt. He had also nearly finished the screenplay of *The Monkey Wrench Gang*. His goal in life was to never have to write another word. He still had a long way to go.

Early winter threatened, and the Abbeys packed up and drove south to Tucson. Jack Macrae wanted Abbey to pare it down by almost half. Which half? What words should go? Every other word? The last four hundred pages? The first four hundred?

To make matters worse, Abbey's intended home site at Vermillion Cliffs in northern Arizona had been desecrated in his own mind by the sudden presence of a house that had been built within line of sight. And even worse, Abbey felt badly because he had not been included in a special edition of *Anteus* magazine devoted to nature writers. As ever, Abbey took solace in Beethoven.

In October, Abbey delivered the keynote lecture at the Western Literature Association conference in Durango.

He dressed for the occasion in a Harris tweed sport jacket, a tie, woolen trousers, and polished boots and delivered a superb lecture that he called "A Writer's Credo." It was later included in his final book of essays, *One Life at a Time, Please*. He had ruminated much on this subject. His audience was spellbound as Ed mentioned the names of those writers he liked and respected and those he didn't. Abbey pulled no punches. He addressed the moral obligation a writer has "to criticize his own society, his own nation, his own civilization." He closed this lecture by saying, "I write to make a difference. . . . I write to give pleasure and promote aesthetic bliss. To honor life and to praise the divine beauty of the natural world. I write for the joy and exultation of writing itself. To tell my story."

In late November 1986 Abbey was invited to be the writer in residence for two weeks at *The San Francisco Examiner,* where he would write feature stories. It was an opportunity for him to visit one of the few cities in America that he enjoyed. Clarke and Becky accompanied him on this journey. His brief tenure was marred only by his catching a heavy dose of poison oak in Big Sur.

He agreed to teach for the winter semester at the University of Arizona. He was facing the rewrite of *The Fools Progress,* and the script for *The Monkey Wrench Gang* was inching toward oblivion. The only immediate solace was to go camping before despair set in. The Abbeys and the Loefflers decided to camp north of the boundary with Mexico this winter and follow the devil's road across the Cabeza Prieta Wildlife Refuge and Gunnery and Bombing Range.

The first day out, as we wandered through Ajo, Arizona, Ed suggested that our families move here, begin a new life as desert bohemians so that we could go into the wilderness at any moment for any length of time. He lauded the beauty of the town plaza and suggested that we could open a public library and a movie house. Neither Kath nor Clarke was eager to move to Ajo. Later, camped somewhere along the Darby Wells road, Ed talked about the dreariness of always having to write, to be accountable. He suggested that he and I go into business together, any business as long as it involved handmade products.

Ed longed to live a more physical, outdoorsman existence. He recognized the same longing in me. There we were, looking into a Sonoran sunset on the one hand, devoted to our respective families; on the other, a pair of atavists standing on the edge of one of the few remaining patches of wilderness left in the contiguous United States. Spiritually bifurcated. At that moment Ed and I were extreme examples of the plight of modern man in America, with the difference that we had both actually spent much of our lives camped under the stars, or at least in the backs of our trucks. We all had fun on that trip. All six and a half of us. Clarke wasn't quite ready to burst with the newest Abbey. But it wouldn't be long.

DEDICATION:

To Benjamin Cartwright Abbey, born 5:00 A.M. by Caesarean section, March 19, 1987, in the dying city of Tucson, Arizona—

*Ben, my boy, you are going to live to enjoy an America at least one half
as uncrowded, open, wild, free, spacious, green, primitive, untamed,
unregulated, unmanaged, unstandardized as the America I have known,
or—*
*Or else! Or else there's going to be trouble. Hell to pay. We'll go down
fighting, balls to the wall.*
This is a threat.

Ben Abbey was born with a mind like a whip—sharp and mobile—even
restless. Thus the Abbey family now numbered five: Ed, Clarke, Susie, Becky,
and Ben. Soon Susie would go off to college. It would be years before the two
youngest would even start school. Ed had just turned sixty, and he was ailing.
He made the strongest resolve of his lifetime—to provide for his family in
advance of his death.

Abbey had queried Macrae about the possibility of a new book of essays.
Beyond the Wall was selling steadily, although it remained hidden from most
eyes east of the hundredth meridian. He wrote to his agent, suggesting that he
write a sequel to *The Monkey Wrench Gang,* which by then had sold about half
a million copies.

He had abandoned the notion of becoming a boot maker.

He finished his final revision of *The Fool's Progress* in early April and took
his three-and-a-half-year-old daughter Becky on a camping trip.

*We camped the first night in Molino Basin beside a trickling stream.
Becky caught a frog and floated it on the pond on a tiny plastic boat.
Later we rode a chairlift to the top of the mountain, played and picnicked
in the snow. We camped the second night at 5,500 feet on a mesquite and
scrub oak ridge down the backside on the mountain along the old dirt
road to Oracle. God, I love that kid. She is so beautiful and can be so
sweet and loving. Every night she cuddled in my arms as I told her stories
of Bill the Bug, Kokomo Joe the Giant Lizard, Joe the Jackrabbit, Eeyore
the Donkey, Felix the Kat, and a dozen others, improvised and invented.
She does love stories. No matter how dumb or dull my made-up tale, she
seems to find it fascinating, always pleads for more. Rebecca, my sweetheart my darling my treasure I love you I love you.*

Abbey was busy compiling his book of essays *One Life at a Time, Please.* Even though he rarely mentioned it, he knew that he was drawing near the end of his life. Nearly thirty years before, he had noted that a preacher had approached Henry David Thoreau as he lay dying and asked him what he expected of the hereafter. Thoreau replied, "One world at a time, please."

In May 1987 Carroll Ballard called to inform Abbey that Paramount Studios had dropped *The Monkey Wrench Gang.* Ballard was still optimistic, but Abbey was mad and called them "chickenshit cowards" and "swine."

Abbey had submitted many queries to different publishers for possible books. He had wanted to make another trip to Australia, perhaps write a book about the beef industry and a book about Mexico. He had managed to regain the hardcover rights to *Desert Solitaire* from a reluctant publisher in Utah, and the University of Arizona published a tastefully prepared edition of this classic with a newly written introduction.

He concentrated his efforts on acquiring a contract to write the sequel to *The Monkey Wrench Gang,* which he had already titled *Hayduke Lives!* Abbey noted that in *The Monkey Wrench Gang,* he had truly found his own voice.

That voice must never, ever be stilled.

In mid-June, Abbey had another bleed.

> *Black ragged clots of shit in the cathole. Black as sin, black as the Congo, black as the heart of darkness. I'm dying again, Gotterdammt. And still haven't quite finished my novel. Or helped Clarke raise our two sweet and wonderful children. Feel weak, tired, trembly. Heart beating rapidly. No doubt about it—the same damn thing I got slugged with two? three? years ago.*

He survived. But the odds were getting worse. Each episode of bleeding took its toll.

The Abbeys moved to Moab for the summer, renting a house on a shady street at the north end of town. It was a good place for Ed to recover and a cool place for Clarke to nurse Ben through his first summer.

In August, Abbey signed a lucrative contract to write *Hayduke Lives!* He would receive the first half of the advance in January and the second half on completion of the novel. This gave him hope for the future of his family and a worthwhile project on which to concentrate over the next year. Nonetheless, he was worn down, and he decided not to even think about the book until they moved back to Tucson in the autumn.

In early autumn 1987 the *Utne Reader* published a letter from Murray Bookchin, a leftist writer living in Vermont who espoused anarchism and the relevance of environmental thinking. The letter accused Edward Abbey, Garrett Hardin, and members of Earth First! of racism and "eco-terrorism." Abbey was appalled by both epithets.

He responded with his own letter to the *Utne Reader* demanding a public apology from Bookchin, whom he held in low regard from that moment onward. The matter was never properly resolved. In truth, Abbey was neither a racist nor an "eco-terrorist." Nor are Hardin and Foreman. All three opposed illegal immigration into the United States, contending that our culture is trying to control human population growth. As to the second epithet, Abbey had long defined his brand of eco-warfare as an attempt to thwart terrorism perpetrated against the natural environment and living organisms by government and industry. Terrorism as he saw it is the threat to commit or the actual committing of violence against humans, other living creatures, and natural habitat. Eco-defense is resistance to terrorism. Abbey wanted this distinction to be made.

He also strongly advocated free speech:

> *I insist on my right to say what I please, no matter whom it may offend. To say what I please even when I may myself be doubtful of its truth. And to say what I please when I am certain of its truth, as for instance crying "Fire" in a crowded theater when the theater is in fact on fire. I resent the current effort to place certain subjects, e.g., racial differences, beyond the pale of permissible discourse, and the constant attempt to intimidate the outspoken and to suppress free speech by hysterical screams of "racism! sexism! fascism! communism! homophobia! anti-Semitism! terrorism! anarchism!"*
>
> *In our taboo-ridden, cult-obsessed, hypersensitive, creed-crazed culture, anyone who attempts to examine tough social questions in a logical, analytic, empiric manner must learn to expect a blizzard of rhetorical abuse from all sides.*

*Anyone with any experience of the other animals takes for granted
the hereditary nature of basic attributes. Only we humans like to pretend
that we are superior to the laws of biology and evolution.*
*Vanity, vanity, thy name is humanism—whether Christian, Marxist or
"secular."*

In October 1987 Abbey, DePuy and I—three old comrades-in-arms—went
camping for several days at Muley Point. We looked out over that awesome
landscape to the south of the Goosenecks that we had all come to know inti-
mately over the decades. Off in the distance were the La Platas, Mesa Verde,
Sleeping Ute Mountain, the Carrizos, the Chuskas, Cañon de Chelley, Black
Mesa, Monument Valley, Agathlán, Navajo Mountain. But the air had grown
dim over the decades, polluted by the pall from the giant smokestacks of the
Navajo, San Juan, and Four Corners generating stations. Power lines marched
across the face of the land. Abbey had first arrived in 1947. DePuy had arrived
in the early 1950s. I didn't arrive until 1957. Still and all, we had each seen it
clean and clear. We had each seen Glen Canyon. We had each fought on behalf
of this land that we loved. This was our home. There was nowhere else that was
home, nowhere else to go.

There was something special about that camping trip. We each knew that
this would be the last time we would all camp in the wilderness together. We
promised that we three would meet there during the first week of October
from thereon, but the truth was carried in the wind.

We stood there on the point. Three old men. Three *compañeros.*

The following month Ed's brother Johnny died in Los Angeles of cancer. This
brought home to Abbey the sense of his own mortality. That January of 1988 he
camped solo out near Granite Tank in the southern Sonoran.

*I want to live. Clarke, Susie, Becky, and Benjamin need me for at least
ten more years. So I must hang on and in there for another decade.*
But how? Black stool again.
*Three days gone and I miss them painfully already, my sweet little
family. That's how they get you. The tender trap. My ball and chain,
which I'm so accustomed to I could not would not live without it. And
why should I? It's natural, animal, human, humane—basic bio-logic—to*

*desire wife and kinder. Only madmen, murderers, and queers attempt to
live without a woman and children.*

When he returned to Tucson, the first half of his advance toward the writing of
Hayduke Lives! had arrived. He was doubly elated because *One Life at a Time,
Please* had just been released.

Thereafter there was nothing for it but to write. For a few months he rented
a room at the Amerind Foundation near Dragoon, about ninety miles east of
Tucson, so that he could totally focus on his book. Every week he would go
into town to visit his family and then return to his rented room to write, intent
on finishing a step ahead of death, thus guaranteeing that Clarke would not
have to forfeit the advance.

Throughout the spring of 1988 Abbey called frequently to talk. In May he
asked me to go camping with him and run the San Juan River. He knew, by
then, that his time was extremely limited. Yet he needed to get away from the
novel for a few days, at least. We met in Bluff. Ed had driven his "new" old red
Cadillac convertible that he had recently purchased in an uncharacteristic splurge
of hard-earned money. He parked it in the yard of DePuy's beautiful hewn-
stone home. DePuy told us that the river would be crowded—like a superhigh-
way full of rafts and kayaks.

We stowed the old raft and river-running gear at DePuy's as well, loaded Ed's
tent and camping gear into the back of my pickup, and went north between the
Bear's Ears to Elk Ridge in the high country. It was a fine trip with many hikes,
many talks, many silences. Ed revealed the plot of his novel. We wandered mile
after mile after mile as we had always done, pretending that we always would.

Then late one afternoon, Ed looked at me and grinned.

"I gotta go home, *frijol viejo*. I miss Clarke and Becky and Ben."

That summer Abbey put all of his attention into *Hayduke Lives!*

On the autumnal equinox of 1988 his fat masterpiece, the result of decades
of work, was finally released. *The Fool's Progress* had finally been published by
Henry Holt. A page appearing in a later edition contained four measures of
music and the following dedication:

"To the spirit and memory of Charles Ives (1874–1954), greatest of all
American musicians."

chapter 8

The autumn was filled with golden light that year. It should have been a time of camping and hiking, river running over low riffles, exploring the abandoned meanders of the soul. Instead Abbey was committed to go on a book-signing tour over a period of four and a half weeks that would take him to sixteen cities throughout the United States. He wasn't displeased because it gave him an opportunity to reverse the silent treatment traditionally afforded him by East Coast reviewers. But it represented a month-long hiatus in writing his final novel. He knew he was racing with death.

He hit the road October 20, 1988, on a tour that took him to Seattle, Ashland, Portland, San Francisco, Los Angeles, Denver, Phoenix, Albuquerque, Tucson, Minneapolis, Chicago, Pittsburgh, Dallas, Boston, New York, and Miami. Henry Holt put him up first class all the way. He called from Albuquerque and invited Kath and me to come down and have dinner with him before his book signing at the Living Batch, then one of the finest bookstores in the Southwest, owned by Ed's old friend Gus Blaisdell.

After dinner, after it had grown dark, we drove Ed from his hotel to the bookstore. We cruised past the University of New Mexico, Ed's alma mater.

"They never did invite me back to speak here," said Ed. "I got two degrees from this institution. Kind of sad, really. I spent ten years of my life here, off and on. I guess they don't like me very much."

We pulled up in front of the bookstore, where a throng had assembled to meet the author, this man whose courage and wit had been an inspiration for two generations.

"Maybe that institution doesn't appreciate you, Ed. But the people do. You're a writer for the people." Kath and I walked him to the door, where his fans greeted him with an enthusiasm that brought tears to my eyes. He gave my shoulder a squeeze, grinned at his fans, and went into the bookstore, where Gus ensconced him at a table piled high with copies of *The Fool's Progress*.

The next weeks were exhausting for Abbey, but there were bright spots. On arriving in Pittsburgh, he was able to drive to Home and visit his parents, Mildred and Paul, and his brother Hoots. His parents had grown old. Paul still spent hours a day with ax and saw in the woods around Home. Mildred was actually taking college courses, ever improving her education.

He left his parents to continue his grueling tour. Soon thereafter Mildred Abbey was killed in an automobile accident. She had driven to a nearby orchard to buy some of Paul's favorite apples. As she pulled out onto the highway, a large truck crashed into her car. She was eighty-three years old. Ed was one of about a hundred people who attended her funeral in the cemetery near the Presbyterian church where his mother had been the organist and choir director for many years.

Ed, Clarke, Becky, and Ben came to Santa Fe to spend Thanksgiving with us. It was a time of mourning. Ed's mother had passed away exactly twenty days after the death of my father. The night they arrived, Ed and I headed out for a long walk in the moonlight.

"It was strange," said Ed. "When I got to my folks' house to visit them before my mother was killed, my father met me at the door, waving his copy of *The Fool's Progress* in my face and saying, 'Why? Why?'"

"Well, Ed. That novel is pretty biographical. And your father dies in it. Maybe that's what upset him."

"That may be true, but that novel and all my novels are based on ten percent truth and ninety percent imagination. That's what a novelist does. He uses his imagination."

"Maybe you'd better tell that to your old man," I said.

"Maybe I will," said Ed.

We walked through the silver darkness.

"Jack. This is a shitty thing to ask, but have you read many of my books?"

"Hell, yes. I've read almost all of them. I couldn't afford the one you did with Muench. And every time I'd open *Jonathan Troy* at your house, you'd ask me not to read it."

"Why don't you ever tell me what you think of my books?" I had ignorantly hurt Ed's feelings. I could hear it in his voice.

"Shit. Ed, I love your books. When I read them, I'm reading the work of an author whom I regard as one of America's truly important writers. When you and I hang out, I'm with my buddy, Ed. I don't think of you as the famous author. I knew you before you were a famous author. To me, you're my friend. Who happens to have become a famous author. But to me, you'll always be my buddy, my partner."

"Well, I write for my friends. That's who I write for. Do you mind telling me what books you like best?"

"That's a tough question. I have to think about that. I'll say this. *The Fool's Progress* is by far your best novel. It's a great novel. It may take people a while to figure that out because they're used to something else. I like *Good News,* a lot. I think it's brilliant. And *Black Sun* tears me up. So does *The Brave Cowboy.* I haven't read either of those or *Fire on the Mountain* for many years. I love *The Monkey Wrench Gang* for a lot of reasons. And you know why. You and I spent a lot of time doing 'research' out there. I never understood why you didn't mention the Central Arizona Project in that book. That was the real villain in my own mind."

"Interesting," said Ed. "You really like *Good News?*"

"Yeah. I just reread it not too long ago. It's hard to say what my favorite is. I guess I like *The Brave Cowboy* because it's about friendship. And *Black Sun* because it's about love. And *Good News* because it's about anarchy. I like wind better than crystals. Don Quixote is like my uncle."

"Until now, my favorite novel was *Black Sun,*" said Ed. "I worked very hard on that novel, writing it, reworking it until it felt right. I also like *Good News.* I'm particularly glad you like it. The reviewers hated it. They've ignored most of my books. New York swine. From their point of view, I was born on the wrong side of the Hudson."

"I think this, Ed. People who live their lives in New York, who take themselves seriously in New York by New York standards, have no idea what's real. Eighteen million people deluded into thinking that they're hip, conscious, aware, when the truth is, their awareness may be well honed, but it's so limited, it's hard to take them seriously, especially if you yourself have spent any time alone in the wilderness. Screw the reviewers. If they've read your work, you've threatened them. From their point of view, it's better to ignore a threat than to actually face it."

"Back to my favorite subject," said Ed. "Me. What do you think of my nonfiction?"

"I think *Desert Solitaire* is an American classic. Like *Walden* is a classic, or *Huckleberry Finn,* or *Leaves of Grass.*"

"I've written better nonfiction than *Desert Solitaire.* When I look back at it, I feel good about it, I'm not ashamed of it, but some of the writing embarrasses me."

"Don't get hung up in the Rimbaud syndrome."

"What the hell is the Rambo syndrome?"

"Rimbaud, not Rambo. You know, where you shoot your literary wad early on and then have to turn to crime for a living. Your writing certainly hasn't deteriorated. But when you wrote *Desert Solitaire,* you set a new American standard. There are really fine essays in all of your nonfiction books. I love your confrontational essays most where you challenge your enemies. To that extent, *Beyond the Wall* is probably my least favorite. I really like *Slumgullion Stew* and parts of *One Life at a Time, Please.* And parts of *The Journey Home.*"

"What did you like about *One Life at a Time, Please?*"

"My favorite of your essays is in that book. The essay on anarchism. Probably because I'm an anarchist and always have been. I also love the essay about the sacred cow and 'The Writer's Credo.' To tell you the truth, I can't really remember all of the essays you ever wrote. But in my opinion, you're one of America's all-time best essayists. The essay is my favorite literary form. You can say what you really think. In my opinion, you are the master of the essay, both contentwise and as an art form. There are a lot of writers who write well. But most of them are bullshit artists. You don't bullshit. You criticize. That's the difference between you and most of the rest of the essayists I can think of. Same with your fiction. Just out of curiosity, what's your own favorite book of essays?"

"I like *Down the River. Abbey's Road* ain't bad. Interesting what you said about *One Life* . . . I have to think about that."

"Do you feel good about *The Fool's Progress?*"

"Yeah. I do. I think it's my best novel, in fact. But it ought to be. I had plenty of years to practice my craft before I wrote it. And it took me a hell of a long time to write it."

"How do you regard *The Monkey Wrench Gang?*"

"I love that book. I had a lot of fun with it. I said what I meant to say with it. Tried to start a revolution with it. Don't think it's my best novel. But I sure enjoyed it. My problem is, people think of me as a naturalist. I'm not a naturalist. I'm a writer, an artist. I'm tired of writing about the environment. I want to write something else. Anything else."

"Well, do it, for chrissake! Who wants to be rich and famous anyway? Might be okay to be rich, but it's a pain in the ass to be famous. Then the telephone never stops ringing."

"That's true. I try to answer all my mail, and it seems like people always want me to do something or other. Good thing I'm not a beautiful virgin."

"Why?"

"Well, I can't say no, that's why."

We both laughed. We walked on into the night, and I wondered how many years Ed had waited for me or for any of his old friends to tell him what they thought of his writing.

"Ed. I'm sorry if I haven't told you how much I appreciate your work. I really do. And I appreciate that you've been so generous with your books. When you sent *The Fool's Progress* a couple of months ago, it really turned me on. I haven't talked about it much because I didn't want to embarrass you. I'm really one of your most devoted fans. I just don't want that to get in the way of our friendship. To me, you and I are members of a brotherhood of old fire lookouts and eco-outlaws. Who knows, we both may be clinically insane. I'm pretty sure you are."

"Fuck you, Loeffler."

"I wonder how many times you've said that to me over the years."

"Not nearly enough."

We reached the edge of the Santa Fe National Forest. The piñon and juniper trees smelled good in the dry autumnal nighttime air. We'd fallen into an easy pace, content to be quiet part of the time, both glad that we'd talked about Ed's work. That was something Ed had wanted to bring up for years, apparently. I'd complimented him on his books over the years. He had given me autographed copies of all of them since the early 1970s. Somebody had "borrowed" my original edition of *The Monkey Wrench Gang*. But Ed had given me a copy from the limited edition with cartoons by R. Crumb and assigned it the number 1. He had also given me the original manuscript for the same book many years before. I had tried to reciprocate by giving him recordings I had made, favored bits and pieces of the jetsam of individual experience. Ed was generous to a fault. A true gentleman.

"Jack."

"Ed."

"There's something I have to tell you."

"What's that?"

"I'm not going to last much longer."

That stopped me in my tracks. Ed stopped, too. We looked at each other in the moonlight.

"How do you know?" I asked.

"I can feel it in my guts. Literally. I've been bleeding off and on for quite a while now. You knew that. But I can feel it, Jack. I'm gonna die soon."

"Aw, shit."

"Black shit. Thinking about writing a novel called *Black Shit.*"

"Christ. How much time do you think, Ed?"

"Don't know. Can't really tell. I know that I have to hang on long enough to finish *Hayduke Lives!* I don't want Clarke to have to forfeit the advance. She's going to need enough money to get by another three or four years until Ben goes to school."

"How far along in the book are you?"

"Two-thirds, maybe. It'll take me another couple of months, at least. Maybe you could come down and visit for a bit. I'd like to spend some time with you."

"Sure, Ed. I'll come down at Christmas. Maybe we can camp out for a night or two."

"Maybe so. But come on down one way or the other. Maybe write me a letter every now and then. It helps, *compañero.*"

Slowly we walked back to where our wives and kids were eating pizza and enjoying themselves. I could feel Ed's burden. It had become tangible.

Abbey went back to Tucson and tried to work on his novel. He rued the reviews of *The Fool's Progress* or the lack of them.

He made an interesting entry in his journal:

> *My final condemnation of existentialism: Obsessive self-obsession. A completely homocentric, egocentric, anthropocentric view of life and*

world. Unacceptable to me now. I think I sensed something of this way back in 1951, at UNM, when I objected, in a course on existentialism, that it was an "indoor philosophy" as jazz is an indoor musick and Christianity is an indoor or man-centered religion. An infantile variety lies at the heart of these enterprises.

Humanity's view of the world as our property, our dominion, our stewardship, is like that of a child who imagines himself as the center of existence, with all other beings having no purpose but to serve the child.

In December, Abbey had yet another bleed. He was weary and gaunt, jaundiced and fragile. No camping trip this year. Clarke was still optimistic and cheerful. Her spirit was carrying Ed. He loved her more than ever and all his children. He told me that he was gravely worried that he wouldn't finish his book in time. He asked me to come in January for his birthday, if he was still to have a birthday.

As soon as he had strength, he went back to work on *Hayduke Lives!* He had been researching a grand finale courtroom scene for his novel, but it was becoming complex. And then in late January 1989 he bled again, this time losing about half his blood.

I drove to their home near Tucson and spent Ed's birthday, January 29, with the Abbeys. Clarke prepared a beautiful ham-and-baked-potato dinner. Ed, Clarke, Becky, Ben, and I sat around the handcrafted dining-room table. We held hands and said grace. That evening Ed and I walked down to his cabin, which had been built by Ed's friend Don Spaulding several years before. Ed pored through the editions of his books that were stored there in a bookcase. He pulled out one of each and piled them into my arms.

"I want to make sure you have them all," he said.

"We still have a thousand campfires, Ed," I said to him as we walked back to the house.

"You're goddamned right," he said. But we both knew that wasn't so.

On February 2 Ed made the following entry in his journal:

On page 423 of Hayduke Lives *today. Have failed the contract deadline, February 1. No matter. Two more weeks will finish the job. May skip the courtroom trial, however, just in case my guts don't hold out much longer. Let Doc, Bonnie, and Seldom escape free and clear from the hijacking of the gigantic Earth mover, get off undetected, unidentified, and therefore never arrested or indicted. This way, we'd still have a complete novel, good enuf to satisfy the contract, and I could croak, if necessary, in peace. Doc MacGregor sez I lost at least half my blood that awful Friday and Saturday, only 10 or 11 days ago. It seems and feels to me I may really not recover this time.*

Rydal Press in Santa Fe wanted to publish Abbey's notes from a secret journal titled *Vox Clamantis in Deserto*. It was to be a limited edition and would contain the best of his one-liners and distilled moments of wisdom.

On February 13 Abbey sent the last pages of *Hayduke Lives!* to Roger Donald, his editor at Little, Brown. He had made it. Abbey's resolve was extraordinary. He didn't let up even then. He immediately went to work on *Vox Clamantis in Deserto,* which he finished on March 4, 1989. That evening he delivered his final speech at an Earth First! rally in Tucson.

He was tired. He called me and asked me to go camping with him. I instantly agreed, loaded my gear, and headed south, feeling great. Ed had sounded better than I had heard him since Thanksgiving. Maybe everything would be all right after all.

I pulled into the Abbeys' driveway late in the afternoon of March 6. Abbey met me on the front porch of his house. He looked me in the eye long and deep and smiled. Then he gave me a big hug. He said nary a word for at least a minute.

Ed insisted on buying me supper at the Mosaic Cafe, a Mexican restaurant a couple of miles from the house.

"Where do you want to camp?" asked Ed.

"Anywhere you want to go," I said.

"The Cabeza, maybe?"

"Sure."

"Clarke's worried that we'll get out there and I'll start bleeding."

"It's up to you, Ed. I'll do whatever you want to do."

"Maybe we should go to Red Rock. That way if I start to bleed, we'll have a couple alternatives."

"That's fine by me." Actually, it was getting heavy, and I seriously began to wonder if I had the strength of character to help Ed face the inevitable. His eyes told me he was soon to die. My heart refused to accept this.

We went back to his house and I visited with Clarke. Then Ed asked me if I knew his friend Dave Petersen, a writer and bow hunter, an ex-marine who later edited Abbey's journals. I'd never met him but I remembered Ed speaking highly of him. Ed asked if it was all right with me if he invited Petersen to go camping with us. I said that it was fine by me. Ed called Dave in Durango but he couldn't come just then. Too short notice. Ed and I decided to leave for our camping trip early the next morning instead of that same evening. The sun was lowering beyond the western range. We had loaded Ed's gear in my truck, but neither of us was anxious to try to find a campsite in the dark. We'd done that before, much to our collective dismay revealed by dawn's light.

Clarke had set me up with the foldout couch down in Ed's cabin. I said good night, borrowed a book, went to bed, and read myself to sleep, as has been my wont for the last half century.

At four A.M. Clarke burst through the door of the cabin and shook my shoulder.

"Ed's bleeding, Jack. You have to drive him to the hospital. Now!"

I swung out of bed, quickly got dressed, and ran up to the house. By then Ed was dressed, waiting for me. Clarke had to stay with Becky and Ben, who were still sleeping.

I helped a weakening Ed out to my pickup, helped him climb into the passenger side, climbed in myself, and fired up the engine. I drove out the driveway to the dirt road a hundred yards down from their house.

"Which way, Ed?"

"Head east on Grant. The hospital's at the other end of Tucson."

We drove in silence for a while. I found Grant Avenue and sped eastward. I remember passing a police car driving in the opposite direction. The cop paid absolutely no attention to us even though I was driving at least sixty miles an hour. We were invisible, in limbo, approaching a major vector.

"Jack, is this a nightmare?" Ed was leaning forward, clasping his gut. I could sense him looking at me.

"As far as I can tell, Ed, this is real."

"Should we go out into the desert and just get it over with?"

"I'll go anywhere you want. Tell me what you want me to do, and I'll do it."

We hung there in space, just the two of us, suspended momentarily in a continuum, waiting for the next course of action to be revealed. Ed was agonized by indecision; I was gathering momentum for I knew not what. It was a time of extraordinary anxiety.

"We better go on to the hospital. I can't leave Clarke and the kids without some kind of a fight. But give me your word you won't let me die there, Jack."

"I already gave you my word a long time ago, Ed. I'll live up to my word. But no matter what we do, it ain't gonna be easy. It's gonna get complicated as soon as we get to the hospital."

"Let's go to the hospital, Jack. I'm counting on you."

What would have happened had we turned back west and headed into the desert wilderness? At that moment it was just the two of us, one-on-one with death. But the moment passed, and we sped on to the hospital.

Ed was admitted to the hospital and was immediately given transfusions. Clarke was able to get a baby-sitter and join us by midmorning. That day Ed seemed to rally. The doctor was optimistic and strongly urged that Ed consider surgery, which would involve installing a "portal shunt," an artificial vein that would extend between his liver and esophagus, relieving the pressure on the tiny cluster of veins that transported blood around the stone-plugged portal vein.

That evening Clarke and I visited with Ed as he lay there in his bed. We were optimistic.

Then Ed said, "I'm not going to make it, guys."

"Don't be silly, Ed," said Clarke. "Of course you're going to make it."

She went on to tell him that he had stopped bleeding, that the doctor had said the time had come for him to have the operation that would save his life.

Ed wasn't convinced, even in the face of Clarke's invincible optimism and cheerfulness.

I remained in the background where I belonged.

The next day Ed wanted to go home. I found a wheelchair in the room of a sleeping patient and stole it. Clarke and I helped Ed into the wheelchair. I started wheeling Ed toward the door of the hospital. Some orderlies and a nurse or two were objecting to our sudden departure. Clarke headed them off at the pass in a superb feint that gave me the extra seconds to wheel Ed into the parking lot. I helped him into my truck and we fled.

We arrived at their house a few minutes before Clarke did. I half carried Ed into bed and pulled off his boots. He was weak and tired. It was the first time I had seen him immediately after a bleed. His body had no strength, but his mind was on fire.

Clarke tucked him in and then went into Becky's room to take a nap. She was exhausted.

Ed looked at me and said, "How about taking me out in the desert where I can die in peace, where it won't be ugly for Clarke and the kids?"

"The doctor said you were doing okay. He said that you were the best candidate for the portal shunt operation that he had ever seen."

"Yeah, but if it doesn't work, and I get only a limited supply of oxygen to my brain like they say sometimes happens, it'll lower my mental capacity. I couldn't stand that."

"Look, Ed. You're not bleeding now. Will you wait a week, during which time you'll talk to the doctor and then make a decision about the operation? He's convinced that it will work. Clarke's convinced, too. If we take off now, it'll be terrible for Clarke."

"You want me to wait a week, huh? Then you'll take me out into the desert if I want to?"

"Yes."

"Okay. We'll give it a week. But then away we go."

"Ed, I think I better go away for a day or two so you and Clarke can work things out. I feel like I'm getting between you."

"What do you mean?"

"Ed, she wants you to live. She loves you. She wants you to help her raise the kids. The doctor has told us that if you have this operation, you'll be fine. She believes that. Christ, even I believe that. If I hang around now, you'll be looking for me to take you out into the desert. It doesn't give Clarke a chance to convince you to have the operation."

"Jack, that operation would bankrupt her. I can't do that."

"The hell with the money, Ed. You've got to try to live, man. Give me a week. Seven days. Then if it isn't going well, I'll take you out in the desert."

"Okay," said Ed begrudgingly.

I left. In retrospect, I shouldn't have. But I did. I couldn't stand to cloud Ed's chances. Everybody was pouring life energy into him. But from Ed's point of view, while I wasn't exactly the grim reaper, I was certainly his ally. Ed wanted me to help him die.

Early the next morning the phone rang in my motel room. It was Kath telling me to call Clarke immediately. I did.

Clarke read me the riot act. I had disappeared while she was taking a nap. Ed was back in the hospital. He had started bleeding again. There had been no one to help. She had called Dave Foreman and his wife, Nancy Morton. Somehow they had convinced Ed to go back to the hospital.

I drove to the hospital. Ed was in intensive care. He was slowly bleeding to death. He felt sick. He felt like hell.

"It isn't going to work, Jack. You gotta get me out of here."

I looked at Clarke. I couldn't cross her. I couldn't cross Ed.

Clarke nodded to me. The tacit permission of hopelessness.

"Okay, Ed. I'll get you out of here. I'll go get my truck."

"Can you get my truck? It's more comfortable in the back than your truck is." That was true.

"It'll take me a while. I have to go back to your house to get it."

I left the hospital to get Ed's truck. It was nighttime, and I drove through Tucson like one in a dream. A very bad dream.

I returned to the hospital, driving Ed's '74 blue Ford pickup. It didn't look new anymore. It had been dented, battered, and scraped. It looked like Ed's truck.

I met Clarke outside Ed's room, and she directed me into a nearby vacant room.

"Peacock's in there with him. He's convinced Ed to have the operation."

Clarke and I both wept.

It took a while to get Ed ready for the operation. We all entered a state of guardedly optimistic limbo. At some point Josh and Aaron came to visit their father, to say hello or good-bye as the case might be. This gave Ed a major lift. Peacock, Clarke, and I rotated sitting with Ed, trying to help him keep his spirits readjusted to having the operation.

The evening before Ed was to go into surgery, Clarke sat on one side of his bed and I on the other. We each took one of his arms and concentrated on giving him the strength to survive his ordeal. We were like that for a long time. Peacock came to the hospital, and then they wheeled Ed away into the preoperative room.

By now Susan, Clarke's sister, had flown in from Salt Lake City. She was at home with Becky and Ben. That evening Susan's husband, Steve Prescott, arrived. Steve is an M.D. His presence heartened us all. Clarke's parents, Tom and Carolyn Cartwright, were coming in from College Station, Texas. Our forces were mounting.

That night the surgery was performed on Ed. It took time, and we all paced the ugly green hospital halls. Sometime in the middle of the night the surgery was completed. It was deemed a success. We all cheered.

The next morning I was sitting with Ed.

"It didn't work, Jack. I can feel myself bleeding."

"The doctor said the operation was successful."

"All I know is that I'm still bleeding."

The day wore on, and tests revealed that there was indeed blood in Ed's guts, but it was arterial blood, not blood from veins. There is a distinction. Ed wasn't out of the woods after all. By now Ed had needles, catheters, hoses, drains plugged into his poor beaten body. It seemed that an artery had started to hemorrhage. It was unrelated to the varices. Ed was still bleeding. No matter what, it was his destiny to bleed to death. There was no way to stop this hemorrhage.

The medical staff agreed that his condition was hopeless. We stood around, all of us. Ed looked at me.

"Get me out of here."

It was time. Ed and I pulled the various devices out of his arms, nose, etc. The hospital staff looked on. This wasn't proper hospital procedure.

"It's time to get him out of here. He doesn't want to die in a hospital. He wants to die his own way."

I'm sure we all remember that time differently. I recall telling the doctor on duty to stay the hell out of my way. The time had come to get Ed out of the hospital. No one was going to stand between Ed and the freedom to die where and when he wanted to. I helped Ed sit up in bed. I figured maybe

Peacock and I could carry him to the truck. The head nurse made a decision.

"I'll help you. I'll get a gurney."

The doctor came to his senses. "Let me give him some more blood. Top him off." That's actually what he said.

As they topped him off, Peacock and I went out to get our vehicles ready. I had Ed's truck, Doug, his four-wheel drive. We made some quick estimations.

"You know this part of the world better than I do, Peacock. Ed wants to die outside. Maybe Red Rock. I'll follow you."

"Okay, Loeffler."

We went back in. By now Ed was "topped off."

We all loaded him onto the gurney and slowly wheeled him out to the back of his truck. We slid him in, and he was able to lie down relatively comfortably, considering that he been under the surgeon's knife all too recently. Steve and Clarke climbed into the back with him. Steve, being an M.D., could minister to him. Clarke would do everything she could to help him through this time.

Ed looked at me. "Did you ask how much time I have left?"

"Yeah," I said. "You have maybe twenty-four hours."

"Twenty-four hours. That's it, huh?"

"That's it, Ed."

"Interesting."

"We're going out to Red Rock. Peacock's leading the way. Is that okay with you?"

"That's fine. Take it as easy as you can. I don't feel so good."

I drove as gently as I could. Peacock drove in front well under the speed limit. By now it was after midnight. We had opened the windows between the cab and the camper. Steve hollered that Ed hurt too much to go all the way to Red Rock. I blinkered my headlights at Peacock. He stopped, and we reconnoitered.

"I know a good place to die," said Peacock. "Follow me."

We continued to head west until we pulled up onto a *bajada* near the base of a small range of mountains. It was beautiful, peaceful. First light streaked the eastern horizon.

We selected a sandy spot in the arroyo near a tree. Peacock built a small fire. It was cool on this March morning. We pulled blankets out of the truck and made a nest. We helped Ed get as comfortable as he could. Then, one by one, we knelt down and said, "So long," to Ed. Everyone but Clarke. She lay down beside him to hold him close while he died.

Steve, Peacock, and I went off to let him die in peace. The dawn blossomed. The morning passed slowly. It got hot. Ed didn't show any signs of dying. We regrouped.

"It's too hot out here to die," said Ed.

"You want to go home?"

"I want to go to my cabin. I want to die in my cabin. That's a good place to die."

We helped Ed climb in the passenger's side of Peacock's vehicle.

Clarke and I took Ed's truck back to the house as fast as we could to make his cabin comfortable for him. By midafternoon he was resting quietly in the cool of his cabin, where a few days before, he had finished writing *Hayduke Lives!* Above his head was his flag, the black flag of anarchism with a great red monkey wrench adorning the black field. There was a buffalo skull, a gift from Ed's friend Ernie Bulow. On the wall was a painting by DePuy. On his desk was his old Royal typewriter, a monkey wrench, a wooden shoe, and a knife stuck in the surface of the desk. There were maps of Big Bend and the Cabeza on the wall. There was a photograph of Ed and Dave Foreman with the Glen Canyon Dam in the background, a great plastic "crack" defacing the enormous, concave face of this tribute to Mammon. There was a "wobbly" poster on the wall and a print of a beautiful nude by Modigliani. There was a broadsheet of a poem by Drum Hadley. There was a portable stereo record player and a woodstove. Ed's rifle, shotgun, and hunting bow were mounted on the wall along with his great hat. There were books in the bookcase. There was a small wooden god with an enormous cock guarding the bookcase—an artifact I had brought back for Ed from Rarotonga. This was Ed's cabin. The sliding glass doors faced west. They were shaded by a portal. It really was a good place to die.

But he didn't seem to be dying. I called his personal doctor and told him Ed seemed to be doing better now that he was out of the hospital. I asked if I could get him some more blood. If we could get it, maybe we could keep him going. Ed's doctor came right over. We got some blood. We plugged him in. Steve Prescott and Doug Peacock became Ed's round-the-clock medical team.

They worked well together. I was the "gofer." I'd gofer blood, gofer a spot of liquid repast through the arm, gofer whatever was needed to keep Ed alive. Clarke poured love and optimism into him.

Ed's sister Nancy arrived from California to visit her older brother.

Ed survived the night. The next day he was downright cheerful. Peacock's wiseass banter bolstered Ed's spirits. Prescott's ministrations kept Ed as comfortable as possible. I kept the blood coming. For a few hours we began to hope that Ed would survive.

That night I took the first watch. I sat by Ed's bed and talked to him. I watched as he slipped into sleep. I listened to his breathing go from easy to labored.

Susie came into the cabin, all the way from New York, where she was a student at Sarah Lawrence. She sat with me, and together we watched Ed truly begin to die. Susie and I have always been close. We gave Ed our best that night.

Nancy came in to relieve us for the second watch. I went off to a motel. Clarke needed room. I needed space. When I got to the motel, I looked in the yellow pages for a source of dry ice. I drank some beer and slept.

Early the next morning I went out to see how Ed was doing. He was dying. His breathing was like a rasp. Clarke and I stood outside.

"He isn't going to make it, Clarke. Don't get your hopes up." She nodded.

Steve told me that Ed needed blood. I headed out to the source. I talked to the man and told him I needed another bag of AB positive. While I was waiting, I called the house. Susan answered. Clarke had held Ed's hand and told him it was okay to die. And he had.

I got a death certificate. I found the ice plant and asked for enough dry ice to keep two hundred pounds of meat fresh for forty-eight hours. I had the dry ice sawn into slabs.

I drove too fast back to Ed's cabin. Steve greeted me and told me that Ed was indeed dead. I backed my truck down to the cabin and went in. There was Ed. I knelt down and touched him. Clarke came in and knelt beside me. It was peaceful. Together we bade Ed release and farewell.

After a bit Tom Cartwright and Steve Prescott came in, and we wrapped up Ed's body in his blue sleeping bag as he had asked and packed him in dry ice. Becky came down to say good-bye to her father. She did this with great dignity, laying a bouquet of desert flowers on his chest. One by one, the family members paid their last respects. I sat down at Ed's typewriter and typed out his death certificate. I couldn't remember his mother's maiden name and had to interrupt Susie in her grief to ask her. I completed the form and signed it. Not totally legal, perhaps, but in keeping with Ed's spirit.

Tom, Steve, and I loaded Ed's body into the back of my pickup truck in the space between the sleeping area and the bed of the truck, where I normally stowed my camping gear. Ed was a perfect fit. If I got stopped, the constabulary would have to really be looking to find Ed's body. I stuck the death certificate in the glove compartment.

Immediately after Ed had died, Peacock had gone off to be by himself for a while. He had been awake for several days and nights by now and had to come to terms. After we had put Ed's body in the back of my truck, Peacock returned, strong as ever.

I said, "We have to get out of here as soon as we can. I can feel it. Who all's going?"

Tom, Steve, Peacock, and I. Susie came up to me.

"Can I come, too?"

"Susie, you can come with me anytime, anywhere."

She looked me straight in the eye, just like her dad. "Maybe I'd better stay here this time."

Peacock and I knew just where we were going. We had been there before. Together and separately. We had camped there with Ed. Ed had agreed to this grave site the day before.

"Peacock," said I. "It's going to be a long day. It's hot. I want to get some beer for this trip."

"So do I. Let's go."

Tom rode with Peacock. Steve rode with me. Ed rode in the back of my old Chevy pickup. We took off. Ten minutes after our departure, there were reporters at the door, asking if it was true that Ed Abbey was dead. But by then we were in a liquor store three miles down the road, getting necessary supplies—jerky, nuts, candy bars, whiskey, and five cases of beer. This was at least a four six-pack trip, and there were five of us, counting Ed. We were a burial team now. It would take all of us to do this job right. But by God, we'd gotten Ed to where he could die in peace. And in beauty. In another day or two, if our luck held, we'd plant him and we'd be done. Peacock advised me to drive just under the speed limit. It wouldn't do to get busted at this stage. Peacock and I both had our pieces. Habit.

We left the liquor store, each having purchased according to his needs. With Ed's spirit in the lead, we headed toward a distant desert fastness far from the reaches of any human society.

It was late in the day when we reached the general vicinity of Ed's grave site. We scouted the terrain and selected a place on top of a rise far from the end of the road. The eastern and western horizons lay far away. It was a perfect vantage from which to contemplate the Basin and Range Province, an enormous area that contains the four deserts of the North American continent. We were near the bull's-eye of a mountain pass situated in one of over two hundred ranges that ripple through this province, each serrated range separated by a wide basin of flatland, each flatland scored by arroyos tracing the course of infrequent waters. We were in the heart of a vast desert wilderness, about to serve the last mortal wishes of our fallen *compañero,* to bury him in a wild desert place where his physical form would slowly transmogrify into the good Earth.

We had brought shovels and pick. We commenced to dig.

"Won't work," said Peacock.

"Why not?"

"There's caprock below the surface of the soil."

"How do you know that?"

"I'm a geologist," he mumbled.

"Come again?" I queried.

"I studied geology, for chrissake. There's fucking caprock beneath the surface of the soil."

About eighteen inches down, there was indeed caprock. Tom and I were digging. We were not to be deterred. We would try to dig down through the caprock. This was a perfect burial site. Aesthetics must be satisfied. We couldn't give up without giving it our best. We dug until almost sundown. Then we decided to camp.

We hiked back to the trucks, taking great care to step on stones to avoid leaving any hint of a trail. This grave site would have to remain secret for a long time.

We gave nary a damn that we were probably breaking several pages of useless laws. We cared very much that Ed remain undisturbed over the next centuries.

We backtracked a few miles to a favored campsite and parked off the road. We built a small fire, but we camped well away from each other. I threw out my sleeping bag near my truck and spent much of the night talking to Ed. It was a beautiful night.

Tom Cartwright later recalled Ed's last night above the Earth:

I thought there was something prophetic when the four of us camped in the bed of the arroyo that night—Ed's last night above the ground. The four of us were bound together in this mission. But somehow we didn't want to sleep right next to each other. We moved out, maybe forty—fifty yards apart. And that night, the coyotes came in amongst us, not on the periphery. They came in to commiserate with us. They howled and yipped and finally went on. Of course it was just happenstance. But I interpreted it as a message. "He was our friend, too. And we'll miss him." That's what I remember most.

The next morning we headed out to the grave site early. Or at least we intended to. My truck was stuck in the sand. True to form. Every time in my whole life I had ever gone camping with Abbey, we had gotten stuck in the sand or the mud. Literally dozens of times. The same with Peacock. For some reason beknownst only to the local deities, this was a requirement of camping with Abbey. Only this time, the lazy bastard wasn't even going to help us get unstuck. There he was, lying down in the back of the truck. I jammed it into reverse. Steve pushed on the left front fender. Tom pushed on the right. Peacock pushed on the grille. Peacock pushed too hard, and the grille exploded into its myriad plastic parts.

Peacock grinned at me along the length of my hood. "Cheap-shit fucking grille, Loeffler."

"Just don't push on the radiator, asshole!" I yelled back at him. A truly remarkable man, my friend Peacock.

They all leaned on the front of the truck with their collective might and I let out the clutch as gently as I could. The truck bounced backward onto the road.

"Sorry, Ed," I said.

We went to the end of the road. This time we decided to take Ed with us. We needed all the help we could get. We slid him out of the back of the truck and carried him on the handles of two shovels, one of us on each corner of this makeshift stretcher. We bore his pall a long way until we arrived at the shallow hole we had begun to dig the night before. We placed Ed in the shade of a large flowering deathbane, a species of flora that sparsely populates that particular desert.

Tom and I started to dig. The tip of the steel pick curled against the caprock. Grudgingly we admitted that Peacock was right. It wouldn't work.

Steve was off scouting an alternative site.

"Holy motherfuck!" muttered Peacock, who was looking through his binoculars back along the road we had come in on. There, maybe ten miles distant, was the telltale cockscomb cloud of dust that revealed a vehicle heading our way.

We hastily formed a plan. Tom would drop down the two hundred or so feet to the other side of the saddle. I would hurry back to the trucks and be fiddling with a bird book and binoculars if the intruder chanced to come to the end of the road. Tom would slowly hike up the trail that continued beyond the end of the road and tell me (in the presence of the intruder) that he had spotted some interesting bird life about two miles beyond. Peacock would find Steve, and they would lay low.

Why should one feel even a tinge of paranoia about burying a beloved friend in the desert? Because it's illegal in the spiderlike eyes of the government, that's why.

You were an outlaw to the very end and beyond, brother Abbey.

I confronted the intruder, who pulled up at the end of the road. He was some poor Joe Six-pack just like the rest of us who actually did want to go bird watching. He had a backpack, heavy-duty binoculars, and a couple of gallons of water.

"Look out for that double-breasted skinny-dipper," I said. One of Ed's favorite birds.

"What's that?" said Joe Six-pack.

"Oh, nothin'," said Tom in his soft Texas drawl. "Have a good time."

We waited by the vehicles for a good fifteen minutes before we started back up to the grave site. When we got there, Steve and Peacock had disap-peared. We followed the rim for a way until we heard the sound of shovel and earth. We looked over the edge. There was Steve, already waist deep in a hole he was digging. And digging. And digging. Steve Prescott has an extraordi-nary amount of brute energy. The dirt and sweat flew.

Peacock said, "There's no caprock here. We can bury Ed good and deep. It's a good place. No one'll find him."

Peacock and I alternately lay in the grave for fit and comfort, made a soft depression here, removed an uncomfortable stone there until it felt good. It was cool and protected. It seemed a fine place to demolecularize into eternity. Looking up from the bottom of the grave, the sky was dark blue, dotted here and there with an occasional buzzard or soaring hawk.

So be it.

We went back to the original grave site and filled it in, piling some stones on top of it to make a mock grave. Then we went over to the flowering deathbane and slid Ed's enshrouded carcass out of the shade, into the light of the sun. We loaded him onto our shovel handles and started the last stage of Ed's funerary procession.

It was hot under the midday sun. The sound of insects was incessant. In my mind's eye, I saw us slowly proceeding along the ridgeline as though from a quarter mile distant. Four men carrying the body of their comrade to the cave beneath the cairn, grave bound for time out of mind.

There really was the cry of a red-tailed hawk. And the sound of a hot, light wind passing through the spines of several species of cactus.

It was tricky bearing Ed the last fifteen feet, but we made it. We lowered him into the grave and covered him over with a ton of desert soil, piling rocks on top. And then it was done. There is no describing what any of us felt. We made final ablutions as we saw fit. We poured beer on his grave in a final toast. Then we left our friend to become one with the desert.

A week later Clarke held a wake in Saguaro National Monument, several miles from their home west of Tucson. It was a beautiful wake, well attended by Abbey's family and friends. It followed Abbey's final instructions as if he had orchestrated it himself. There was beer and wine and tequila. There was bagpipe music. Peacock provided a magnificent slow-elk stew. Susie read a passage from Abbey's essay "Theory of Anarchy." I played taps on the flügelhorn. There was gunfire and laughter and tears and love. Bobby Greenspan and the boys played music, and there was dancing. DePuy, looking like Zorba the Greek, danced in the desert sand. Earth First!ers honored the passage of their friend and spiritual adviser. And finally, in the waning hours of the afternoon, someone put on a tape of Ed's last speech, which he had delivered only two weeks earlier. Everyone listened as Ed expressed his thoughts concerning the protection of the planet and wilderness against the interlopers of capitalism.

Ed was there at his own wake.

Awakening!

Adios, muchacho . . .

bibliographic essay

I selected to write a short bibliographic essay in lieu of a regular bibliography. Since the book is not a biography but a biographical memoir, it seems appropriate that footnotes be excluded.

I'll begin by saying that I have a copy of Edward Abbey's Journals IV through XX and have read them, made notes on them, quoted them, and used them to establish the chronology of Ed's life. The first three volumes of his journals were lost long ago. I have also used files prepared by the FBI available through the Freedom of Information Act to fill in certain chronological gaps.

I read or reread each of the twenty-one books and a few articles written by Abbey that I have in my possession, to which I referred frequently.

I have selected from journals kept by Ed's mother, Mildred Abbey; referred to the Abbey family tree prepared in April 1981 by family members Kathleen Osmund, Ida Abbey Crawford, and Howard and Paul Abbey; consulted notes on life during the earlier twentieth century in the Abbey family prepared by Ed's aunt Ida; and read miscellaneous letters, poems, and other papers that were stored by Paul Revere Abbey in Home, Pennsylvania, that came into my possession.

I conducted personal recorded interviews with Ed's father, Paul Revere Abbey, his brother Howard "Hoots" Abbey, his sister Nancy Abbey, and his widow, Clarke Cartwright Abbey.

I also conducted recorded interviews with friends and others who had known Ed or corresponded with him at various points in his life, including Malcolm Brown, Fred Black, Archie Bahm, John DePuy, Douglas Peacock, Tom Cartwright, Dave Petersen, Alan Harrington, Bill Hoy, Jim Stiles, Renée Downing, Gary Snyder, William Eastlake, and David Brower.

I referred to a recorded interview I conducted with Abbey on January 1, 1983, and a recording I made of a lecture he delivered at St. John's College in Santa Fe in the mid-1970s. All of the above recorded interviews are in my aural history library in Santa Fe, New Mexico.

I included an excerpt from a letter from Gary Snyder to Edward Abbey dated 10:XI:82.

I referred to E. J. Hobsbawm's book *Bandits,* published by Penguin in 1972, which includes a chapter on Haiduks, and my own book, *Headed Upstream: Interviews with Iconoclasts,* published by Harbinger House in 1989.

And to a great extent, I referred to my own journals, the correspondence that survives between Ed Abbey and myself, and the recollection of our myriad conversations conducted while hiking, driving, river running, or just staring into campfires.

acknowledgments

This book owes its presence to many people who nurtured it through a ten-year gestation period. It began in the minds of my old friend Dave Foreman and his editor, Michael Pietsch. Our dear friend Clarke Abbey gave the project her blessing and has provided her wonderful energy throughout the process. Becky and Ben Abbey have been of special delight to me. Ed's oldest daughter, Susie (who once wrote a biographical sketch of me), is dear to me and provided a special spirit to the project. Ed's father, Paul Revere Abbey, recalled memories of young Ned and provided me with papers that had been in the family's keeping for many years. Ed's sister Nancy and brother Howard were generous with both time and information.

The staff at the University of Arizona Library Special Collections, where Edward Abbey's papers are located, provided invaluable support.

I am grateful to Ed's friends and acquaintances who were willing to share their recollections of Ed, including Malcolm Brown, John DePuy, Archie Bahm, Fred Black, Doug Peacock, William and Marilyn Eastlake, John Nichols, Gary Snyder, Dave Petersen, Alvin Josephy, Bill Hoy, Jim Stiles, Renée Downing, Tom and Carolyn Cartwright, Steve and Susan Prescott, David Brower, Stewart and Lee Udall, Alan Harrington, Ken Sleight, and Starr Jenkins.

My close and brilliant friend Bill Brown made a skillful editorial pass through the manuscript somewhere about the midway point.

Author Luís Urrea introduced me to Joanna Hurley, whose knowledge of the publishing industry helped me regain my manuscript.

My pal, attorney Daniel Yohalem, did regain my manuscript with a swift, single stroke of jurisprudential genius.

My good friend Beth Hadas from the University of New Mexico Press edited my manuscript, refining and streamlining it, and elicited the book that lay within the words. Copyeditor Karen Taschek cleaned up myriad errors throughout the book and demonstrated an understanding of the comma far superior to my own. Mina Yamashita provided the design for this book with the ease and elegance for which she is distinguished.

Finally I want to thank my wonderful wife, friend, and partner, Katherine, for her wisdom and perseverance, and our superdaughter and pal, Celestia Peregrina, for her spirit. Without their support and input, this book would have remained unwritten.

index